GITTINS

Other books by Ross Gittins

Gittins' Guide to Economics
Gittinomics
The Happy Economist
Gittins' Gospel
How Australia Compares
(with Rodney Tiffen)

GITTINS

A life among budgets, bulldust and bastardry

ROSS GITTINS

to Jo
Power behind the throne
Ross Gittins

ALLEN&UNWIN
SYDNEY • MELBOURNE • AUCKLAND • LONDON

Page 110: Letter to the editor reproduced with permission of the *Sydney Morning Herald*.
Page 185: Cartoon reproduced with the permission of Michael Leunig.
Page 263: Cartoon reproduced with the permission of Alan Moir.

First published in 2015

Allen & Unwin
83 Alexander Street
Crows Nest NSW 2065
Australia
Phone: (61 2) 8425 0100
Email: info@allenandunwin.com
Web: www.allenandunwin.com

Cataloguing-in-Publication details are available
from the National Library of Australia
www.trove.nla.gov.au

ISBN 978 1 76011 287 5

Set in 12/17pt Adobe Caslon by Midland Typesetters, Australia
Printed and bound in Australia by Griffin Press

10 9 8 7 6 5 4 3 2 1

FSC www.fsc.org MIX Paper from responsible sources FSC® C009448

The paper in this book is FSC® certified. FSC® promotes environmentally responsible, socially beneficial and economically viable management of the world's forests.

For my boys—male and female—who laughed at my jokes, learnt from my hoary anecdotes and encouraged me to write them down

CONTENTS

CHAPTER 1
OLD-SCHOOL JOURNO TELLS ALL

The fact that a man is a newspaper reporter is evidence of some flaw of character.

Lyndon Johnson

It takes quite an ego to imagine the story of your life and work could be of much interest to anyone but your family and friends. Well, here's my first startling revelation: I have quite an ego (though I've learnt to keep it hidden). Of course, as a journo that hardly makes me unique. Though journalism isn't badly paid, it isn't particularly well paid, either, so what motivates journos is their egos. From the first thrill of seeing your name in the paper—and having your mum see your name—to the daily contest to get a better story than your rivals at other news outlets and the struggle for a more prominent place in the paper than your own colleagues, it's an oversized ego that drives you on. That, plus the occasional win.

Out of the office, my life's been pretty ordinary. No escaping from wicked stepmothers or starving in garrets. So what have I got to offer? An insider's story of what goes on behind the veil at the headquarters of the largest remaining independent news media company, Fairfax—one whose survival a lot of people care about.

And the viewpoint of an old-school journo. During my 40 years at Fairfax Media, lots of people have left and lots have arrived. Most of those have been and gone while I've soldiered on. So my time stretches from the antediluvian period of hot metal and linotype machines, the largely effete but paternalistic ownership of Sir Warwick Fairfax and his family, the fast-flowing rivers of classified-advertising gold and the stodgy journalism they permitted, through decades of ever-growing competition from every angle and the resulting ever-increasing commercialism, to the present day of rapidly declining circulations for the paper editions of the *Sydney Morning Herald* and *The Age*, advertising-revenue rivers that have become thin streams, ever-multiplying digital 'platforms', reading the paper on your phone, seemingly unending rounds of staff redundancies, and a great big question mark over where the digital revolution will leave the future of quality journalism.

I'll tell you about the good old days and how we got from there to here. But old-school though I am, journos spend their lives keeping up to date with the news and so can't escape living in the world as it is, and wondering where it's going. No one knows better than I that the past is dead and gone. So I'll give you my best explanation of the interplay of economics and technology that got us to where we are now. Then I'll give you my battle plan for securing the future of quality journalism. It won't be back to the future but it will emphasise that, in our battle for survival, there's no point giving up the very things that make journalism a job we can be proud of.

In 40 years I've had a ringside seat as the economy has changed and become only just recognisable to some awakening Rip Van Winkle. I've seen and written about those changes. I've seen a cavalcade of treasurers, treasury secretaries, central bank governors and prime ministers come and go. I've covered 40 federal budgets, 16 federal elections, 13 treasurers, eight prime ministers, five changes of government, three major recessions and one global financial crisis that could have been a bad recession but wasn't. I've seen the management of the economy shift from Canberra to Sydney without any Canberran wanting to admit it. I'll tell you my economic and political highlights. Is this one of those memoirs full of blatant dropping of the names of the famous and powerful? Yes.

Most memoirs—particularly those from politicians—are about staking the author's claim for a place in the nation's history book, to which end the pollies do their damnedest to rewrite history in their favour. I hope I won't be judged guilty of the latter; rather, my goal is to shed a little ringside light on some of the happy fictions that have emerged. But I suppose I'm guilty of the former motivation—that overblown ego again, though journos' egos are no match for politicians'. *They* only ever did what they did for the good of the nation; I'll spare you that dubious claim on my part.

The most sales-conscious of the political memoirists make sure their book has its share of revelations, indiscretions and tales out of school. I wouldn't sink to that level, surely? Let's just say that after decades in the business I hope I've learnt how to make a story interesting. And I do have a reputation around the office for being overly blunt. I've found it to be a handicap in my personal relations, but an asset in journalism. If it's controversial I've steered towards it rather than away from it. Similarly, a journo should have the ability to tell a story about some minor character—me, in this case—that nonetheless holds the reader's interest. You be the judge.

I admit to being an old-school journo, but the emphasis in that phrase should be on old. I've been around for a long time, a living link with journalism in the olden days. I hope I'm old-school in the sense of believing journalism is about seeking and revealing the truth, of believing in the importance of spelling and grammar, hating Americanisms and American pronounciations, conforming to the style book and always presenting the subeditors with 'clean copy'. I come down hard on youngsters who write that people have 'passed away' rather than died.

But I'm not old-school in the sense that I'm typical of all the practices and principles of the old boys. My career is far from typical. Most journalists start as reporters and never progress to opinion writing; I went almost straight to opinion writing and did only a smattering of (undistinguished) reporting. I've always been a bit of a loner in journalism, never one of the in-crowd at the pub. And, as you'll see, there's a host of traditional beliefs and practices I've never thought made sense. This, I hope, will add a little interest, even controversy.

In journalism, as in many professions, there's an important element of what I suppose I must call showpersonship. On ABC radio's *Journos' Forum*, we see the questions in advance so we can think of something less than obvious to say, but we know never to admit that fact. In print the goal is to make what you do seem effortless, concealing from the customer how furiously you're paddling under the surface. A little showmanship? Sure.

But that being so, this is a tell-all book. I don't just retail anecdotes, I spell out how I do my tricks. I do this hoping the reader will find it of some interest, but also as a guide for journos to come, including the small school of economic journalists whose contribution I've worked for so long to promote. It would be a sad thing for that expertise to be lost in all the upheavals of the digital revolution.

Of all the challenges and changes in journalism over the past 40 years and longer, one many Melbournians feel most keenly is the ever-tightening incorporation of *The Age* into the Fairfax empire. To be frank, I regret it too—even though I could be seen as part of the growing influence of the Sydney-based owners. It was a great day in my career when, in the early 1990s, *The Age* decided to start running my columns. There has only ever been one paper I'd want to work for apart from the *SMH* and that's *The Age*. Even had *The Age* remained totally free of its Sydney owners, the two papers have far more in common than, say, the *SMH* and *The Australian*.

True, *The Age* was the first of the Fairfax twins to modernise, under the still-revered editorship of Graham Perkin, supported by the broad-sighted management of the Syme family's Ranald Macdonald. And *The Age*'s record of political independence—of determining its election support for Liberal or Labor strictly on the parties' merits—is much better than the *SMH*'s.

But permit me to make this painful point: *The Age*'s ability to survive as an independent, Victorian-owned paper was lost well before I joined the *SMH* more than 40 years ago. If you accept that, then I think you also have to accept that being taken over by Fairfax was—and remains—the least-worst of the available options. Whatever the Sydney–Melbourne frictions, I'm sure that was always the view of the Syme family. Whatever their misgivings, it was always the Fairfax family—not the Murdochs, the Packers or the executives of the old Herald and Weekly Times—they preferred as their white knight.

As Gavin Souter records it in his book *Heralds and Angels*, whereas John Fairfax Ltd was controlled by only three Fairfaxes, the terms of David Syme's will meant control of David Syme & Co. Ltd was shared by many members of the Syme family. In

1966, at the behest of Syme's Colonel E.H. Neill, Fairfax entered a partnership agreement with the family that enabled those family members wishing to sell their shares to sell to Fairfax rather than other suitors. By 1972, this had taken Fairfax's holding in Syme above 50 per cent. In 1983, Fairfax bought the last of the family's shares at the request of Macdonald, who had decided to move on to other interests. Soon after, Fairfax took its holding to 100 per cent.

More recently, the Fairfax management's need to find cost savings following both papers' dramatic loss of classified and other advertising revenue has involved much of the copy written by journos in Melbourne, Sydney and Canberra now being run in both papers (and the *Canberra Times*). While this is a pity, it's similar to the economies of scope being pursued by News Corp's six capital-city tabloids, and hasn't affected each Fairfax paper's primary focus on fully reporting developments in its own city—an important element in both mastheads' bid for survival in a threatening age. I'll give you my best advice on how to pull it off.

CHAPTER 2
EARLY LIFE OF A CHRISTIAN SOLDIER

It cannot be emphasised too strongly that balanced, well-adjusted, stable and secure people do not, on the whole, make good writers, including good journalists.

Paul Johnson

The main thing you need to know about my early life is that I was an OK—an officers' kid. Both my father and my mother were officers (ministers) in the Salvation Army and until I left home at 21, the Army and its strange way of life dominated mine. For 45 years my father was in charge of a succession of small corps (churches) around Queensland and New South Wales. This meant our family moved every two years, sometimes after only one year. Every second Christmas holidays was spent packing and I ended up attending five primary schools and three high schools. All that moving meant I have few friends from school days, but it was the only life I knew and I've yet to meet an OK who felt it did them any harm.

Especially for a corps officers' kid, the Army was an all-consuming religion. The whole of every Sunday was taken up attending prayer meetings ('knee drill'), open-air meetings on street corners, holiness meetings in the morning and salvation meetings in the evening, plus, for 'junior soldiers', directory meetings in the morning and company meetings (Sunday school) in the afternoon. At all these meetings I'd wear the appropriate uniform, of course. Most were held at 'the hall' (my father was rarely in charge of corps big enough to call their meeting place a 'citadel'). On weeknights there'd be 'legion' (a kind of boys' brigade) and, as I grew older, band practice and songster (choir) practice.

The Gittinses are an Army family. Of his 13 siblings, three of my father's brothers and three of his sisters also became officers. An aunt and an uncle of my father's were officers, and six of my cousins are officers, plus a couple of their kids, making four generations of officers in all. My parents were strict, but never stern or preachy. They did their duty to God faithfully (my father's favourite word and highest ambition) and cheerfully, never questioning their superiors' arbitrary decisions to shift them hither and yon. But they lived for their children and though, as products of their age, they were undemonstrative, I was never in any doubt that I was loved. I was, in any case, the baby of the family.

Even among other Salvationists my parents were rather old-fashioned in their disapproval of 'worldliness'. Like all Sallies they disapproved of drinking, smoking and all forms of gambling (we were allowed to play Happy Families or snap, but never with ordinary playing cards for fear people might think we were gambling), but they also disapproved of makeup, jewellery, dancing, doing anything much on Sundays bar attend meetings, and even going to the pictures.

This last was the one that pinched a little with me. I remember wandering the streets alone on Saturday afternoons while my mates were at the matinee, rolling Jaffas down the aisle and watching serials and such exciting flicks as *Smiley*. But no one in my family was rebellious, and nor was I. It wasn't until I was a full-time student at Newcastle University that I began sneaking off on Wednesday afternoons to see a movie at one of the picture shows in Hunter Street. I suspect the experience has left me with an addiction to cinema going. People at the *Herald* will tell you little has changed except the day: I still sneak off to the movies on Tuesday afternoons (what they don't know is that, these days, I usually see three films in a row).

I think my parents' objection to worldliness had as much to do with conservatism as spirituality. Their views had been formed long before the advent of television, so it escaped their strictures. When TV arrived in 1956 their problem with it was purely the prohibitive cost of buying a set. I was never discouraged from joining the throng on the footpath watching telly in the windows of department stores and often went down to see the latest episode of *Robin Hood* outside the electrical store near our house in the inner west Sydney suburb of Leichhardt. When my parents retired my sisters bought them their first telly, on which they happily watched reruns of all the movies they had disapproved of for so long.

All this may help explain why my own kids were deprived of television throughout their school years. My wife, Claudia, rang me at work one day when our first child was still very young to say our house in Redfern had been broken into and our TV stolen. Don't worry, I said, I'll pick up another set on my way home. Don't bother, she said, let's try life without it. I explained to my son, Sandy, that we no longer had a television because someone had stolen it, and he accepted that. We let our kids watch TV at their friends' houses, I took care to buy them the books or toys associated with TV crazes, gave them an unlimited book-buying budget and occasionally rented a telly so Sandy could watch the Rugby World

Cup, but we didn't buy another set until the day our second child, Katie, finished her last HSC exam. Our lack of TV was something I kept dark during the two years I was on a huge part-time retainer to Frank Lowy's Ten Network, but I never felt my inability to watch current affairs television left me at any disadvantage professionally. I got on with my work most nights. As for Claudia, it was her idea. As for the kids, I doubt it did them any harm and may have meant they read and studied more.

At this late stage I'm proud of my Army heritage, proud of my father's contribution, proud of the mark the Army and my parents have left on my values and happy to talk about it—though when I do I quickly become emotional, a trait I inherited from my dad. But growing up as an officers' kid in such a small, strangely behaved and attired sect does make you feel a bit of an oddity and an outsider—not one of the gang. Whenever my kids were embarrassed by the doings of their parents I'd say, until your father turns up at your school wearing a uniform from the Crimean War, you don't have anything to complain about.

Such an upbringing *could* lead to just one ambition in adult life, to fit in and be one of the guys. For me, however, it left me with a distain for the gang and a desire to prove I was better than them, to make *them* envy *me*. As a journalist I've never seen myself as normal nor wanted to be normal. Have I been more ambitious than most? Yes, I guess I have. Why? I think it goes back to my years as a teenager in Newcastle. My father's corps were so small I had few friends my own age and at divisional (diocesan) gatherings was very much on the outer. Looking back, I suspect it left me determined to become someone of note.

Leaving aside the 'social work' of the Army that so many people know and admire, as a church it's just another Protestant denomination, formed when William Booth broke away from the Methodists in London in 1865. It adopted the military metaphor in 1878, also exploiting the huge popularity of brass bands at the time. Just as the Catholic Church is run from Rome, so the worldwide Army is run from London, also as an autocracy, only its general is elected, in much the same way as a pope. Though it administers no sacraments and adheres to no formal liturgy, Army meetings do follow a standard pattern, with much singing of songs and choruses and items from the band and the songsters. The Army were the original happy-clappies.

It is thus a very musical religion, which helps make it more of a subculture. I was taught to play a brass instrument at the late age of 13 and for the first few weeks my father selected the songs (hymns) for his meetings from those few whose second-cornet part the band-master considered I could manage. I played in successive small Army bands until not long before I became a journalist. I haven't played since then, but these days wish I'd practised harder. Although I've long been what the Army would call a backslider, all those tunes, songs and choruses have stayed part of me. I often listen to Army music as I sit up writing at night and the words can move me almost to tears. On the census I still put myself down as Army.

All my family are Queenslanders except me. Before he went to the Army's training college at Petersham at the age of 20, my father, Harold Gittins, grew up on *his* father's dairy farm, *Mechan-burri*, at the end of Gittins Road near Withcott in the Lockyer Valley, not far from Toowoomba.

He came from an extended family that first arrived in Queensland in 1849. My first Australian-born ancestor was my grandmother's grandmother, born at Breakfast Creek, Moreton Bay, when it was still part of New South Wales. Thomas Gittins, my great-grandfather, was a law clerk from London who arrived in Brisbane in 1862 and became a pioneer settler on a farm near Beaudesert. One of his sons, Arthur George, became an Army convert while on a holiday in Sandgate. My father, his fourth child, was born not long after Arthur left Beaudesert to set up his farm in the Lockyer Valley.

My mother, Catherine (Katie) Lennox, the youngest of eight children, grew up on her father's 300-acre cane farm near Home Hill on the Burdekin River in North Queensland. Alexander (Sandy) Lennox had been born in Glasgow in 1859. He put up his age to 'take the Queen's shilling' and join the Northumberland Fusiliers, serving in the second Afghan war before joining his brother Jack in North Queensland. My grandmother, Margaret (Maggie) Algie, also born in Glasgow, came out to marry Sandy at Mount Morgan in 1890. Her sister Isabella was already here, married to Jack. Sandy, who'd worked as a manager of small gold mines and had travelled with Andrew Fisher, a fellow Glaswegian and Australia's fifth prime minister, was one of the district's pioneers. But he died when my mother was 10 and her mother died when she was 14, so she went to live in town with Auntie Bella and Uncle Jack.

Like my father, my mother left school at 12. She worked for a tailoress and for the rest of her life was an accomplished dressmaker, making all our uniforms with their intricate braid and piping. Her aunt was a Salvationist and it was at an Army meeting that she met young Lieutenant Gittins. She too travelled down to the Army's training college at Petersham and in due course was commissioned as an officer. In 1931 my parents married.

Whereas my farm-boy father would have struggled with his studies, my mother was dux of her session. She was an intelligent woman and over the years read widely and undertook many correspondence courses for officers, sent from the Army in London. When I was a boy at Paddington, in inner-city Brisbane, one of my jobs was to go to the local library and select the six or so books she would read in the following week. I was a book-worm—much to my father's disgust—reading all the English series popular at the time: Enid Blyton, *Jennings*, *Billy Bunter*, *Biggles* and Richmal Crompton's wonderfully erudite *Just William* books. For years my ambition was to be a librarian.

My parents' marriage was one of strange mutual dependence. My mother was highly intelligent, but painfully shy, with no sense of direction. She left all the grocery shopping to my father (which suited him because he wanted to patronise the shopkeepers who made weekly contributions to the Army's 'shop league') and when she needed to shop for clothes, or more likely clothing material, he would take her. Every day he cooked breakfast for the family, organised the school lunches and gave my mother breakfast in bed.

My father was a simple, trusting, hard-working, gentle man who saw looking after 'little women' as one of his callings. He was the most saintly man I ever expect to meet simply because, unlike the rest of us, he never harboured an uncharitable thought about anyone. We saw plenty of him because, though he worked long hours, he did so from home, the Army 'quarters' (manse). My mother did all the worrying and decision-making. Despite his limited schooling, my father never used bad grammar. Why not? Because, I realised, she had long ago beaten it out of him.

When we were appointed back to the Newcastle area, my father's name would occasionally appear on a roster of ministers whose sermon the previous day would be reported in the *Newcastle Herald*'s Monday morning 'From the Pulpit' column. The minister was required to submit his sermon notes, which (presumably) the most junior cadet reporter would cut down for the column. The first time my father submitted his sermon, what appeared in the *Herald* bore no resemblance to anything he had said nor anything any minister would have thought made sense. So my mother stepped in and, on future occasions, she would write out a sermon, giving one copy to the paper and another to my father. He would preach an approximate version of it, but what appeared in the *Herald* would be virtually unchanged. That's how I know any skill of mine as a journalist comes from my mother. As it happens, her sister Bessie had been a reporter on the *Ayr Advocate*.

My father was too young to go to the First World War and not at all keen to go to the Second when he had a shy wife and three children he needed to look after. My mother was appalled at the thought of being left to fend for herself. Eventually, and despite his occupation, my father was called up, but after two or three weeks was sent home because he had flat feet.

The great event of his life was the Depression of the 1930s and I used to hear about it at breakfast most mornings. What I didn't know until my sisters told me later was the lengths to which he, as the Army officer in successive Queensland country towns, went to help men passing through, as required by the rules of the government's meagre 'susso' (sustenance) payments. Many knew to come to the back door of the Army quarters, where they'd get any help he could give. He made billycans with a tin and some wire, filling them with dripping he'd saved and potatoes he'd grown. He had a shoemaker's last he would use to repair their boots with rubber soles cut from old tyres. And he had an enema kit he'd use to give a clean out to anyone who needed it.

I'm an early baby boomer but, as you will have gathered, not because my parents married soon after my father returned from the war. My brother, Clyde Lister, was born in 1934, 14 years before me. My sister Ruth Glenda came soon after and my younger sister Lynnet Dawn arrived in 1941. Coming almost seven years later, was I a mistake? Not at all, my siblings assure me. My mother wanted a big family, the problem was affording another mouth to feed. My father was often unable to draw his full, though meagre, salary. Things looked up when Clyde started helping my father collecting at a speedway but, even so, my father's boss, the divisional commander (or bishop), gave him £5 out of his own pocket to help with the cost of the new baby, Ross Roderick, who arrived late and with two teeth on Friday, 13 February 1948. How did my parents manage such remarkable family planning, I asked. Abstinence, how else?

In my names and my brother's you can detect shades of my mother's lowland Scottish patriotism. She had Orangemen on both sides of her family and faithfully passed on their prejudices. Only much later, when visiting Ireland and Scotland, did I realise the Irish were terribly friendly while the Scots could be dour and bad-tempered.

Novocastrian boy

I was born in the Newcastle suburb of New Lambton. Almost a year later we were appointed to Cessnock, where we stayed for three years while my brother completed the leaving certificate. Then it was on to Hornsby and Waverley, where Clyde took up a bursary at Sydney University. He went off to work for the Commonwealth in Canberra, where he eventually became a government actuary, while the rest of the family spent just a year in Albury—where my sisters and I got up at three in the morning to watch the Olympic torch go through—because the winter cold contributed to my mother's ill-health. Then it was up to the warmer climes of Brisbane for two years, two years back in Sydney at Leichhardt, one in Bathurst (too cold for Mum) and finally four appointments in the Newcastle district, at Lambton, Merewether, East Maitland and Shortland. It sounds madly peripatetic but, even so, whatever requests family considerations caused my father to make to his bosses were always granted. My first year at high school was spent at Fort Street Boys and then a year at Bathurst High before third year at Newcastle Boys. I decided three high schools were enough and got my father to ask his boss to let us stay in the Newcastle area so I could complete my schooling at Newcastle Boys. In the end we stayed long enough for me to go on to Newcastle University. Since I'd been born in Newcastle, spending most of my teenage years there allowed me to think of myself as a boy from Newcastle rather than a religious nomad, something I value.

I suppose I could also see myself as a working-class boy. My parents' income was certainly low enough to qualify and most of the 'comrades' in our corps were workers, but my parents' values didn't fit. My mother esteemed education and saving—the great middle-class virtues, both requiring delayed gratification—my father's instinct was to see the boss's point of view and, like almost all the Army officers I knew, their politics were conservative. Mum described Joh Bjelke-Petersen as her pin-up boy, and when one of my uncles in Queensland heard he'd acquired a new grandchild he said, 'Ah well, another vote against the Communists.'

Newcastle Boys High was the selective school my brother had been attending when I was born. Although I was smart enough to make it to my second selective school, I wasn't diligent enough to get anywhere once I'd arrived. I was always well down in the year and usually in the E class—in the days when all classes were 'streamed' (graded) and teachers made no effort to protect your fragile 'self-esteem' by disguising how poorly you were doing in the competition. At the Intermediate I just scraped through English and failed maths. I can't remember doing much study for the Leaving Certificate, and the results I got were pretty undistinguished—two As and four Bs—but in those days that was enough to get you into uni.

I guess I'm proof that there's life after an undistinguished academic career. But there's a lot about my school days I can't remember. For instance, I can't remember ever playing any sport at Newcastle Boys. I guess I must have, but it's just a blank in my mind. All I can remember was being keen to be a Library Boy because they were allowed to skulk in the library on Wednesday afternoons. And I would much rather have been covering library books than playing sport. The only school prize I ever got was for being a Library Boy.

But it's not just that I've forgotten so much, it's also that my memories aren't always accurate. When I attended my 20-year reunion at the Newcastle Rugby Club in 1984, I was looking forward to meeting our old headmaster, Harold Beard, and was completely nonplussed when the principal in our final year was introduced as Mr Richardson. Who was he? Where had he sprung from? It took me a long time to remember that Mr Beard had retired in our second last year and been replaced in our final year by the much less memorable Mr Richardson.

I do remember our modern history teacher, Mr Carter (Orsen Carter, we called him), who said something one day I never forgot: that for an exemplary example of written English we should follow his lead and read the editorials in the then *Newcastle Morning Herald*. I thought of that many years later when I was writing editorials (or 'leaders') in the *Sydney Morning Herald*. I guess my prose wouldn't have been up to Mr Carter's standards, but I hope I knew a bit more about the subject matter than most editorial writers did. Seeing the leader-writing process from the inside is like watching sausages being made—it's better not to know what goes into them.

My last English teacher was Mr Kerr (Cat's Eyes). I was in the E class, but one day I put up my hand and asked him if he thought it was worth me trying to get an A in English. He unhesitatingly told me not to bother—but as it turned out, I got one. Some tiny inkling of my future career was starting to peep through. Mr Kerr was also the careers adviser, but I don't blame him for the careers advice I got, which typically in those days was uninspired and uninspiring. I probably told them I wanted to be an accountant (which was true), they looked at my academic performance, saw I was quite good at a subject called accountancy but not much else, and grudgingly suggested that, if I tried really hard, I could probably manage a part-time tech course in accounting. Perhaps all the tough love we got from teachers in those days—all the negative comments on report cards—had a useful effect in making us determined to show we were better than our teachers assumed. I enrolled in accounting at uni rather than tech, and had no trouble doing well in it. It was only the economics that gave me trouble.

But Mr Kerr ended up doing me a favour. A local chartered accountant, Ray Patrick, came to the school saying he needed to employ a junior audit clerk. Mr Kerr recommended me, I took the job with alacrity and worked for Ray Patrick for two years before going to uni full-time and then moving to Sydney to work for one of the big chartered accounting firms.

Another teacher, Lyle Abell, taught me both accountancy (in which I got my other A) and economics (only managed a B). It took me a long time to see the point of economics. Many years later, after I became economics editor of the *Herald*, I was invited back to a lecture day to talk to HSC economics students from various schools in the main lecture theatre at Newcastle Uni, one I had sat in many times as a student, the fragrantly named BO1. As I held forth to the schoolkids it suddenly struck me that, when I was studying economics at school, I wouldn't have understood a word of what I was saying to those students. The modern HSC is a lot more intellectually demanding than the Leaving was in my day.

Everyone is supposed to have a memorable teacher who inspired them with ambition or a love of learning. But in the eight schools I attended, only one heroic, outstanding teacher sticks in my mind: the long-time headmaster of Boys High, Harold Beard. He was probably the most eccentric man I've ever observed—not in his dress or demeanour, but in his beliefs and practices as a teacher. He had his own ideas—his own educational priorities—and he was in charge of exactly the right school to implement those ideas, not caring for a moment that others may have considered him odd, as I'm sure many did. In this he set a great example to us boys. He was a pioneer in the field of sex education, with his endlessly repeated showings of the battered and scratchy film *Human Reproduction*, from which kids, by the time they were in fifth year, could recite long passages by heart.

He was a great believer in current affairs and public speaking. Two days a week would be divided into nine periods rather than eight, and the last period of the day would be devoted to this purpose. The senior or junior half of the school would go to the assembly hall to listen to a guest speaker, while the other half would go to their roll teacher who would take them in 'speech training'. Sometimes we'd do debating, other times we'd each give two-minute speeches in front of our schoolmates on a topic we'd been given only a few minutes to think about. I think that was excellent training for boys likely to end up in positions of leadership. Nothing could be better calculated to help people overcome their fear of public speaking.

Mr Beard did all he could to encourage our interest in current affairs. We would memorise the names of Asian political leaders for his regular current affairs tests—Lee Kuan Yew, Tunku Abdul Rahman, Sukarno, U Thant and many more. He conned many of us into subscribing to Sydney University's *Current Affairs Bulletin*, and every month or so the school corridors would be awash with bulk copies of the latest *CAB* that none of us were keen to read. Then there was his enormous faith in the ability of the United Nations to deliver world peace. We had a loudspeaker system in every classroom and, at times of international tension, Mr Beard would listen to the radio and then excitedly break into our lessons to bring us the latest uplifting news from the world. Years later I realised how few people shared Mr Beard's faith that the UN would solve all our problems.

My favourite guest speaker at the assemblies was Professor Brinley Newton-John, the vice principal of Newcastle University, who'd been in the British secret service during the war. He used to tell us he was sworn to secrecy about his wartime exploits, but still managed to say enough to keep us interested. Only later did I realise we should have been more interested in seeing and hearing his daughter Olivia.

As a boy I thought the Second World War had happened in the olden days. Later I realised how recent the war was when we were growing up in the 1950s and early 60s. Most of our teachers were 'returned men'—and by today's standards it's remarkable to think how many of them were men. In my first two years at Boys High there was only one woman on the staff, the music teacher, Mrs Hindmarsh. But by 1964 she'd been joined by three other women. Perhaps that was Mr Richardson's doing. I note that whereas Mr Beard was always referred to as the headmaster, Mr Richardson was the principal. When you remember how comparatively rare university degrees were in those days—a lot of returned men had the qualification ASTC (associate of Sydney Technical College)—it's surprising that almost all our teachers had BAs. Perhaps that was Mr Beard's doing—or perhaps in those days, unlike today, the Education Department accepted that a selective school needed highly qualified teachers.

When the guest speaker didn't turn up to school assemblies, Mr Beard, who was a pianist, would lead us in community singing from a special school songbook he'd had printed. These events were riotous fun. Mr Beard's problem was that, from the piano on the stage, he needed one pair of glasses to see the music and another to see us. So while he was frantically juggling his owlish glasses, the fifth years would be up the back demanding to sing our favourite, the 'Drinking Song' from the *Student Prince*: Drink, drink, drink! Let every true lover salute his sweetheart—let's drink!

One event that sticks in my mind was when, in 1963, the minister for education, Mr Wetherell, came to open the new library. I've never seen a place so on edge; the staff were beside themselves. The school had been cleaned and polished from top to bottom and a collection of potted aspidistras had been acquired from somewhere and distributed strategically along the corridors. It was all so pristine that any boy who dared set foot in the school was roared at and we were kept out in the playground for the whole day until the minister arrived. But then it rained during the opening ceremony and everyone had to rush inside. I often thought of that day 11 years later when I was a cadet reporter in the press gallery at Parliament House in Macquarie Street. The then minister for education could have been an old Labor lag, a drunk and a buffoon, a figure of derision around the House, but were he to visit a particular school, everyone from the principal down would quake in their boots.

I was sorry not to be able to make it to my 40-year school reunion in 2004, but I did find the 20-year reunion quite memorable. I know that only those confident of their success are inclined to show up to reunions, but even so I was struck by how many people in my year seemed to have ended up as barristers and medical specialists. I suppose I shouldn't have been surprised—when you take the brightest boys in a city as big as Newcastle it's not surprising a lot become professionals—but I guess I hadn't realised what a high-powered bunch we were. Our year, and every year at Boys High.

But the thing I found really disconcerting that night at the rugby club was the way the whole show was taken over and run by our prefects, with the school captain presiding, wearing his school blazer, lovingly preserved by his mother and into which he could still fit. What disconcerted me was that this arrangement instantly re-established the social hierarchy that had existed in my last year at Boys High: prefects on top, followed by the first XIII, then the first XI, and so on down to the misfits, choir boys and Library Boys. I'd spent the previous 20 years fighting to get myself a bit of social status and here I was cast right back to the bottom of the pecking order.

In the years since leaving Boys High I've often considered the rights and wrongs of selective schools. They're hugely popular with parents these days—and no politician would dare do anything other than add to their number—but the Teachers Federation has long been implacably opposed to them, and there was a time when that opposition was in the ascendancy and some selective schools were deselected, so to speak. I still remember the disappointment I felt when I learnt that Boys High was now nonexistent, with Waratah High taking its place. As I pondered this over the years I realised that most of the big-name Sydney selective schools had been left intact—Sydney Boys, Sydney Girls, North Sydney Boys, North Sydney Girls, although the two Fort Streets had been merged. Indeed, just about the only other selective school to bite the dust that I heard of was John Howard's old school, Canterbury Boys. How come we got the chop when so many others survived? My theory is that many of our most influential old boys rose in the ranks of BHP and so were all down in Melbourne and thus unavailable to do what I suspect the influential old boys of the surviving schools did—have a quiet word with the premier: 'Of course, Premier, the new rules won't be applying to my old school will they?' 'Oh no, Sir John, not to your old school.'

I once met a university education lecturer who was very much opposed to selective schools, arguing, among other things, that they were bad for the confidence of the kids selected. These kids had come from being first or second in the class at their primary school, only to discover that at high school they were well down in the year, and this would lead them to doubt their abilities and stop trying so hard. I don't accept that. I didn't see much evidence of it at Fort Street or Boys High, and it ought to be counteracted by the fact that you're thrown into a whole group that's travelling much faster than the individual kid would be travelling back at the comprehensive high school, as well as having a lot more expected of them by their teachers at the selective school. If anything, I think going to a selective school frees bright young kids from the peer-group pressure at comprehensive schools not to act brighter than the others and not to do nerdish things like bringing a violin to school.

I think kids in selective schools are more tolerant of individual differences—you can be a bit odd and no one thinks much about it. Certainly, that was my experience at Boys High. I realised this later when I went to work for a big chartered accounting firm in Sydney, which was staffed by a lot of private school boys. They just couldn't help themselves, remarking continually on the respects in which I differed from all of them: my oddball religion and even what they regarded as my odd political opinions.

What we had at Boys High was a good mix of classes. There must have been plenty of middle-class boys, the bright sons of bright fathers who were the town's business and professional people, but there was also a high proportion of boys who were the bright sons of fathers who were just ordinary workers. We had a mixture of classes but we weren't terribly conscious of it. People were different in some way, but what of it? The denizens of the New South Wales Right look on the Labor Party not as a party trying to advance the interests of all the battlers and disadvantaged, but as a ladder the bright sons of workers can climb to achieve their overwhelming goal in life: to escape the working class. I think Boys High filled that ladder role for many of the boys who attended it.

How well did the experience of starting your career through life at a school like Boys High equip you for the fight to get ahead in the world? Did going to Boys High heighten your ambition? Well, I suppose it must have provided a good base and made many of us more ambitious. Although we didn't have famous old boys constantly paraded before us as they had been at Fort

Street, you can find running through the rhetoric of Mr Beard and Mr Richardson the expectation that we were bright, intellectually privileged boys who would go far and had an obligation to contribute to the advancement of our nation.

Growing up in the working-class town of Newcastle left many of us feeling we were outsiders with something to prove, many of us with a burning desire to prove we could make a better fist of material advancement than our fathers had. We didn't have the natural self-assurance, the born-to-rule mentality of the kids attending private schools, but we did have a belief that we lived in a meritocracy, where those who were bright enough and worked hard enough could get ahead. It was the very opposite of the Old School Tie. Perhaps it was this positivity that Boys High added to our attitudes as boys growing up in a working-class, anti-boss town like Newcastle.

Hanging on at uni

I arrived at Newcastle University in 1965, the first year of its autonomy from the University of New South Wales and its last year at the old campus at Tighes Hill before moving to its new bushland site at Shortland. I was quite overawed as I walked around the old campus—I thought I was surrounded by people who were much brighter than I was—so I resolved to work a lot harder. It worked for the first year, but then I eased off. I actually failed macro-economics at my first attempt (and failed commerce stats twice) but in those easy days failing a few subjects earnt you only the minor inconvenience of having to 'show cause' as to why you should be allowed to repeat.

I was active in the Evangelical Union—our heroes were the bright young sparks who came up to speak to us from the Anglicans' Sydney diocese—and once got co-opted at the last minute into the uni's undergraduate debating team, which went to the national intervarsity competition at the University of Queensland and, despite losing our first debate, won the repechage and survived as far as the final. I spent much of my time in the students' union drinking coffee and arguing with friends, and remain convinced it taught me as much about how to handle myself intellectually as most of the lectures I attended.

My brother-in-law, several of my uni friends and many Novocastrians worked for BHP and its steel-related subsidiaries in Newcastle, and I did, too. In the uni long vacation I got a holiday job, where they set me to work sweeping the dirt yard beside the coke ovens. But it was impossible to tell whether you'd made any progress with the dirt, it was blazing hot and at the end of my first day I went home exhausted. On the way home after the second day I rang my old boss Ray Patrick and asked if he needed any help doing tax returns over the holidays. He did, so next day I resigned, taking what little pay I'd earnt. My glorious career at BHP was over so fast I was out of there before the chit for the cost of my safety boots had reached the pay office.

I knew I'd need to get a job at the end of my second full-time year at uni and, as my twenty-first birthday approached, thought getting a job in Sydney presented an ideal justification for leaving home and escaping parental controls, even though I hadn't quite completed my degree and would need to finish it part-time at the University of New South Wales. But hoping one of my cousins would organise a job for me, I discovered I'd left it very late to find myself a berth.

So one day I caught the train to Sydney and went straight to the office of the Institute of Chartered Accountants, where they supplied me with a list of the big firms who might be hiring. In what remained of the day I managed to get around to three or four firms, walking in off the street and asking to speak to the staff partner. Each of them offered me a job. I retired to my big sister Ruth's house in the suburbs to make my decision and next morning rang the firm that had offered me the highest starting salary, Spry Walker & Co.—later to be known by the name of the American firm with which it was affiliated, Touche Ross & Co.—and accepted, before travelling back to Newcastle. My girlfriend at the time, a nurse at Newcastle Hospital, was hugely impressed by my pay of $4000 a year—almost $80 a week! I've told this story several times, to mixed receptions. The point was not what a desirable catch I was but rather the remarkable state of the labour market in the era of 'over-full employment' in the closing years of the postwar Golden Age before everything fell apart after the first OPEC oil price shock in late 1973 and the advent of 'stagflation'. Never again would it be so easy for university leavers to find a job.

I leave the Big Smoke for Sydney

I moved to Sydney early in 1969 and have stayed there ever since, apart from a brief stint in Canberra. A rev I knew from the Evangelical Union, John Chapman, got me a place at a students' hostel near the Uni of New South Wales, a rundown former mansion in Randwick overlooking Centennial Park, owned by a relic from the war, the CENEF—the Church of England National Emergency Fund. I threw myself into the Army, soon becoming secretary of the Paddington corps and secretary of the Salvation Army Students Fellowship, or Studflip as my mother christened it.

As a senior accountant at Spry Walker I tried to get interested in the junior auditing jobs they gave me, including a factory making pneumatic valves, a factory making glass containers and a local distributor of Wolf power tools, but my main duties were two subsidiaries of the Bank of New South Wales, one selling unit-trust investments and another superannuation schemes open to the public. The latter was undemanding, repetitive work but plenty of it, all performed in a labyrinthine building shaped like a multi-layered sandstone slice of cake called the Wales House, at the corner of Pitt, Hunter and O'Connell streets. I'd have taken a lot more interest had I known it was formerly the purpose-built head office and printing plant of the *Sydney Morning Herald*. Fairfax left it in 1955 to move to its newly built headquarters at Broadway, a building said by journos to have been designed by the journalist managing director of Fairfax, 'Rags' Henderson, without air conditioning, 'the oldest new building in Sydney.'

After I'd completed my commerce degree the next step was to qualify as an associate of the Institute of Chartered Accountants in Australia. In my later years at high school I'd thought about careers, but within the very limited horizons of an officers' kid. As leader of the Inter-School Christian Fellowship at Newcastle Boys I was going through the most intensely religious period of my life (an experience that served to inoculate me against religiosity in later life). For a time I thought I'd like to be an Army corps officer like my dad, but this was because I'd been watching him closely and was convinced I could do it a lot better than he did. Not quite a call from God. By rights I should have become a teacher. I was from the teaching class—my sister Lynne and many of my friends at uni became teachers—but it didn't appeal. My father had terrible trouble doing the corps books and stood in awe of other officers who were good at book work—'office johnnies'. I was having no trouble doing accountancy at school, so it was obvious: I'd become an accountant.

When I started working for Ray Patrick I realised there was a class structure among accountants, with *chartered* accountants at the top. If I was a *chartered* accountant I'd have so much status I'd be entitled to address my corps officer by his first name no matter how much older he was. Those were the days before the institute instituted a professional year of tutorials and regular tests for uni graduates with accounting degrees. It developed a syllabus and reading list, issued past papers and conducted twice-yearly examinations at Paddington Town Hall. With no lectures and pass marks set well above 50 per cent, it was a diabolical system. It was hard to come home at night and make yourself work, especially because, with exams twice a year, it was so easy to tell yourself failing an exam didn't matter much. As a commerce graduate, however, I had only to pass the last three subjects.

The old Sydney Showground was within the boundaries of the Paddington corps and many of the comrades helped to collect donations at the Easter Show. I was on the gate one fine night, resplendent in my bandsman's uniform and cap, shaking my collection box, when a gang of my mates from work rocked up for a night out. I don't know who was more embarrassed, me or them.

I hadn't been at Spry Walker long before they introduced a scheme where the best of the senior accountants were sent to help out for a few months in the audit rush-season at branch offices of the American firm of certified public accountants we were affiliated with. It was dogsbody work, poorly paid by American standards but well paid by ours and a great privilege to be selected. The firm paid your return airfare, but you could give them the extra to convert it into a round-the-world ticket and, after the work in America had finished, spend three or four weeks touring Europe and spending all the money you'd made before returning to work in Sydney.

Thanks to my parents' political conservatism, I must have been the last uni student in Australia to oppose the Vietnam War, even though I could have been conscripted. By early 1971, however, I was ready to join a Vietnam Moratorium march down George Street. But what if one of the partners saw me and ruled me out of the American job? To my shame, I walked on the footpath beside the march, with my moratorium badge in my pocket.

I did get selected and was sent to the San Francisco office for a few months in the northern winter of 1971–72. It proved a turning point in my life. It was my first overseas trip—first time in an aeroplane—and San Francisco was an exciting place. For the first time in my life I was under no obligation to attend the Army. I sampled a few of the corps—one in an upstairs room in Chinatown, one in the Mission district where, though the meeting was conducted entirely in Spanish, I knew every song and felt I recognised every cliché in the sermon—but mostly I just enjoyed the hitherto unknown pleasure of having Sundays to myself.

The little half-day job I enjoyed most was one the Californians flicked to me because it had been referred from my office in Sydney. Max Newton—the man who'd done so much to develop the *Australian Financial Review*, as well as virtually manage Arthur Caldwell's campaign in the 1961 election, when Fairfax had utterly uncharacteristically turned against Bob Menzies—was trying to establish himself as a newspaper proprietor and had acquired a small daily commercial newspaper in San Francisco. The Sydney office was his auditor, and my job was just to go down to the docks and establish that the paper really existed. I spent an afternoon lapping up the grandiose stories of the young Kiwi cowboy journo Newton had sent to run the paper.

I spent much of my spare time writing to or phoning my girlfriend back in Sydney, of whom I'd become very fond. To my amazement I received word from home that I'd passed my last exam and was now a qualified chartered accountant. I was elated, but soon found it disillusioning. Over the many years that this had been my goal I'd built up quite unrealistic expectations: once I was qualified I'd be good at my job and filled with the personal assurance such an exalted status would carry with it. But I felt not one whit different. What's more, I knew from the impatience of the American managers I was working for that I wasn't much good as an auditor. I was good at passing accounting exams, but no great shakes as an accountant, a job from which I derived little sense of achievement.

I had a mate from the Sydney office, Ranald Stewart, who'd been sent to the Denver office. When the work was over we were going to meet up in London and tour the Continent together. I got there first and received a letter from my girlfriend breaking it off. Ranald was short of money and wanted to cash in the remainder of his ticket and buy a cheap flight back home from a bucket shop. But the approval for this from our firm took a long time to come through, so we organised our trip around the Continent to go from one Qantas office to the next, where he would inquire whether the permission had come through. Eventually it did.

It wasn't until we got home that we discovered what the problem was. Newton had been running ads for Qantas in his Australian newspapers, which it paid for with 'contras'—Qantas tickets.

Newton, hard up, had used Qantas tickets to pay his audit bill. Our partners hadn't actually bought tickets for us, but had used some of the tickets they'd acquired from Max. So my mate's decision to cash in his ticket had cost the partners money.

Back in Sydney I went through a particularly low period, still upset about the breakup with my girlfriend and realising there was no future for me in chartered accounting, but uncertain about what to do next. At the premature age of 24 I had my midlife crisis. I could do what most non-partner-material auditors did and take a job as an accountant for one of their audit clients, but I didn't have any client I wanted to work for. I considered working as an accountant at Army territorial headquarters, and wrote to the commissioner (the archbishop) offering my services at bargain rates. He thought of me as a young troublemaker from the students' fellowship and quickly declined.

Meanwhile—and I know this hardly fits with that last dashed ambition—I told my corps officer at Paddington that I'd lost my faith (what kind of God would let your girlfriend drop you?), a proposition he knew he couldn't refute by argument, and stopped going to meetings.

Then I had an idea: I had about 40 years of my working life left; how much difference would it make if I took just one of those years and wasted it? None. So I'd take a year off, have some fun, then resume my career. There was a shortage of accountants so, after the year was up, I'd buy a copy of the Saturday *Herald*, pick an accounting job I liked the sound of and ring them up: 'I've got good news for you, I'm accepting your offer.' I figured I could probably survive as an accountant if I was working for a firm with a product I could get interested in. As a reader, I wouldn't mind working for Angus & Robertson, the publishers, or maybe John Fairfax.

A normal person taking a year off would have spent it beachcombing, but I wanted something more intellectually satisfying. I'd go back to uni for a year, but this time I'd pick a subject purely for interest, not for a meal ticket. At first I thought I'd do an MBA, and passed the Princeton test for admission to the MBA course at the Uni of New South Wales, on the strength of which the commerce department offered me a job as a part-time tutor of first-year accounting. I accepted.

But then I realised an MBA would get me deeper in the commercial world, whereas I was trying to pull back. I'd been attending a night course at the Workers' Educational Association on trends in contemporary journalism, run by the journo-turned-novelist Frank Moorhouse. I loved it. One night he advised that if any of us were thinking of doing the New South Wales Institute of Technology's new degree in journalism and public relations we'd better get on with it because applications closed next week. I thought it sounded a lot more interesting than an MBA, so I applied—while keeping the part-time tutoring.

The course, which was to become the BA (Communications) at the University of Technology, Sydney, involved smatterings of psychology, sociology, economics and journalistic writing. The writing class was run by Terry Mohan, formerly an English teacher at Sydney Tech. I owe Terry much. One day he announced that the students' union was trying to start a student newspaper and needed an editor. I had dabbled in amateur journalism in various Army publications for years, so I volunteered. So did another member of the class, Jane Richardson, an experienced subeditor at Fairfax. We became the co-editors of *Newswit*, each paid $50 a week. Jane did all the subbing and layout, and dealt with the printer; I wrote most of the copy, with help from other members of the class. I had no time for student newspapers banging on about Marxism and foreign affairs, and figured it wasn't what our mainly part-time students were looking for. Our focus should be on the running of the institute and whether students were getting good treatment. Jane livened up my copy, changing the name of some administration heavy from McMillan to McVillain, Ron Werner became von Werner and the representative of the non-academic staff on the institute council became the non-academic Mr Soandso. We had a lot of undergraduate fun.

Terry knew I was only staying for a year and as the year was drawing to a close he asked me about my plans—had I thought of going into journalism? I hadn't. I'd assumed I was too slow a writer and too bad a speller to be a journalist. But he got me thinking. I'd been writing articles solidly for a year, they'd been subbed by a professional sub and she'd changed very little of what I wrote. She'd corrected any spelling mistakes without thinking it worthy of comment. Maybe I *could* hold down a job as a journo. Terry said he knew the cadet counsellor at the *Sydney Morning Herald*, Kath Commins, and would get me an interview. Meanwhile, I applied for a cadetship at the ABC (not interested) and went for the obvious: an interview with the editor of the *Australian Financial Review*, Peter Robinson (ditto). Decades later Peter told me he'd wanted to hire me but his boss, managing editor V.J. Carroll, wouldn't let him.

And years later I realised Terry hadn't just got me an interview at the *Herald*, he'd given me a very big tick. I arrived with a sheaf of issues of *Newswit* over my arm as examples of my work, but Commins showed no curiosity. She said the editor of the Hobart *Mercury* had asked her to keep an eye out for potential cadets so, if the *Herald* wasn't able to use me, would I be interested in a job with the *Mercury*? I said I didn't fancy having to move to Hobart, but if that's what I had to do to get into journalism, I would. Much later I realised it was a trick question. The *Mercury* wasn't part of Fairfax, why would its editor be crossing party lines? And why would he ever want to hire any young person who wasn't a local? But I had given the perfect answer, demonstrating how keen I was to be a journo.

From the hundreds of school leavers and graduates who'd applied—in those days the annual intake of about six was spread roughly equally between the two groups—I made the short list. The next step was an interview with the news editor, Alan Dobbyn. Again, I discovered many years later he'd checked me out with a neighbour, Norm Hilton, one of my supervisors at Touche Ross. Dobbyn told me he couldn't believe a qualified accountant would stick it out long as a cadet journalist, but he was prepared to take the risk. I'd beaten off the competition and made it in.

While I waited to start the new job, a mate and I took a holiday in New Zealand. We stayed a few nights with a Sally couple I knew, Roger and Wendy Cresswell, who were running a two-teacher school in the country. Roger, who'd worked briefly as a reporter for New Zealand Associated Press before escaping to teaching, couldn't believe I'd be so foolish as to exchange the high status of chartered accounting for a lowly job as a reporter. But I saw journalism as a highly enviable, even glamorous occupation and couldn't wait to get started.

CHAPTER 3
A FAST TRACK THROUGH THE OLDEN DAYS

If a person is not talented enough to be a novelist, not smart enough to be a lawyer and his hands are too shaky to perform operations, he becomes a journalist.

Norman Mailer

My career at the *Sydney Morning Herald* has been radically different from the norm. In journalism, as in most occupations, you have to walk before you can run. The *Herald* had me running in no time, so much so that I never really learnt to walk.

Newspapers and all news media are fundamentally about reporting the news. Almost everyone, from the newest recruit to the editor, is involved with reporting. Every young journalist starts with news reporting, and only as their reporting skills strengthen are they promoted to the supervision of reporters or moved to the subeditors' desk where they check the reporters' copy for incisiveness, grammar, spelling, length and legal risks, writing the headline to put on the story and laying it out on the page. Only the most experienced reporters—and only a few of these—are invited to leave reporting and write opinion and analysis in features, columns or unsigned editorials ('leaders') on the editor's behalf.

When I joined the *Herald* in February 1974 as a graduate cadet journalist on $100 a week, at what was then considered the very old age of 26, I was put straight to work in the newsroom. But not for long. Within a week or two I was summoned to the office of the editor, Guy Harriott. He'd been told I was an accountant, but what was my ambition in journalism? I said I hoped to become a political journalist. He replied there was no shortage of young reporters wanting to write about politics, whereas those with the desire and ability to write about economics were scarce and in great demand. Accounting and economics were much the same thing, weren't they? I thought only an idiot would imagine so, but kept my mouth shut and decided it was good advice, resolving on the spot to be an economic journalist.

He would like me to have a go at writing some economic features for him. He'd speak to the news editor and get me moved under his wing. So that was the end of my stint in the newsroom, except that on Mondays I was to go down to state parliament in Macquarie Street and act as offsider to veteran state political correspondent John O'Hara, because Mondays were his young assistant's day off.

I liked my weekly visits to state parliament, liked the political milieu, liked meeting the other journos in the press gallery—including a confident young chap working for Radio 2UE and *Nation Review* called Malcolm Turnbull—and liked working with the avuncular O'Hara. He was always calling a passing waiter to bring him some buttered toast and a bottle of Seppelt's Moyston Claret, which he used as a kind of fuel.

One Monday a good-looking young woman came into our room. She was a solicitor working for the Aboriginal Legal Service in Redfern. The staff of the ALS were visiting parliament to protest against the Whitlam government's threat to cut off their grant because they hadn't been keeping good enough records about how the money was spent. She seemed a bit embarrassed by the lobbying, so stayed quite a while chatting with O'Hara. When finally she made to leave, he said, 'Don't go yet, Ross was just about to ask you out.' To my amazement, she stayed. I thought this suggested the chances of rejection were low, so I did ask her out. She was Claudia Sloan, and four years later we invited O'Hara and his good lady to our wedding.

You may not think of journalism as a particularly creative pursuit, but I assure you it is compared to accounting and, particularly, auditing. It may be non-fiction writing, but still you take a blank sheet of paper and a full vocabulary and you paint a picture. The pictures are different from day to day and some are prettier than others. But every time you write, the challenge is to be as creative as possible. It took me no time to realise I got more satisfaction from a day of journalism than from a year of auditing. And I'd been having trouble convincing myself that what accountants did—measure and report profits as accurately as possible—was a particularly valuable contribution to the world. By contrast, I had no trouble believing the big issues with which economists grappled—inflation and unemployment—were matters of both great interest and great importance.

Reporters don't do research, they phone an expert and get a quote. In my early days I was so shy I hated having to phone people I didn't know, or hated having to get past telephonists and secretaries who thought their job was to stop me speaking to the boss. In truth, talking to the press is such a risky business most bosses would want it done by someone pretty senior, if not themselves. Eventually I realised I was calling as an agent of the mighty *Sydney Morning Herald*, and though many people didn't want to talk to Ross Gittins, they did want to talk to the *Herald*, so why should I hesitate? I also realised that just as I'd usually been dealing with people well above my pay grade as an auditor, so it was in journalism.

There was one reporting job I remember, even though the short piece I wrote hit the spike (wasn't published). The chief of staff sent me to cover the annual meeting of the Boys' Brigade. Not the real Boys' Brigade but another one, the personal charity of Sir Vincent Fairfax and his son, John B. Fairfax. This Boys' Brigade had just one meeting place, a two-storey building in Riley Street, Surry Hills. It did, however, have a full-time manager, who had an office somewhere in the city. Huh? How was that possible? Well, it also had another asset: a huge chunk of shares in John Fairfax Ltd. The annual meeting was held in the last remnant of the *Herald*'s presence in Hunter Street, where several of the Fairfax directors had their offices. I was amazed to see these great men of business earnestly debating whether the age of admission for boys should be lowered from eight years to seven.

It took an extraordinarily long time for me to write the features Harriott assigned—only partly because I was always sneaking out of the office to conduct accounting tutorials at the University of New South Wales at Kensington—but the first one I produced, about the fashionable topic of tax indexation, impressed the *Herald*'s economics editor, Alan Wood. He sought me out and from that time became my mentor and effective boss. He sent the blacks (a carbon copy) of another early feature I wrote to the executive editor, David Bowman, for his perusal. Bowman sent the blacks back with the comment 'Mr Gittins is a natural' written in fountain pen at the end. I wasn't sure what a natural was, but it sounded like a compliment. I realise he was right. I hadn't learnt how to report—and would never learn—but from the very beginning I just knew how to write an interesting, readable, understandable feature. Thanks, Mum.

My distinguished predecessor

For about 17 years, the outstanding business and economic writer on the *Herald* had been Tom Fitzgerald, the financial editor. He was a pioneer of investigative journalism, particularly in the financial area, writing columns that exposed the misdeeds of particular Australian companies, making himself as unpopular with the executives of those companies as he was celebrated by our share-owning readers. He also wrote the *Herald*'s economic leaders. And he started his own fortnightly magazine, *Nation*, as a freer outlet for his and his friends' opinions. But in 1970 Fitzgerald was lured away by Rupert Murdoch to write for *The Australian*, a move he came to regret.

The vacuum his departure left at the *Herald* had to be filled by two people. A Kiwi mining writer, J.N. Pierce, took over as financial editor. To find someone to write the economic leaders the *Herald* had to dragoon a young reporter for the *Financial Review*, Alan Wood, who'd recently been sent to report from the London office in recognition of his sterling service in the Canberra press gallery. No doubt he was induced to return and move to the *Herald* with a decent pay rise, plus the title of economics editor, making him opposite number to the *Fin*'s economics editor, Padraic Pearse McGuinness. Even so, his primary task was to write one editorial a day.

Woody had been the *Fin*'s first cadet, joining from school. He gained a BA with a major in economics at the Australian National University while working for the *Fin* in Canberra. He was a far more accomplished journalist than I'll ever be, with a far deeper understanding of economics. In Canberra for the *Fin*, he led its long-running crusade against protectionism, earning him the gallery nickname, A. Tariff Wood. Long after he'd left the gallery his contacts among politicians and senior econocrats were still first-rate. I'm probably the only person to remember that, from Sydney, he broke the story of the Whitlam government's 'loans affair' before the running was taken over by other papers.

And few would remember or ever have known that Woody got wind of the Whitlam government's top-secret plan in 1973 for a 25 per cent across-the-board cut in the rates of all tariffs (import duties), cooked up by an adviser (and subsequently good friend of mine), Professor Fred Gruen, and others as a way of reducing protection and inflation pressure at the same time. But Gruen's collaborators dissuaded Woody from writing the story on the grounds that, were the plan to become public, the tumultuous opposition to it would almost certainly stop it from happening. One reason few old journos know this story is that most political journalists—indeed, most journalists—would regard it as shameful; a failure of courage, even ethical standards. The story comes first; other loyalties be damned. But I'm with Woody. I decided it encapsulated the ultimate ethical test of an economics editor: willingness to put good policy ahead of a good story. More proof I'm not a real journo.

For decades the bureaucratic leader of the fight against protectionism was Alf Rattigan, head of the Tariff Board and inaugural chairman of the Industries Assistance Commission, one of the Whitlam government's least acknowledged but most influential economic reforms. Rats enjoyed Whitlam's confidence, but as prime minister he was subject to many contrary pressures. In Rats' memoir, *Industry Assistance: The Inside Story*, he often recounted battles that had arisen and what he'd rushed across to the PM's office to tell Whitlam. Then he'd record at some length the judgement that great and independent authority the *Sydney Morning Herald* had passed on its leader the next morning. Just how the *Herald*'s leader writer had become so consistently well informed on the issues and so sound in his views, Rats didn't say. But I think I know.

As boss and mentor, Woody was neither tutor nor micromanager. Whenever I'd finished a piece or needed advice I'd have to go across the road and interview him in the pub, where he'd be ensconced with his old *Fin Review* mates—Paddy McGuinness, Maximilian Walsh (known to journos as Thanksamillion for the alacrity with which he accepted junkets) and maybe Max Suich (the first man I heard described as a legend in his own lunchtime, though many senior journos of the time fitted that bill) or Fred Brenchley. They'd be drinking, but mainly they'd be conducting a friendly argument about the latest point of economics or politics. It was a never-ending seminar they used to keep their thinking sharp and take an idea for their next column on a test drive.

In those days daily journalism was a pub-based culture. Journos on morning newspapers worked what a boy from Newcastle would call afternoon shift, starting at 3pm and finishing at 11pm. In practice, they got their copy in much earlier, then repaired to the pub to be on hand while they served out their shift. The pub across the road from the Fairfax building in Broadway was *The Australian*. Printers occupied the front bar, journos the back. In a booth in the back bar was an extension from the Fairfax switchboard. When the phone rang the nearest journo would pick up the receiver, listen, then shout, 'Subs want So-and-so!' and So-and-so would come to the phone to answer their queries. Coming from a long line of teetotallers, hanging round in a pub wasn't my idea of fun.

The unsociable hours journos worked greatly restricted their ability to meet the opposite sex so, although the men outnumbered the women by about six-to-one on the *Herald* at that time, there was a tendency for journos to marry journos—and, I don't doubt, a tendency for long, late hours in the pub to break up marriages. I always thought I was blessed to have a wife from another profession to help keep my feet in the real world. These days, deadlines are much earlier, with 7pm being a late departure from the office for most reporters, so social life is pretty much unaffected. Young journos are better educated and better dressed, with similar numbers of male and female reporters (though not editors). The office pub is long gone.

Newspaper jargon

- head = headline
- lead = first sentence in a news story
- intro = first sentence in a feature or column
- spill = the part of a story continued on another page
- leader = unsigned editorial
- splash = main page-one story with head right across the page
- masthead = name of the paper across top of page one; the newspaper and all its digital platforms
- puff box = strip under masthead promoting stories inside
- woff = 'write-off' summing up a feature or column under the head
- breakout = shorter subsidiary story to a main story; sidebar = ditto
- widow = last line of a par (paragraph) containing a single word
- caption = line of words under a photo
- H&J = a column of type that has been hyphenated and justified
- ragged-edge = a column of type that has been left-justified but not right-justified or hyphenated; often used to distinguish comments from news reports

- circulation = number of newspapers sold
- readership = circulation multiplied by average number of readers per paper
- newsprint = the paper on which newspapers are printed
- beat-up = an exaggerated story
- run = a story being used rather than spiked (discarded). Some runs are better than others
- round = topic area covered by a reporter
- sub = subeditor, who checks a story for spelling, grammar, conformity to house style and possible defamation, writes the headline and places it on the page
- race calling = how parties are performing in the polls or during an election campaign; the ups and downs of the economy, particularly speculation about changes in the official interest rate
- op-ed page = the page of opinion articles and columns opposite the page containing the unsigned editorial

On my way

When I wasn't writing features for Woody and the editor, the news editor would seek my help on special projects. I wrote the whole of the *Herald*'s tax-time guide to filling in your return—did it for at least 10 years, as I recall—and, as the 1974 election approached, was asked to produce a version of Malcolm Mackerras' electoral pendulum based on his invention, the two-party preferred vote. It was just a matter of getting the official voting figures from the last election, doing the calculations and arranging them in order—except that, in those days, the electoral officials would cease distributing preferences as soon as a candidate had attained an absolute majority. To get the two-party proportions you needed full distribution of preferences, and if this hadn't happened you had to do it yourself, using your own reasonable assumptions about, for instance, the way the DLP vote would distribute between Labor and the Coalition. This, of course, was where the great psephologist had knowledge I didn't. So I made assumptions, did the numbers and then compared my results with his. If mine weren't too far off I left them as they were; if they were well off I 'tortured the data' until they weren't.

This was a time when, under the Whitlam government's inexpert economic management, wages were rising rapidly. When the shop assistants' award took their pay to just over $100 a week, it drew much notice. Goodness, that's what I was getting. I went to see the chief of staff, John Rich, to make my case: when I'd switched from chartered accounting to the bottom rung of journalism, I'd assumed my commercial qualifications and experience were of little relevance and so was willing to take a big pay cut. But in the few months I'd been here the *Herald* had done little but take advantage of my professional skills. That being so, shouldn't it be paying me more appropriately? Rich told me to put it in writing and he'd pass it on. So, after just four months of my one-year cadetship (and with no shorthand), I was made a graded journalist. Formally, I was raised to the lowest, D grade, but in reality I was paid as a C. The grades went up to A and then A1 ('super A'), which I reached when I was made economics editor four years later.

Perhaps I should explain that, among journos, to be comfortable with figures was—still is—comparatively rare. Journos tend to be literary not mathematical. Soon after I joined the *Herald* I bought one of the first pocket calculators, a huge, clunky thing sold by Bell & Howell. It hardly did anything more than simple arithmetic, and cost $40. I used it for my work and had reporters coming up and asking me to work out percentage changes for them; they could never remember whether the change went over the starting number or the finishing number. So I asked Rich if I could claim it on expenses. He thought that might raise eyebrows in the pay office, so told me I could claim for two lunches instead. Those were the days before they required receipts.

That was my first lesson in the dark art of journos' expenses. My second came when the assistant chief of staff came to see me waving my expense claim and with a worried look on his face. 'You say here you took a taxi down to police headquarters and a taxi back. You can't justify using a taxi just to pick up your police pass . . .' Oh dear, I thought, now I'm in trouble. I'd actually gone by bus. '. . . so I changed it to say you went to a press conference.' The next lesson came a few months later when I first arrived in the Canberra gallery. At a certain time each week all the journos would sit down and fill in their expense claims. We were each entitled to claim a living-away-from-home allowance. Some would also have been claiming amounts they'd been awarded 'under the table' in lieu of a formal pay rise. What else? I asked Hamish McDonald, who was soon to start making his name as a distinguished foreign correspondent. 'Well,' he said, 'who did you take to lunch?' Didn't take anyone. 'Well, who would you *like* to have taken?'

Finally, the old journos' story about the time there'd been a palace revolution, with rumours that some people might lose their jobs and others be moved. The new boss gathered the journos in the newsroom to explain the new arrangements and settle down the worriers. Any questions? 'Yes,' said an old hack at the back, 'who'll be signing my expenses?'

I may have been glad to be out of accounting, but I still had an accountant's tools in my kitbag. And I make the immodest claim to be the person who invented the 'what you save' tax-cut table. Incredible as it may seem today, in those days the treasurer would announce a change in the income-tax scale and simply give one example of the weekly saving of someone on average weekly earnings. I knew I could do better than that. I would whip up a table for the second edition which allowed you to look up your own weekly wage. It showed how much tax you were paying now, how much you would pay under the new scale and, hence, what your weekly saving would be. When the *Herald* ran such a table, our stablemate, *The Sun*, would run it in its afternoon edition and Murdoch's *Mirror* would simply lift it. I did this only two or three times before the treasurer and Treasury got wise and started doing their own. Today it would be unthinkable for the treasurer to announce a tax cut without producing what-you-save tables for reproduction by the media.

When I attended my first federal budget lockup in August 1975, I discovered we were in the habit of taking in with us someone from Fairfax's auditors. 'He can't do anything for you that I can't,' I said, and we've never taken the auditors in since. I haven't missed a budget lockup since that first one.

Woody wasn't terribly happy with the services of the *Herald*'s economics correspondent in Canberra at the time, Alan Thornhill, and so towards the end of my first year he began urging I be sent down to replace him. The Canberra bureau chief, Brian Johns, objected that I was too inexperienced as a reporter and he was dead right. But Woody prevailed and late in December I moved into the bureau, a small room housing about eight journos as part of a long wooden hut perched on the roof of the Senate side of the old parliament house.

Thorners was away on holidays on the day I arrived in the bureau, so I asked to be shown his files. 'They're over here,' some heavy replied, 'but what business is it of yours?' I've been sent to replace him as economics correspondent. 'Well, no one told us. Does Thornhill know?' He did when he got back from holidays and read the letter from the news editor waiting for him at home. I was extraordinarily grateful Thorners didn't hold it against me, and we became friends. I have a theory that extroverted journos stay as reporters, whereas introverts gravitate to the subs' desk, where they're able to have less contact with people. When chief subs become news editors, as was common in the old days, a lot of people who deserve to be told things to their face aren't.

In my first week in Canberra I had to come in on Christmas Day to help the senior chap manning the fort, Chris Snow. Before an uneventful shift was over we learnt that Darwin had been struck by a cyclone, but all communications were down. I wasn't much help, but Chris frantically called everyone he could think of until he stumbled on a colonel at a military base in Townsville who'd had brief radio contact with the military in Darwin. Chris' story next morning was by far the most well-informed but, as usual, we soon lost leadership of the story to other papers.

Back in reporting, my performance was as undistinguished—unsatisfactory—as might be imagined. It wasn't helped by the fact that only the tiniest handful of reporters on the paper were entitled to a byline. The rest of us were 'by a Staff Correspondent'. So no one I talked to had heard of me, I had no track record and they had little way of monitoring how faithfully I used the information they gave me. Much better to talk to the bylined guy.

One day in question time, Bert Kelly, the *Fin*'s Modest Member, a lifetime campaigner for free trade with a well-developed sense of humour, asked the new treasurer, Jim Cairns, whether, if printing money was such a good idea, he'd go down into the basement and print a lot more. Cairns replied that he just might. I phoned Woody in Sydney and he was very keen on the story, but then I spoke to the economist in Cairns' office who convinced me it wasn't a story because the boss had been joking. Next day every other paper went big on it. Lesson learnt: treasurers aren't allowed to joke about serious matters.

An important innovation at the time was the Bureau of Statistics' move to provide 'seasonally adjusted' estimates of its main indicators of the state of the economy, thus allowing valid comparisons to be made between successive months. Since they were so new, I took care to label the seasonally adjusted figures whenever I used them. The chief sub, Alan Peterson, informed me I was to make no use of these estimates because 'the *Herald* only reports the real figures'. It would have helped if he'd had the humility to let me explain seasonal adjustment to him before he made his ruling. These days we quote only the seasonally adjusted figures, not even bothering to label them as such.

In my 15 months in the gallery—which encompassed the very best year to be an observer, 1975, culminating in the Dismissal—I probably wrote only one piece of note, one giving the lowdown on the confidential security checks ASIO performed on ministerial staff and others in sensitive jobs. I knew a bit about it because a mate from Newcastle who was working for Clyde Cameron, Milton Cockburn, had given my name as a referee—yes, the gents claiming to be from the Attorney-General's department did want to know if he was gay—and because a Sally mate who was a reasonably senior bureaucrat slipped me a document.

My undistinguished performance as a reporter couldn't have gone on for many more months before I was pulled back to Sydney and given a more menial task. Fortunately, something turned up to make me the exception that proves the Peter Principle's contention that people rise to their level of incompetence. I got promoted beyond my level of incompetence to a job I was better at.

Back to head office

Woody got an offer to work for a former *Fin Review* colleague, David Love, who was now proprietor of a highly successful private-subscription economic newsletter, *Syntec*, which specialised in knowing the mind of Treasury. Woody wanted to leave as soon as possible, but the *Herald* was in no hurry to let him go because the award required him to work out three months' notice. Woody thought finding a suitable replacement was the key to his early release, so he began pushing me as his obvious and highly satisfactory successor.

I was excited and frightened by the prospect in equal measure. It had been my ambition to succeed Woody one day, but I'd thought it would happen sometime in the next decade. The economics editor, author of a daily editorial, was the *Herald*'s in-house authority on economics with a well-formed opinion on every topic. I couldn't remember much of the economics I hadn't properly learnt at uni up to a decade earlier; there was this furious fight between Keynesians and monetarists, and I hadn't decided whose side I was on.

I thought the chance that I'd fail in the job was high, but decided I'd be a mug not to take the risk. If I did fail I'd beg them not to sack me but just strip me back to the ranks and throw me in the finance section, where I'd use my accounting background to attempt a more low-key career as a business journo. The one advantage I had was that Woody had given me plenty of notice of what might happen. I had to acquire some opinions in a hurry, and I thought of a great shortcut: I would read and re-read Woody's daily editorials, internalising all his opinions as my own.

Meanwhile, I was summoned to Sydney for an interview with the editor and boss of the leader-writers, Harriott. He was terribly right wing, having presided over front-page editorials thundering for the removal of the Whitlam government. What if he asked about my political sympathies? What if he quizzed me to determine the depth of my economic knowledge? I needn't have worried; neither subject arose. Woody had assured him I was 'sound' and that was good enough for him. When could I start? They'd raise my pay and start me off as economics writer, promoting me to economics editor once I proved myself. He didn't mention it but another advantage was that, as Woody's successor, I would automatically inherit his place on the tiny, board-approved list of people entitled to bylines.

I arrived back in the Sydney office in Woody's last week, which was only a week or so short of his full three months' notice. The first leader I had to produce was a full-length job written on the fly in comment on the Fraser government's first mini-budget, delivered that day. Woody was too busy attending multiple farewells—none of which I had time to attend—to give me much help. But I survived and, as the weeks passed, realised I was doing OK.

The leader-writers consisted of three old boys—Harriott, his deputy, Harry Kippax, responsible for foreign affairs leaders and formerly the *Herald*'s distinguished theatre critic, and Harriott's Kiwi mate, Bob Bell—and me. We ran two leaders a day; my job was to write one of them so the other three had only to write one more between them. Harry would see some figures for retail sales or overseas trade in the morning's paper and suggest I write about them. I'd patiently explain that they didn't prove much. His stock reply was, 'Well, shouldn't we say that?' But when some foreign disturbance was brewing he'd say, 'Want's watching.' Harry could never write on any topic until his copy of *The Economist* had arrived. And when a few years later Bowman made him share his subscription with a rival, Peter Hastings, he almost went on a one-man strike. Every night we'd get the leaders down the chute by seven o'clock, when a *Herald* driver would take Harriott and Bell to their dinner at the Macquarie Inn in Macquarie Street. I'd duck home to Paddington for dinner, then we'd all come back to check the proofs before leaving for the night.

I blush to think of many of the leaders I wrote. I was travelling rapidly up the economic commentator's learning curve and much of what I had to learn was stuff that's supposed to stay unseen beneath the bonnet. I'd have a long phone call with someone from the Bureau of Stats about how the trade figures were put together, and that's what I'd put in the leader.

But my strongest emotions at the time were amazement and guilt that someone as inexperienced as me could have his ill-formed opinions broadcast to the world. My mates back in accounting had identical educations to mine, but their opinions on economics and politics were spread no further than the bar room. What a fraud I was. And how slaphappy newspapers were to trumpet the opinions of people so ill-equipped. On that latter charge, not a lot has changed in the past 40 years. But for myself I no longer feel guilty. I've spent the intervening years studying my topic—even reading textbooks on my holidays—and now am confident I know more about it than most of my readers.

My strategy of internalising Woody's highly rationalist views worked well. The great beauty of the simple neo-classical model is that it offers a straightforward (though not necessarily palatable) solution to every problem. The old boys would ask me what I thought about some issue, I'd reply and I could see their minds working: 'I've heard that before somewhere. Where have I heard it? Oh, that's what Wood used to say. Oh well, in that case the young fella must be right. Very sound.'

Whatever his politics, Harriott proved a good boss. He was unfailingly courteous and appreciative, trying hard to get me promoted to economics editor just as soon as he realised I was doing well. Querying me about an item on my expense claim, he prefaced it by saying, 'Speaking as one who has always relied on the office for all his stationery needs . . .' His office contained this 1950s building's only fireplace, though he never used it. Much of his time was spent reading thrillers, which he reviewed in the Saturday book pages using the pseudonym of his two middle names, Edward Warre.

Just as there was a time when the governors of New South Wales and Anglican archbishops of Sydney were always recruited from England, so editors of the *Herald* were once always recruited from Fleet Street. Harriott replaced the last of the English editors, John Douglas Pringle, who left after incurring the chairman of the board's displeasure by publishing an Easter editorial devoid of religious sentiment.

Harriott's first act on my arrival among the leader-writers was to instruct me to read *The Economist* each week. His second was to tell me to have lunch with John Valder, now a broker and boss of the stock exchange, who'd been a *Herald* journo in the Canberra press gallery. It may have been the naive questions I asked, but Valder was distinctly unimpressed and urged me to find a job to which I was more suited. It must have been the arrogance of youth that protected me from taking his advice.

My first palace revolution

I hadn't been writing leaders all that long before I witnessed the first of many palace revolutions in my time at Fairfax. In March

1977 the elderly chairman of the board, Sir Warwick Fairfax, great-grandson of the original John Fairfax, was deposed by the board in favour of his son from the first of his three marriages, James Fairfax. Journos believed the other family members had been steeled for it by management. Wocka had been interfering in management decisions and giving some editors a hard time. And everyone feared that, should Wocka die, he might be replaced on the board by his third wife, Lady Mary. The immediate consequences of the coup were favourable, but it intensified resentments that would eventually cost the Fairfaxes the business they'd owned for almost 150 years.

Following a model copied from the *New York Times*, Wocka had installed a rigid bifurcation of the *Herald* between news and opinion. The editor, who effectively reported to the chairman, was responsible only for the editorial page, the op-ed features page and the Saturday book pages; the news editor was responsible for all the other pages and thus the great majority of the staff. As the new chairman, James' first move was to end the bifurcation by installing David Bowman as editor-in-chief over both the editor and the news editor. Bowman's job was to arrest the *Herald*'s falling circulation by making the paper more modern and lively.

He had a lot to work with. The *Herald* I joined was terribly set in its ways. I used to think the chief sub saw it as his job to drain the 'colour' out of every story before putting it in the paper. I remember Harriott railing against some misguided souls who'd started referring to people as Jim Smith rather than Mr J.M. Smith, thus turning the *Herald* into an RSL sub-branch newsletter. One of Bowman's first reforms was to make bylines freely available. Columnists even got *picture* bylines. It was the story of my life: just as I arrived in big-city chartered accounting the practice of not coming back from Friday lunch gave way to the filling in of hourly timesheets; just as I'd got myself onto the exclusive byline list it was abolished. And just as I was getting used to the feature-writers' darg of one a week, a talented young woman named Geraldine Brooks arrived and started doing one a day.

Bowman was a great writer of office memos. Indeed, he was known as Captain Memo. He was the last of the editors who believed in the *Herald* as a 'paper of record' and was always trying to 'shoehorn in' some small story about something, a practice that made our pages look terribly messy. But every editor is looking for a new star performer who could be promoted on his watch and thus help demonstrate how much better the paper had become. As a writer, you can only be discovered and pushed by one editor; to every subsequent editor you're someone he inherited and so can't be part of his big improvements.

Bowman discovered me and became my patron, gradually shifting me from leader writing to column writing. In 1979 he gave me a weekly column—with a picture byline—on the coveted op-ed page, initially with the title 'Principle and Interest', later dropped when titles for personal columns became unfashionable. Apart from leave, I've written that column every week since, establishing my claim to be by far the longest-lasting columnist in the *Herald*'s more than 180 years, and quite possibly the longest-lasting columnist in the country. Two years earlier Bowman had given me a column on Mondays in the business section. Later I took over a Saturday column in business. My steady shift from leaders to columns was made possible by the move into economic leader writing by a former *Herald* deputy business editor, Alan Mitchell, who was my age and became a close friend. Alan completed an economics degree by correspondence while writing leaders. He became the editorial page editor, was poached by John Alexander to do the same job at the *Fin* and is now my competitor as its economics editor.

Bowman urged me to use more 'homely' examples in my columns. Homely wasn't a word that made my young heart race, but now I realise he meant examples from everyday life, and it was good advice. The more high falutin' the economic concept you're explaining, the greater the need for a concrete, utterly familiar example of what you're on about. In June 1978 Bowman put through my promotion to economics editor.

Captain Barbara Bolton was another person to whom I owe a lot. As an officer in the Sallies' editorial department in Melbourne in the 1960s she'd done a lot to encourage me to write for the Army publications she edited. We became lifelong friends, but when she 'left the work' in the late 1970s she fell on hard times. Alan Dobbyn, the news editor, was a churchgoer, so I was hopeful I could persuade him to give Barbara a job as a sub. He hired her as our 'church reporter' and for a couple of years she flatted in Forest Lodge and came to our place for dinner every Sunday night. But before long she felt called back to 'the work' and eventually was transferred to the editorial department at the Army's international headquarters in London. I saw a lot of her while I was there on a British government junket. Too soon, however, she contracted multiple sclerosis and came home to die. If I had my life over I'd be a better friend to my friends.

Bowman once explained to me how to handle 'guidance' from Wocka. When Bowman had been news editor Wocka would occasionally phone to say his friend the premier, Sir Robin/Robert Askin, had just given an important speech and we should run it on page one. 'Well, Sir Warwick,' Bowman would reply, 'that's not my judgement. But if you're instructing me to do so, naturally I'll comply.' Wocka would invariably go to water. The Fairfaxes were so many generations removed from having to make their own decisions and live with the consequences they'd become quite effete.

First taste of 'new technology'

In the late 1970s and early 80s the *Herald* began a painful adaption to the wonders of new technology. At first this was about the computerisation of the processes of producing daily newspapers. Much later it was the advent of the internet and the digital revolution, a threat to the survival of newspapers and a challenge to the traditional practice of journalism still far from resolved.

Fairfax's printing process moved from 'hot metal' to 'cold type'. The old printing process began with a compositor operating a linotype machine that moved trays of metal type, heating each line of type so the letters melded together. Each page would be reproduced as semi-cylindrical metal cast to be strapped onto the drum of a printing press. When a whole page of type and metal photo negatives was assembled on a metal table called 'the stone', it would be inspected by a 'stone sub' journalist, who was permitted to point to, but not touch, anything he wanted changed. Somewhere between the metal page and the end of the sub's finger was the line of demarcation between the work of members of the printers' union and the work of members of the journos' union. If a proofreader discovered that a comp had celebrated his last day on the job by slipping a four-letter word into a classified ad, it might be too late to reset. A printer would hold a chisel over the offending word and hit it with a mallet so it could no longer be seen on the printed page.

The new cold-type printing process began with a computer spitting out at breathtaking speed endless single columns of words. These would be pasted onto a newspaper-sized piece of cardboard, then photographed to make a plastic cast for the press. Under the old process, all subbed, typed copy of reporters was retyped by compositors using the linotype machine's non-qwerty keyboard. Cold type permitted 'the single keystroke': unless it had to be changed for some reason, each letter typed by a reporter would not need to be retyped. (This also permitted ordinary office typists to be used to continue the printing process during a strike.)

Cold type required far fewer printers to be used to get papers out, greatly reducing the company's costs once all the redundancy payouts had been covered. It signalled the end of the printers' many 'old Spanish customs' (or, in the language of Labor's Accord, restrictive work practices) and a marked decline in the printing union's power and militancy. Computerisation meant the journalists and the printers no longer needed to be in physical proximity, so the company seized the opportunity to move the printing from the lower floors of the CBD Broadway office to a new plant in the outer suburb of Chullora. This made it much easier to get paper trucks in and out of the city. More subtly, the move to a 'greenfields site' allowed the company to draw a line under the manning levels and industrial practices at the old site and start with a much tighter regime at the new one. I don't think I've heard a peep from the printers' union since.

The journalistic side of computerisation proceeded far less smoothly. It involved the journos moving from typewriters and carbon copies to keyboards and what were called VDTs—visual display terminals. Essentially, word processors. In a move that proved far too ambitious, the company commissioned a Dutch small business, appropriately called Arsycom, to pull off a technological coup no other newspaper in the word had yet managed.

Unsurprisingly, it failed. But there was much frustration, delay and expense before it and Fairfax gave up. When journos were first asked to write their copy on the new system, each new story would be assigned an eight-digit number. The system would crash several times a day, causing all unsaved work to be lost. Once the system was back up, if you'd lost the eight-digit number or copied it down wrongly there was no other way to recover your story. The only choice was to start again from scratch. When the company decided to try again, it sought a tried and proven system, picking one called Coyote, which was widely used by American newspapers. Worked like a dream.

Early in the computerisation process the journos' union, anxious to get its cut from the cost savings, went on a strike that lasted almost a month. It was the longest strike I've been on; every one since then has lasted just a day or two. It was a disaster, but taught me a lot. My wife was working, so I wasn't worried about the loss of income, but I did come to resent the loss of my time. We'd meet every second day in the Lower Town Hall. I attended most of the meetings, enduring all the speeches by amateur industrial relations experts, and all the self-delusion about how the handful of editorial executives back at Broadway still getting the paper out were drinking heavily and couldn't keep it up much longer, in the hope there'd be a vote to go back and I could throw my puny weight in with the sensible souls. We told ourselves the quality of the paper had collapsed, it had become an antipodean echo of the *New York Times*, and the readers would surely notice. They didn't.

After we'd been out for almost a month someone on the employers' side got smart. They made us the same offer they'd made two days into the strike, but threw in a face-saver: three days extra annual leave, taking our total to six weeks and three days (remember, journos work on public holidays). When you think about it, it was an illusion. We'd be paying for the extra leave ourselves in the form of work intensification because, in any given week, more of our colleagues would be on leave and needing to be covered for. But it sounded nice, so we leapt at it. We had nothing to show for all but the first two days of our strike. A real industrial relations expert told me that once striking workers had 'gone to grass' it was terribly hard to get them back. That by then they would have lost their dispute was obvious.

I resented that, by attending all those meetings, I'd wasted a month. If I'd had more sense I could have been writing a book, reading economics texts, getting my library in order—anything useful. I resolved that, next time, I'd plunge straight into a project and rely on the ABC news to be told when to go back to work. If a strike looked brief, I'd at least get some joy out of it by going straight from the office to the movies. Meanwhile, I'd waste no more of my life attending union meetings to listen to windbags. Years later, when the management and direction of Fairfax became dependent on an ever-changing cast of know-nothing blow-ins from the corporate world, I became a lot more sympathetic to union action. These grossly overpaid cowboys would happily roll over the journos unless we showed 'em we had the gumption to stand up to them.

Bowman's overthrow

The next palace revolution came in 1980 with the retirement of Fairfax's general manager, Bob Falkingham. The Fairfax family acted like lords of the manor, who left all tricky decisions to their estate manager. Wocka's first estate manager had been R.A.G. Henderson who, promoted from the journalist ranks, was managing director for a quarter of a century until 1964. It was Rags who had built the Fairfax empire, acquiring a Sydney afternoon paper, *The Sun*, the Macquarie radio network centred on 2GB, and several members of the Channel 7 television network, centred on Sydney's ATN-7. He also had a hand in acquiring the *Newcastle Herald* and the *Illawarra Mercury*.

Rags was succeeded by his eternal offsider, Angus McLachlan, in 1965. McLachlan, too, had started out as a journalist and worked his way up. I've always had mixed feelings about this tradition of having the company run by journos. It's reassuring to know the decisions are being made by people who, presumably, share their journalists' commitment to ferreting out and trumpeting the truth. But it's worrying that managerial decisions are being made by people with no better experience of good management than a journo. I've always thought that, administratively, newspapers are surprisingly badly managed. Be that as it may, when McLachlan retired in 1969 to join Rags on the Fairfax board, his successor, Bob Falkingham, was no journo. He'd been chief accountant at the Bank of New South Wales before joining Fairfax as its chief financial officer.

The revolution came when Falkingham retired in 1980, to be replaced by two people: Greg Gardiner as general manager and Max Suich (pronounced Such) as chief editorial executive. So? So among the warring tribes of Fairfax journos, this was an upset win for the lefty wild men of the *Fin Review* and *National Times* over the housetrained gentlemen of the *Herald*. Those who'd quietly defied chairman Wocka's 'guidance' on politically sensitive matters—in particular, the Vietnam War—triumphing over those who'd knuckled down. The leader of the rebels was Max Suich. The man who, as executive editor, was responsible for attempting to enforce the will of Wocka and the equally conservative Falkingham was Bowman. After years of doing Falkingham's dirty work, Falkingham's last act was to betray Bowman and his ambitions, delivering him into the hands of his enemies. From the moment Bowman heard of Suich's appointment he knew he was for it.

Why had Falkingham—with the board, of course—made such an uncharacteristic decision? The official reason was that Bowman had failed to revive the *Herald*'s circulation and it was time to give someone else a go, perhaps with a more adventurous approach. To the extent this argument is genuine, there was merit in it. The *Herald* needed more radical reform and, when it came, circulation improved.

But everyone knows the real reason. That year Bowman had left his wife and taken up with his secretary. The gentlemen of the *Herald*, who knew and liked his wife, were scandalised, none more so than that upright Methodist R.P. Falkingham. Bowman was struck out of the will. He believes he was fitted up by Suich, who presented the board with a fat dossier of his manifold failings as editor. One of them, I was told, was that he made too much use of 'sans serif'—modern typefaces with no curly bits. This was calculated to play on the prejudices of old Angus McLachlan.

I was close to Bowman. He told me 1980 had been quite a year: he'd turned 50, left his wife and lost his job. But in the gentlemanly world of Fairfax, no one is sacked. Editors judged to have failed are regularly moved on, but always with a parachute and often with 'blue-water treatment'. Bowman had been offered a year's leave on full pay, but his pride was wounded and he knew there was no future for him under Suich, so he declined and resigned. At the time I hoped that, in the same circumstances, I would have been more hard-nosed. The pity is that, at that stage, the Fairfax super scheme was unreformed. Bowman left with far less than his due and had to earn what he could as a freelancer.

Vic Carroll's tough love

Perhaps fearing I might leave in sympathy with Bowman, Suich called me into his office—Harriott's former office, the one with the fireplace—for a chat. Bowman's replacement would be V.J. Carroll, Suich's mentor and a man who'd done much to develop the *Fin Review* and the *National Times* as their managing editor. 'You'll like Vic,' he told me, 'he's the great journalistic teacher.' Great, I replied, I'll take all the teaching I can get. But for months I couldn't see it. For a writer, the man seemed utterly inarticulate, utterly unable to tell you what he wanted or why he wanted it. Eventually I understood: it was up to you to watch what the great journalistic teacher did, then figure out for yourself why it worked.

I like David Bowman and to this day I know I owe him a lot. I didn't like Vic Carroll until he'd moved on and I'd realised all *he'd* done for me, all of it more with a kick than a pat on the head. So it pains me to admit that Carroll was the better editor. Undoubtedly the best editor I've served under in 40 years at the *Herald* and, as far as I know, the best editor the *Herald*'s had. Under the spur of his tough love, I was equipped to move up to a higher level in my career.

When I first became a leader-writer I justified working for such a conservative paper by telling myself that if I could move the *Herald*'s position just a few degrees away from the extreme right

I would have achieved more than most people. But the trouble with internalising someone else's worldview is that the very act ends up making it your own view. By the time Carroll became my boss I saw myself as guardian of the *Herald*'s conservative economic line. I knew the *Herald* would be supporting the Coalition at the next federal election, so it was my job to ensure everything we said during the term was consistent with what we'd be saying come the election.

But in that post-monetarist era, Carroll was an old unreconstructed Keynesian. The powerful critique of Keynesianism—the parts of the monetarist attack that had been conceded by 'reconstructed' Keynesians—had passed him by. Equally, he shared with Emerson the belief that consistency is the hobgoblin of little minds. As I was to observe, his approach was much more larrikin: we'd say what he felt like saying throughout the term, but then on the Saturday before the election, he'd wheel out Harry Kippax to write a leader telling people to get out there and vote Liberal. That Harry's leader bore little resemblance to what we'd been saying for the past three years was a matter of little moment.

Carroll was a highly experienced financial journalist, but he'd never edited a big general newspaper like the *Herald* before and I suspect in the early months he found it pretty tough. My guess is that he regarded the daily leader-writers' conference as a pleasant break from the real work, where he could have a happy argument about economics and politics. I argued hard to maintain 'the line'. Once I got so exasperated I called him a f—wit at the top of my voice and in front of the rest of the conference. With another editor such an outburst could have got me into big trouble, but Carroll was unfazed. In fact I think I remember him suppressing a smile. I've never met anyone so self-assured. He knew he wasn't one of those, he knew no one else thought he was one and, indeed, that even I didn't really think it. I was just a young fellow with a lot of potential who was a bit too passionate, but I'd grow up.

So I have Carroll to thank for liberating me from my self-imposed conservatism. If he wasn't worried about sticking to the Fairfax family's line, why should I? From then on I reviewed all the positions I'd inherited from Woody, dropping or modifying any I didn't really agree with. In future I'd say only what I really believed, and if it happened to be a little unorthodox or controversial, so much the better.

But one respect in which I've never departed from Woody's line was his implacable opposition to tariff protection. In this I'm merely embracing the paper's long-held position. Going back before Federation, New South Wales was in favour of free-trade while Victoria was protectionist. In consequence, this disagreement goes back to John Fairfax and David Syme. And you could see it in the positions of the *Herald* and *The Age*, and their respective economics editors, until very recent years.

One thing I—and most economists—believe is that inheritance taxes are good taxes because they do little to distort people's choices. At a board meeting in July 1983, Sir David Griffin had taken exception to a leader I'd written which he thought was advocating the re-introduction of death duty. He didn't think many *Herald* readers would fancy the idea. Suich replied that, to be fair, I had only been discussing the idea. Carroll had been seeking to develop a style of editorial which was more an essay than a statement of opinion. I learnt of all this only years later in the second volume of Gavin Souter's history of Fairfax. And that is as it should be. The duty of Fairfax editors is to shield their staff from political pressures, whether from vested interests or from higher up in the company.

Carroll, a north Queenslander, was a tough character. His nickname was The Cobra. A staff member, stirred up about some perceived injustice, would come into his office to make her complaint. When she'd finished Carroll would just stare at her, saying nothing. Embarrassed by the silence, she would elaborate on the complaint. Carroll would just stare at her, saying nothing. After a minute or so she'd rush from his office in tears. Once one of the leader-writers went in to demand a pay rise. When he emerged a little later he was so disconcerted the editorial page editor sent him home.

Not long before his removal, I persuaded Bowman to make me the business editor's boss. He wasn't much interested in business—few editors are—so I'd monitor it for him. He agreed provided I kept up my work as economics editor. My title would be assistant editor (business and economics). Unfortunately, however, Suich wouldn't let him give me a pay rise. He knew it would be of little consolation, but he'd hunted around and got me into some obscure non-contributory super fund intended for the printing staffmen downstairs. (That little extra is now worth several hundred thousand dollars to me. So thanks, Max.) I soon realised I simply couldn't muster the interest to read all three rival business sections, then compare and contrast every day.

When Carroll arrived at the *Herald* he must have decided he'd start by cleaning up the one part of the paper he really understood, the business section, and he was mighty unhappy with it. Every day or two the business editor, Vickie Smiles, and I would be paraded before him to have our many failings pointed out yet again. This went on for several weeks and I got more and more unhappy. One night after another bollocking I went home and was watching an old Time-Life doco on telly that consisted mainly of the famous

American foreign correspondent Harrison Salisbury sitting at his desk pontificating. What a heavy, I thought. I imagined him phoning the editor of *The Times* to say, 'Hold me a space on the front page, I've got a story coming.' 'Yes, Mr Salisbury, thank you,' the editor would reply. It struck me there were two ways to get ahead in journalism: one was to get pay rises and promotions by slowly climbing the rungs of the management ladder, the other was to be a star writer who had to be paid a fortune so he wouldn't be poached by rival editors. I decided I'd shoot for the star track.

Next day I told Carroll I no longer wanted to be the business editor's boss, I just wanted to write my columns. He said he wanted to think about it and he'd get back to me. I waited and waited, but he didn't. It may have been some sort of benign neglect. But by now I was starting to think like one of the wild men, so I just went round to Vickie and told her I was no longer her boss. So ended my first and last attempt to climb the management ladder. Once I'd abandoned my ambition to be editor I stopped wearing ties and began dressing purely to please myself.

Carroll kept up the pressure on Vickie, but she told me she knew what he was trying to do and was determined not to succumb. Eventually, however, it all got too much, so she went to Carroll: 'OK, you win, I'm resigning.' Carroll was genuinely surprised and not at all happy. Sometimes even a boss as smart as he was can miscalculate the effect he's having.

Carroll had strong opinions about headlines. He wrote the strongest headlines, and headline writing was one of his great strengths. Whatever I know about headlines I learnt from him. One of his rules was: statements, never questions. Another was: no gerunds (verbs ending in -ing). One day Carroll put a list of his headline rules on the subeditors' noticeboard. Underneath it the chief sub had typed:

'These are general rules, there will be exceptions, of course.' But under that was written by hand: 'No there won't. V.J.C.'

Once at a staff meeting someone asked Carroll if his goal was to move the paper down-market. His reply is one I've never forgotten and have quoted to many subsequent editors: 'I want to make the hard harder and the soft softer.' It's the perfect objective and I knew it was indeed what he was after. Unlike the oh-so-earnest *Oz*, the modern *Herald* has never forgotten that even a 'quality' paper needs a mixture of hard news and soft news, the serious and the light and fluffy. The hard part is getting the mix right—as well as making the hard news more informative and the soft news more entertaining.

Not long after he arrived Carroll brought in the former editor of *The Sun-Herald*, Chris Anderson, to be his deputy. I was kicked out of my little office on mahogany row to accommodate him, but the news editor, Peter Bowers, who'd been brought up from Canberra by Bowman, felt his position was being undermined by Anderson. If they didn't want him he was prepared to go—but only on his own terms. Contrary to his nickname in the gallery—Daffy—Bowers was a canny operator. And he solved his problem in a way I never expect to see again. He simply announced that he'd been sacked, then hung around the newsroom. Every time some young journo would express her concern to him he'd say loudly, 'Don't worry about *me*, love, *I'll* be all right.' He kept it up for two days as the young journos got more and more anxious and the interlopers' nerve cracked. They called him in to ask what they had to do to get him to unsack himself. He wanted to go back to Canberra and write a weekly column. *Fine.* As a columnist Bowers earnt my eternal envy by popularising the phase 'the Easter-Island face of Malcolm Fraser'.

Sometime after he became editor of the *Fin*, Paddy McGuinness asked if I was interested in moving across. Without pausing for thought I declined the offer. Why? Because, as an economics writer, I'd rather be a big fish in the small *Herald* pool than a small fish in the big *Fin* pool. Ha ha, he said, now what's the real reason? That was it. It's a decision I've never had cause to regret. What I've always wanted to do was explain economics to non-economists and I seem to have developed some skill at doing so. Why would I want to work for a paper whose readers at least maintained the pretence they already knew it all?

My job today is almost identical to what it was when Carroll arrived in 1980: three columns a week, each on the same day in the same section of the paper. The problem with my career—if you could call it such—is that I achieved the pinnacle of my ambition at 30 when I was made economics editor. In all that time I haven't been able to think of another job I'd prefer to do, nor paper I'd prefer to work for. Since they began running my columns in *The Age* in Melbourne sometime in the 1990s I've been in the two best and biggest-circulation quality papers in the country. Unbeatable. For many years all my ambition has been horizontal rather than vertical: to be better than my competitors.

But equally, my greatest motivation has been to emulate my hero Horace Rumpole of the Bailey (or my father): to go on doing the job I love for another week, hoping for more wins than losses.

CHAPTER 4
GETTING OLDER AND GETTING ON

You cannot hope to bribe or twist,
thank God! the British journalist.
But, seeing what the man will do
unbribed, there's no occasion to.

Humbert Wolfe

I don't know about you, but for me the most instructive and formative times in my career came early on. Watching the Fraser government taught me most about politics, just as Guy Harriott, David Bowman and Vic Carroll taught me most about journalism. I've worked for many more editors and editors-in-chief in the 30 years since then, but they've tended to flash past ever faster, leaving just the odd anecdote to remember them by. On the palace-revolution front things got much more momentous. But since these machinations have been well covered by other book-writing Fairfax journos, I'll spare you the corporate history.

I've got on well with all the editors I've worked for. Being my father's son, I've always trusted them to deal with me honestly, always tried to deal with *them* honestly and always wanted to please them. But I think their main motivation has been to keep me happy and not wanting to go elsewhere. My picture-byline has been appearing in the *Herald* for so long that a lot of our readers are conscious of me, I've become a big part of the paper's personification, and at least some of them would notice if I ceased to appear. When I told my then editor, Alan Oakley, I'd had an offer from Alan Kohler to work for his online paper, *Business Spectator*, Oakley's instant reply was that I wouldn't be leaving on his watch, even if he had to come round to my house and wash my dog for me.

Carroll was the last editor to feel free to offer me helpful suggestions on topics for my column, many of which I didn't take. These days, no editor would dare—nor see any need to. The old rule in journalism is that as long as you're seen to be doing well, no one interferes. Only if you're slipping will they intervene. Over the years I've become more confident of my own judgement in picking subjects and taking an approach my readers will be happy with. Presumably, my bosses agree. Never in 40 years have I had them decline to run a column, no one tells me what I can or can't say—this isn't News Corp, you know—and there's no 'house line' I have to conform to. I haven't written a leader in decades and any similarity you detect between my column and an editorial would be explained by the fact that the leader-writer asked for my opinion before he wrote the paper's.

Because I mainly just write my three columns a week and pick my own topics, I don't have a lot of contact with the editor. In any case, since about 1990 I've been permitted to work mainly at home. Most of my contact is just a friendly exchange as we pass each other in the office. Sometimes I think I've got the ideal combination: almost freelance in terms of direction, but with a wad of money hitting my bank account without fail every fortnight.

Chris Anderson succeeded Carroll as editor-in-chief in 1984. He was a smart operator whose manipulative skills were later to serve the journos well when things got rocky under Young Warwick

Fairfax. I remember overhearing him say to someone: 'Be reasonable, you can't hold me to that. I said that in negotiating mode.'

Out for a duck in multimedia

One day, sitting in the business section, the phone rang and a secretary's voice said portentously: '*Mister Lowy* would like to speak to you.' Sure, I said, wondering who this great man was.

'I don't know you,' he said (what kind of lightweight was he?), 'but I've just bought the Ten Network and I'd like you to work for me as an economic commentator.' I could start off working part-time provided I'd come full-time if things worked out. The idea of leaving the *Herald* to work for a TV station appalled me, but fortunately I agreed. One of his sons would be in touch to work things out. He didn't say so, but he'd already hired half the big names in journalism: Chris Masters, Kerry O'Brien, Paul Kelly, Bob Gottliebsen, Max Walsh and more.

For weeks I heard nothing more, then I got a call from the boss of the network. Would I come over for a chat? At the chat he said he wanted to put me on a two-year contract, with an annual retainer of $X. Would that do? I did my best to hide my amazement and said I supposed it would do. I'd do no interviews with other channels and he wanted a letter from the *Herald* saying it was OK for me to work part-time for Ten. Anderson didn't hesitate to give me the letter.

At first I imagined I'd become a multimedia personality like Norman Gunston, but though I was on the budget of O'Brien's Sunday morning political program, *Face to Face*, I never heard from him. I was used once on the Ten Network news, then never again.

Very occasionally I'd be asked to come out to North Ryde to be interviewed by Kerri-Anne Kennerley on *Good Morning Australia*. They always wanted me to talk about some company in the news, not the economy, but I wasn't game to say no.

So much for my multimedia career. I was disappointed, but then realised that had I been required to fly to Canberra on Saturdays to prerecord O'Brien's show, this would have wrecked every weekend. I thought that if you divided my retainer by the amount of time I was actually on the box, I was being paid more per minute than Elvis. I decided second prize—the money but not the box—wasn't so bad. I suspect I'm someone who can quickly reconcile himself to second prize.

I had plenty of time to speculate on how this strange thing had occurred. Lowy had decided he wanted me, his network manager knew it wasn't a good idea and dragged his feet until Lowy had reviewed his to-do list and told him to get on it. O'Brien was already having to share his show with Kelly; he wouldn't have wanted a third inflated ego competing for the camera. But why had Lowy wanted me? He hadn't heard of me, but maybe his mates at the Hakoah soccer club were readers and told him I'd be good. But businessmen buy into the media to enhance their political clout. Maybe he'd asked Paul Keating who he should hire.

I used the Ten Network money to pay for alterations to my house—we built a room over the carport that became my home office—and then pay off the mortgage. By the late 1980s we were mortgage-free. Lowy had done his dough and moved on by the time my two-year contract expired. There was no way it would be renewed. All the same, thanks, Frank.

Just a few years ago I attended the launch of a book by Professor Ross Garnaut—who I'd first met when he was Prime Minister

Hawke's economist—at the Lowy Institute. I was talking to Ross when Lowy arrived with his sons. He looked at me and said, 'I'm Frank Lowy, do you remember me?' I certainly did. Then he looked at Garnaut and said, 'Bob told me to hire him.'

Brief brush with Beecher

Carroll had recruited a go-ahead young chap from *The Age*, Eric Beecher, who established for us what *The Age*—being many years ahead of the *Herald* in entering the age of modernity—already had, something my mate Alan Mitchell called 'the silly sections' and others, 'lifestyle journalism'. If you're tempted to think you don't get much for our cover price, remember there was a time when newspapers came without restaurant reviews and recipes, sections about health and fitness, weekend magazines and gig guides. When Anderson stepped up to be editor-in-chief, Beecher became editor.

Beecher started a cricket magazine while still a schoolboy. As his long and illustrious career—and hefty bank account—since then well demonstrates, he is the most innovative, future-knowledgeable newspaperman of the modern age. If there's a future for quality journalism beyond the lumbering behemoths of Fairfax and Murdoch, my bet is Beecher will be first to find it.

But back when I worked for him, Beecher had much to learn. We learnt a few things together. While the Canberra press gallery was agog waiting for Keating to unveil the draft white paper on tax reform he'd take to the tax summit of 1985, I thought I'd figured out how he'd offset the regressiveness of his broad-based consumption tax and wrote a column explaining it. Beecher read it and got very excited, saying he wanted to run it on the front page. Oh,

OK. He really knew how to give something a visual drumroll and when I saw it in the paper next morning he'd made it look like the exclusive of the decade.

The Canberra press gallery exploded with excitement. Obviously, Keating had leaked the white paper to Gittins, who was well known to be in Keating's 'tax-reform cart'. I heard one kid from the ABC reporting that I'd been seen with the treasurer's press secretary last week leaving Parliament House by a back door. (It was true. Tom Mockridge had worked with me when he was on the *Herald*, and I tried always to have lunch with him when in Canberra. I doubt if the subject of tax was mentioned.)

It proved to be the worst day of my career. A saying of Carroll's was that an ounce of inside information was worth a ton of analysis. My ton of analysis was worth a lot less than that. I spent the morning trying to hose people down. Mockridge told the gallery my report was wrong—as indeed it proved to be. At lunch my mate Mitchell tore strips off me for being so foolish. I went on the then equivalent of the ABC's *7.30 Report* to explain myself and, when it was over, heard Gerry Doogue's producer chip her for going too easy on me. Until that day I'd never worried much about the consequences of what I wrote. I knew that, should I stray too close to the precipice, some older and wiser boss would grab me by the scruff of the neck and haul me back. But Beecher was younger than me, and he'd pushed me over. From now on I was on my own.

My parents had taught me never to lie, especially not to authority. There was no lying in my family. If Mum thought your bum looked big, Jesus wouldn't want her to deny it. At least in that respect I've tried to live up to my childhood training. But in newspapers, 'merit' pay rises are sparse unless you get an offer from a rival employer, whereupon editors suddenly realise how highly they value your services. No system could be better calculated to encourage staff to trail their coat. I've never misled my boss on anything other than 'offers'.

These days the *Herald* can rarely afford to match the offer, but editors do what they can and they probably realise not many of us are keen to swop teams from the Fairfax Gentlepersons to the Murdoch Cowboys. Murdoch will pay well to attract a name from Fairfax, and I've known for decades I was effectively paying a healthy premium for the privilege of working for an employer who wouldn't tell me what to say. Except that, knowing this, I've tried to get my money's worth by saying exactly what I think—meaning, of course, the premium would have disappeared long ago. It's a long time since I've had an offer from over the road.

But in those far-off days, a mate who was leaving *The Australian* said he'd tell his editor I was interested. His editor called and I went to Holt Street for an interview, knowing full well I'd be observed walking through the enemy newsroom and that this news would be back at Broadway before I was. I told Beecher I was dissatisfied and considering an offer from the *Oz*. Except that within a few days I got a letter from the *Oz* editor saying he wasn't making me an offer because he wasn't sure I was genuine. Beecher was taking it very seriously but—though I don't know how he got in on the act—Carroll came around to my office to check my story. I looked him in the eye and told him how unhappy I was. I don't think he fell for it. But Beecher wanted to be sure so he responded to my demands, pulling Fairfax-group strings to get me a paid daily interview with John Tingle on 2GB and a weekly interview on Channel 7's 11am news program with Clive Robertson. There were less than a handful of secretaries on the *Herald*, but Beecher got the women's section secretary to answer my phone. (I'm not sure she appreciated the extra task. She'd pick up my extension and bellow, 'Women's!')

Anderson reaches the top

By the late 80s, Anderson had become chief executive and begun the search for more stable funding to prop up Young Warwick's shaky ownership. He embarked on a frantic round of networking, particularly with bankers, which often involved inviting them to lunch at Fairfax, where they could meet the editors of the Fairfax papers. I was usually invited, too. One day in the lift on the way up to the directors' dining room on the fourteenth floor, the editor of the *Fin*, Gerry Noonan, told me he resented being used as a performing bear.

I didn't; I loved it. The editors would stand in a circle while Anderson introduced them to the honoured guest. There'd be perfunctory handshakes until he got to someone whose name the guest recognised. His face would light up: 'G'day, Ross!' That's why I was there, of course. Fairfax had provided the platform I'd used to become well known. If it wanted a little back in return, that was fine by me.

It must have been much earlier than this that I happened to attend a lunch of the ever-more-elderly Fairfax directors. They began debating whether the planned *Times on Sunday* should be tabloid or broadsheet. I was just about to air my opinion when Anderson cut in and abruptly changed the subject. Later I asked him what the problem was. 'You don't think we'd let those old buffers make an important decision like that, do you?' Though the *National Times* had been tabloid, its replacement was broadsheet.

The decision was based—correctly—on which would bring in the most advertising revenue. Most people judge papers and magazines by their editorial content, but I like to judge them by their advertising. The *National Times* seemed pretty anti-establishment, always seeking out corruption among the high and mighty, but most of its ads were for flash foreign cars and $5000 watches.

My relationship with John Alexander, who became editor-in-chief in 1988, was one more of mutual respect than friendship. I knew he had a remarkably good nose for the sort of stories our readers were interested in; he knew a lot of readers liked me. Alexander had started at the *Herald* as business editor—recommended to Carroll by Max Walsh—and we'd been wary colleagues. Although we were very different in many respects, I suspect in some respects our characters were too similar for us to like each other.

Alexander always had a coterie who, as we were later to discover, tended to follow him from paper to paper. A few of them thought they'd be able to do my job better than me, but he never yielded to their entreaties, and always gave me what I asked for. In 1991, in the early months of 'the recession we had to have', business was complaining bitterly about the economy's parlous state, but I stuck with Treasury's insistence it would be no more than a 'soft landing'. I was proved badly wrong. But my dereliction in failing to castigate the Hawke government seemed to have been viewed with great disapproval by Peter Smark, a senior journo formerly on *The Age*, who fancied himself as an éminence grise. One Saturday I was surprised to see Smark observe in his *Herald* column that, in his opinion, the nation's best economic commentator was *The Australian*'s Alan Wood. Though I thought this a strange thing to say in our paper, and though I privately agreed with him, I didn't think many other people did, so thought no more of it. Only many months later did a mate tell me this had been part of Smark's campaign to persuade Alexander to replace me with Woody. Obviously, Alexander wasn't buying.

Once I went in to see Alexander to inform him I'd just declined an (in no way tempting) offer to work for the *Sunday Telegraph*. 'Oh,' he said, 'then I guess I'd better organise you a pay rise.' Thanks. At that stage he was the last of the big-spending editors and budget-ignorers. Only after he was working for Kerry Packer did he become the great cost-cutter.

End of Fairfax paternalism

Young Warwick's departure after the company was put into receivership in late 1990 ended the family's association with the company—or so we imagined at the time. As befits lords of the manor, the Fairfax family had been highly paternalistic proprietors. The company established its own superannuation scheme, private health insurance fund, staff lending library, retired employees' association and the Fairfax Foundation, charged with assisting former employees' widows and orphans. To this day the foundation owns holiday homes in Port Macquarie available to employees at reduced rents. We had a medical centre staffed by a full-time doctor and nurse, as well as a barber shop. The children of employees were often given jobs as printers or journos. But with the departure of the Fairfaxes these many benefits have slowly disappeared.

Although economists set great store by 'the mobility of labour' in moving between employers, the company's super scheme was originally designed to reward and encourage those who stayed with Fairfax until retirement. When I joined the scheme in my first week with the company, it contributed 5 per cent of my salary and I was required to contribute 4 per cent. Those who left before retirement would get back only their own contributions plus interest. The trick was that the company didn't keep the contributions it had made on behalf of the many people who stayed just a few years, but put them into a 'general fund' to be shared by those who did last the distance. So the longer you stayed, the more you had to lose by leaving; you were held captive by golden handcuffs.

Before they were ejected by the arrival of Young Warwick's men in 1987, Fred Brenchley and Max Suich got wind that those men had designs on all the money in the super scheme. Almost their last act before leaving was to change the scheme's rules, introducing a form of 'vesting': for every year a member had spent with the company they'd get to keep 10 per cent of their company contributions, plus earnings. Anyone leaving after 10 years or more would get 'full vesting'. Not much later, Treasurer Keating's introduction of compulsory employee superannuation imposed reform on existing company schemes. All employees would get to take with them all employer contributions and earnings. What's more, companies would be permitted to have only one scheme.

Ah. As part of their paternalism, the Fairfaxes were always setting up additional, non-contributory retirement schemes to reward their loyal employees. These additional schemes would have to be closed and their proceeds added to their members' accounts in the main scheme. There was some method in the family's mad generosity. It didn't quite own 50 per cent of the company's shares and felt vulnerable to a hostile takeover. Most of these additional schemes held most of their funds as shares in the company, as did the main scheme's general fund. The trust deeds of all these schemes provided that the trustees were not required to sell their shares to the highest bidder, but were free to act in their members' best interests (by telling the raider to sod off).

So all those schemes were part of the family's defence against takeover. In Young Warwick's case, however, he amassed so many shares that company law permitted him to compulsorily acquire all the remaining shares—at $8.50 a pop, far more than they were worth. Thus it was that existing members of the super scheme—including yours truly—did very nicely out of Young Warwick's discharge of Lady Mary's revenge. When the various subsidiary schemes were wound up, their continuing employer contribution arrangements were added to the main scheme's 5 per cent contributions. Thus it was that my employer contributions were well above Keating's compulsory 9 per cent of salary long before that level was reached in 2002. And thus it is that I've been well placed to retire since I turned fifty-five. Wocka, James, Young Warwick—thanks a few million.

Early in the post-Fairfax period David Hickey was appointed editor-in-chief, with Milton Cockburn as editor. I met Cockburn at his brother Lance's twenty-first in Newcastle in the late 1960s. I remember him saying he'd got his driver's licence that week. We became friends later when he moved into the hostel I lived in at Randwick. Cockburn had a successful career as a Labor ministerial adviser before deciding to switch to journalism. Would I help? Had Bowman remained editor-in-chief Cockburn would have needed my help, but Carroll wasn't put off by a Labor pedigree. Cockburn came in as a leader-writer but before long moved back to Canberra as a political reporter, eventually becoming chief of our bureau.

Now the editor was an old mate of mine. Somehow a rumour got started that I'd been seen at News Limited and might be leaving. There was no truth to it, but by then I knew better than to scotch it. Cockburn took it very seriously, however, and organised a pay rise for me. I wondered about this. I remembered that, a year or two earlier, he'd been threatening to leave and I'd put a fair bit of work into persuading the trumps we'd lose him if we didn't pay him more. But maybe Hickey wanted to give me a rise to secure my loyalty; he'd also given one to Max Walsh, who by then was a senior columnist of ours. If so, it worked with me but not with Walsh.

Whenever he saw me near his office, Cockburn would pull me in, close the door and proceed to tell me things I wasn't supposed to know. I figured he needed someone to unburden to, someone he could trust not to spread it round the office. I did enjoy being mates with my boss.

Various moves later, Greg Hywood became the *Herald*'s editor-in-chief. I'd known Hywood since we were both in the Canberra gallery. Once we were talking in the middle of the newsroom when we heard the news of some mutual acquaintance taking a big step up. 'Gee,' Hywood said more to himself than me, 'and to think I'm still only editor-in-chief of the *Herald*.'

In all that time I never hankered after an overseas posting, but I've rarely said no to an overseas junket—a tour of somewhere funded by some outfit hoping for coverage. Bowman once sent me on a five-week tour of the five main capitals of ASEAN to write editorial for an advertising supplement, but that's the only time I can remember the *Herald* paying for an overseas trip. I tend to be offered government study tours—of the United States, West Germany, Britain, Japan and the European Union. Citibank sent me on another US study tour, but the junket to end all junkets was something I applied for myself: a Nuffield press fellowship for a term at Wolfson College, Cambridge. Three months swanning round the home of Alfred Marshall, Keynes, Arthur Pigou and the rest. I attended lectures by Amartya Sen, John Hicks, John Kenneth Galbraith and a bright young American called Joe Stiglitz. I heard an ancient Lord Kahn refer to 'my multiplier' but, like a fool, failed to attend the memorial services for Piero Sraffa and Joan Robinson.

Captained by an All Black

In 2005 Fred Hilmer decided he'd had enough and installed David Kirk to succeed him as Fairfax chief executive. Kirk had been captain of the All Blacks and an advisor to New Zealand prime minister Jim Bolger. He immediately set about reducing Fairfax's dependency on the *Herald* and *The Age* by acquiring other businesses. His most successful purchase was New Zealand's hugely profitable eBay equivalent, Trade Me.

In September 2006, on my last day before taking off for a four-week holiday in Italy, I received a copy of a note to a reader that Kirk had handwritten to clear his in-tray before going on his own holiday. The reader had complained to him that I, and another *Herald* journo, had failed to reply to several of his letters (which were trying to persuade me to join his crusade to save the old quarantine station at North Head). Kirk told the reader he completely concurred with his view that communications from readers should be 'promptly, courteously and comprehensively' replied to.

I was beside myself with anger. In all my years at the *Herald* neither I nor any other journo had been given the time or secretarial assistance to allow us to reply to more than a few letters from readers. Did Kirk not know this? Did he know it but still chose to shift the blame from management to us? Why hadn't he sought our side of the story before dobbing us to a reader? I dashed off an email to Kirk saying it was management's fault not ours and that I thought his role was to protect his journalists from unreasonable outside pressures, not amplify them. I sent a copy to my boss, Oakley, and then, because I regarded it as an attack on all of us, put a copy of his letter and my email on the office noticeboard. Then I flew off on holidays.

While at Lake Como I got an email from Oakley. Someone had given the two documents to the *Crikey* website and *Crikey*'s story had been run (without attribution) by the *Oz*. Why had I decided to go public with what should have remained confidential? In a subsequent email he said he'd given me a lot of support but felt I'd let him down badly. He'd like me to apologise to Kirk for the way I'd behaved. I replied—from Venice— that I didn't give a fig for Kirk and his feelings. He was just the latest in a long line of grossly overpaid chief executives who knew nothing about newspapers. However, I did regret doing something that might get *my* boss into trouble with *his* boss. So I'd use my skill as a former leader-writer to find the 'form of words' that would come as close as I could to the appearance of an apology. In my email to Kirk I said I'd been asked to apologise to him, explained that I had a fiery temper and acted in the heat of the moment, explained various other things and advised him that newspapers traded on the egos of their journalists. 'When you're in the business of trading on egos, you have to know how to handle the stock in trade,' I wrote. Kirk replied that he appreciated my email and conceded that he'd handle such matters differently in future.

The joke is, when finally I got back to work I discovered Kirk had replied promptly to my original email saying, in effect, that we'd have to agree to differ. It dawned on me that you don't get to be captain of the All Blacks without learning how to handle a lot of big egos. The episode raised my opinion of him enormously.

In 2008 when I got a gong in the Australia Day honours, Kirk sent word he'd like to put on a boardroom lunch for me and I could pick the guests. At first I thought I'd invite a selection of my protégés, but then I thought: these bosses think I'm some sort of shootkicker around the place, I'll show 'em otherwise. So I invited the secretary to the Treasury, Ken Henry, the secretary of the New South Wales Treasury, John Pierce, the governor of the Reserve Bank, Glenn Stephens, the federal shadow treasurer, Malcolm Turnbull, and various other heavies.

They all turned up. Henry flew up from Canberra just for the lunch. They assumed the purpose of the lunch was to say nice things about me, and Henry had come prepared. Back in 1985, the draft white paper on tax reform on which he'd worked was being opposed by everyone—the rest of the cabinet, the ACTU and the Business Council—but my unflinching support for tax reform had kept it alive until the tax summit. He quoted some of the pieces I'd written that Treasury found particularly helpful. Wow, really? I had no idea. But then Turnbull, arriving late, took over the conversation, reminiscing about his role in the Kerry Packer/Conrad Black bid to take over Fairfax. I got the feeling the econocrats weren't terribly impressed by his performance, but I had a whale of a time.

Finally facing up to the dread digital

Two likeable bosses—Oakley and Peter Fray—moved out or up before the appointment in January 2011 of Amanda Wilson as the *Herald*'s first female editor. She treated me as a confidant. I liked her and gave her all the support I could, including defending her against unreasonable criticism at a staff meeting with her boss,

Jack Matthews. She worked hard to ensure Hywood's decision to save money by outsourcing the *Herald*'s subbing wasn't the disaster it could have been. She already knew what I told her: journos thought 'quality' meant lots of exclusives and stories that led to royal commissions, but readers thought quality meant no spelling, grammatical or other silly errors. If there were such errors, the editor would be the one who copped the blame. It's been far from perfect—particularly when copy is whacked straight on the website in the middle of the day—but could have been a lot worse.

I actually started to respect Matthews, believing his anti-paper militancy the sort of unreasonable toughness an ancient empire like Fairfax needed if it was to have the ghost of a chance of surviving in the digital world. Whoever decided to retain his services—I suspected it was Roger Corbett, now chairman of the Fairfax board and another prickly customer I quite liked—had made a smart decision. And with old print-journo Hywood above him and not-so-old print journo Garry Linnell below him, the risk of him doing something stupid to our 'legacy assets'—newspapers—was small.

The integration of the newspapers with our ever-expanding 'digital platforms'—the website, the tablet apps and the app for smart phones—demanded a complete reorganisation of Fairfax editorial effort. The operation needed to be reoriented from writing for the papers and then letting the digital people take anything we'd written for their 'platforms' to making the production of news 'digital first'. Journos would write first for the digital platforms—and increasingly would produce little videos and graphics, not just words on a page—and the editors of the paper platform would be free to 'reverse publish' anything they fancied. This was possible because there was so little overlap between our digital and paper readerships.

There was nothing about the attitude or behaviour of Fray or Wilson that suggested they would be unsuitable to stay on as bosses in the reorganised editorial world. But you don't have to work for big organisations for long to know that when new brooms arrive they like to sweep clean: new big boss, new underling bosses. Matthews and Linnell offered Fray and Wilson sideways shifts, but they declined.

The first *Herald* editor-in-chief of the new era—in charge of all the *Herald* platforms—was a quite young Sean Aylmer. His 'news director' was a journo with long experience at News and the *Herald*, including much experience on the digital side, Darren Goodsir. Goodsir told me he'd relied on my columns to get him through economics for the HSC many moons ago, then had enrolled in economics at Sydney Uni before getting a job offer from the *Telegraph.* It wasn't long before yet another radical reorganisation saw Aylmer move up to bigger and better things and Goodsir become editor-in-chief.

Aylmer, who had an honours degree in commerce from the Uni of New South Wales, had worked as an economist at the Reserve Bank before I hired him for the *Herald*'s business section in 1997. He was soon lured to the *Fin* to be their economics correspondent in Canberra, the start of a long and successful career at the *Fin* in which he rose to be editor of the magazine, *BRW.* Missing out when Michael Stutchbury returned from the *Oz* to be the *Fin*'s editor-in-chief, Linnell put him in charge of one of the early exercises in knocking Fairfax into digital shape, combining the *Herald*'s and *The Age*'s two business sections as the website-oriented BusinessDay. (At about this time the two papers' bureaus in the Canberra press gallery were combined, later to be joined by the *Canberra Times*' bureau.)

Ever since I'd seen Alexander as editor-in-chief looking after Max Walsh, the man who'd recommended he be made business editor years earlier, after an unfortunate property investment had put a hole in Walsh's retirement savings, I'd dreamt of the day when as an old and failing columnist I'd have one of the people I'd hired as my boss. Now the day had arrived. Whenever I was in Aylmer's company he'd tell anyone who happened along that I'd been his mentor.

He liked retelling the story of our first interview: I'd told him the other two candidates only got interviews, but he was getting lunch—'don't muck it up!' (or words to that effect). Then, when he'd had second thoughts about coming because Simon Crean had offered him a job in his Canberra office, I'd phoned him demanding to know if he was a complete nitwit (or something like that). I'd said if he became a journo he could get a job in a minister's office anytime he liked, but if he passed up this chance to get into journalism there mightn't be another. After he'd become editor-in-chief he recounted that story to Crean, who said, 'Seems you jumped the right way.' When Aylmer became my boss I was pleased to be free to offer the frankest assessment of his performance.

Fairfax has had repeated rounds of voluntary redundancies among journos since it closed *The Sun* in 1988. But these were small compared with the redundancy round of 2012, announced by Hywood as part of a sweeping program of cost-cutting needed to restore Fairfax's profitability as advertising revenue—from display ads as well as classifieds—continued to plunge. The *Herald* and *The Age* would move from broadsheet to tabloid. Linnell said this was in response to readers' requests—which had probably been true for at least 50 years—but the real reason was that the classifieds motive for broadsheet had gone, and going tabloid would permit the two papers to be printed at various Rural Press printing plants, thereby allowing Fairfax to close its relatively new broadsheet plants at Chullora and Tullamarine, which were now running at about 40 per cent of capacity.

The redundancy round was by far the biggest we've had and Aylmer and his boss Linnell weren't at all sure they'd get all the volunteers they needed. It coincided with the radical reorganisation of the newsroom, and a lot of people held off applying for redundancy until they discovered how they'd fared in the shake-up. The trumps needn't have worried. Indeed, with hindsight they accepted a few offers they shouldn't have. Pay David Marr big money to stop writing for us and write for an online rival instead? Pay to lose the services—and disrupt the big fan club—of Adele Horin?

Previous redundancy rounds were aimed at dislodging older journos who were highly paid but had stopped pedalling. They had the perverse effect of discouraging the old and tired from retiring until they were bombed out of their chair with a big bag of money in the next redundancy round. That wasn't true of everyone, of course. When I asked Oakley why he'd granted redundancy to the legendary Alan Ramsey, he said: 'Since he'd turned 70 I didn't think I could knock him back for a third time.' As a reasonably rationalist economics editor I notice occasions when decisions in the private sector are, shall we say, less than profit-maximising. The truth is that redundancy payouts have, by mutual consent, become a fallback for baby boomers who've neglected to save enough for their retirement.

But by the time of the 2012 redundancy round—there've been others since—the oldies had been cleaned out. This one was aimed at middle-aged journos, many of whom were presented with a proposition that, in effect, was this: if I were to halve your mortgage, would you be prepared take your chances at finding another decent job? More than enough were. But to help the process along, the bosses arranged for the pay office to calculate for everyone—not just those who inquired—the payout they'd be entitled to.

I meet readers who say what a terrible thing it was for so many people to lose their jobs. I tell them not to be too sorry for the dear departed. They were all volunteers and were all rewarded handsomely for their sacrifice. Indeed, a lot of them took the shilling because they feared the present arrangements were too generous to last. My problem is I haven't run out of things I want to say. I didn't want to retire and, in any case, didn't think my offer to go would be accepted. But they did me the dubious favour of telling me exactly how much they weren't prepared to pay me.

CHAPTER 5
ADVICE TO BOYS

News is anything you haven't written for a fortnight.

Dennis Warner

It may be terribly fashionable these days, but journalists don't 'mentor' people. Journalists don't; I do. And I don't just take an interest in the young people I find around me in the office. Most of the 15 journos I've mentored over the years I also hired and trained.

Journalism is too competitive for mentoring to be common. As a reporter you're not just competing against rivals at other papers and news outlets, you're also competing against your own colleagues for space and prominence in the paper. Old-school journos say never kick a copyboy, he might end up as your boss. Some young kid you helped could end up taking your job. And reporting tends to be a singular activity—one reporter, one story. It's not always true, but when you see a story with the bylines of more than one journo at the top it's usually because a subeditor has taken two stories and combined them. Sometimes readers ask me if I have an assistant. No, and I've never wanted one. Why not? Because under the egalitarian rules of the journos' union, I'd have to share my byline with them.

But if mentoring is so out of favour among journos, why have I put so much effort into hiring, training and mentoring young people? I could tell you it's because I've wanted to make a wider contribution to the paper and the profession. I certainly believe economic reporting is too tricky for a respectable paper like the *Herald* to let be done by someone without economic qualifications. When I joined the *Herald* it was still committed to the 'universal journalist' model: no topic required any special knowledge to be reported accurately provided the reporter was well trained and well edited. This was why reporters didn't need bylines. All the reader needed to know was that the report had been written by a *staff* correspondent—that is, by a reporter trained in the *Herald*'s high standards.

If the universal journalist assumption was *ever* justified it certainly wasn't by the time I joined the *Herald* 40 years ago. And the economy's become a lot more complex since then. But the sad truth is most Australian papers and electronic news outlets don't go out of their way to hire economics graduates, nor to give reporters training in economic reporting. I got into hiring and training young economic journalists because I believed the *Herald*'s economic reporting needed to be done by people with qualifications and, as economics editor, I didn't want to be obliged by Canberra bureau chiefs to agree to the appointment of economics correspondents who, though they knew no economics, were 'a great little story-getter'. I'd train my own in Sydney and have them on the rank ready to fill any vacancy that arose in Canberra. And since so few news outlets bothered to hire or train, I'd have to do a fair bit because, to an extent, I'd be training for the rest of Fairfax and even the industry.

Does that sound virtuous? The deeper truth is I do it because I love it. When I was a part-time tutor in accounting I realised how much I enjoyed performing in front of a blackboard. From the start I've been a frustrated teacher—sometimes I think I'm the most overpaid teacher in the country. I like explaining things to readers and I like explaining things to young journos even more. I like having a fresh audience for my hoary anecdotes. And the kids I hire are smart enough to know they should suck the old boy's wisdom dry and then move on.

These days, trainee journalists are chosen and hired by human relations departments and selection panels of mid-level journos. But I'm still allowed to select my own, parade them before the editor for final approval and then turn them over to the HR people for processing. Why? Perhaps because editors know HR departments and panels of journos with BAs aren't much good at attracting and selecting economic and business types. Perhaps because editors feel they have to humour me. But I'd like to think it's because—as I'll seek to demonstrate—I've had a pretty good strike rate. Touch wood.

Selecting boys

So what do I look for when hiring? An economics degree, obviously. But that's just base level. Like most employers I'm less impressed by high marks than by extracurricular achievements such as Duke of Edinburgh, debating or getting elected to the SRC. Editors of student newspapers go to the front of the queue. I do try to judge whether the person looks like they can write fluently. That's why evidence of a pre-existing interest in (amateur) journalism wins big points. Once, early in my career, I asked for examples of a chap's writing but he didn't have any. You must have tute papers, I insisted. I read a few and concluded he was almost illiterate. He'd used a lot of big words but didn't seem to know what they meant. I told Chris Anderson not to hire him, but he did anyway. That chap went on to be chief sub at the *Oz*, editor of a couple of country papers, night editor of the *Fin* and is now a columnist on the *Herald*. He's also written a couple of books. Whoops. I don't ask for tute papers anymore.

After assessing ability to write I look for hunger, for people who've been called by God to be a journalist, not people who think a stint working on a newspaper might look good on their CV. A good test of hunger is willingness to drop money to get in the door. The standard trainee's wage is the highest I'll go. Another good sign is having done a part-time master of journalism, not because of what they've learnt about how to report—they'll pick that up in a few months on the job—but because of what it says about their determination to break into journalism. I've been a part-time student and I know hanging around an empty campus at nine o'clock at night after a day at work isn't a lot of fun.

Once, after we received a sheaf of replies to an advertisement, I thought the thing to do would be throw them in a filing cabinet and see what transpired. Those who rang to inquire what was happening about their application would get an interview. Journalists are pushy people; the more someone hassles me for a job the more impressed I become. Similarly, journalists are people who ask questions; how many has this person asked me? And journalists have to be able to handle the unwilling interviewee. I often play the hard cop to see how they handle it.

Unlike some of my bosses, I never ask questions on how they'd go about reporting this or that event. I don't expect people to think like a journo before their first day on the job. Rather, I look for people who are super-smart. If you're smart enough it won't take you long to figure out how the reporting trick is done. On the other hand, I do ask questions about economics—what's your response to some economic controversy in the news? I used to have a standard question: what's the relationship between bond prices and bond yields? The one-word answer is: inverse. As a matter of arithmetic, if one goes up the other goes down. Only one person has got that correct, a kid who'd worked for a merchant bank in the holidays, but I didn't hire him. Matt Wade gave me the second-best answer: 'I don't know, but I do know who I could ask.' That's a journalist's answer.

I'm looking for an interest in politics because economic journalism is a specialty within political journalism. And I always extract a promise that the person will move to Canberra whenever it happens to suit the paper. But I'd never hire anyone who was a member of a political party unless they agreed to resign immediately. And, in case they're misled by the kind of work *I* do, I always stress they're being hired as a reporter and will be given zero opportunity to express their personal opinions.

When people are asked why they want to be a journo, the most common answers are 'because I love to write' and 'because I love working with people'. Sorry, journalists are cynical souls and they hate answers like that. The perfect answer is: because I'm a stickybeak and a gossip. Why? Because that's what reporters do—find out things about other people's business and then tell the world.

It's probably true that I'd never have hired Ross Gittins. But economic reporting is a lot more sophisticated today than it was in the early 1970s. And if my recruiting standards are higher than they need to be, I've never had much trouble finding good people. A favourite editor's interview question these days is: who are your favourite *Herald* columnists? (Hint: he's fishing for perceptive observations, not compliments.) I'm glad no one asked me that question because I'd never read the *Herald* before it gave me a job. One of the ways my parents saved money was by not buying newspapers.

I could call all the journos I've mentored mentees, understudies, protégées, apprentices or offsiders, but I prefer to call them my boys. Most have been male boys, but just under a third have been female boys. I like to run a family where we stick together and the older boys help the younger ones. It's only a matter of time before my boys leave home, but they stay part of the family.

A rollcall of good 'uns

Greg Bright was a reporter in the *Herald*'s business section before he was sent to the Canberra gallery as our economics correspondent and, as the *Herald*'s new economics editor, David Bowman put him under my care. I don't remember being of much help to him, but Bright remembers it more fondly. He moved to the *Fin* in Sydney before leaving to achieve his long-held ambition to be his own boss, a successful publisher of trade magazines.

Tom Mockridge, who began his journalistic career on the *Taranaki Daily News*, succeeded Bright as our economics correspondent. He switched to Paul Keating's office and when, after quite a few years, he left to work for Murdoch, he sent me a note saying the three biggest influences on him had been 'the two PKs and you'. The other PK was Paul Kelly. Mockridge climbed to the top of News Corp. He was head of Sky Italia in 2011 when called in to replace Rebekah Brooks as chief executive of News International. In June 2013 he became chief executive of Virgin Media in Britain.

Ian Cassie, who came from the Reserve Bank, was the first boy I hired—making him my guinea pig. I foolishly decided it would be good grounding for him to spend a year in the general newsroom before moving into economic reporting. Fortunately, the business editor, John Alexander, rescued him and installed him in the business section. He tried to transfer Cassie's loyalty away from me, but Cassie had been attracted to the *Herald* by my presence.

Cassie became a favourite of mine. He had double honours in economics and econometrics and was the only one of my boys to teach me economics, rather than me him. His trouble was his surprising lack of hunger. Once I threw him a press release from an employer group, saying I thought it would make a story. Next morning our rivals gave it a big run, but we had nothing. What happened? I didn't write it. Why not? Their fundamental premise was wrong. I was flabbergasted. They're a lobby group so of course their fundamental premise was wrong—it's always wrong. The real question is whether it was a good story. Cassie became the *Fin*'s economics correspondent in Canberra before leaving to join Alan Wood at Syntec. He ended up where most young economists who leave the Reserve go first: the financial markets.

Karen Maley applied for a job, but though we gave it to someone else, she rang me for weeks trying to talk her way in. Eventually I decided someone so keen had to be a good bet, so persuaded the boss to let me hire her. She became our economics correspondent in Canberra, moved to the *Fin*, then made a lot of money as a political consultant before returning to the *Fin* as a business feature writer and columnist. She's hosted a couple of parties for my boys.

Stephen Ellis was the first of many graduates from political economy at Sydney Uni I've hired. Whereas conventional economics has become more and more mathematical, PE remains essay-based, which is a better fit with journalism. We don't have much call for equations. Ellis, too, was lured to the *Fin* where he worked for some years before going to America to do an MBA. Back in Australia, he's long been a policy adviser to Malcolm Turnbull.

Anna Bernasek is half Czech, half Australian and half American. Her father was an economics professor at Macquarie Uni before returning to the University of Michigan. John Alexander hired her for the business section, but I took her under my wing. Soon after she arrived in Canberra as our economics correspondent, someone asked her to write a little comment. Next day I told her I didn't like it much. It was criticising for the sake of being critical rather than criticising from a fixed-values position (which, to be fair, was hardly surprising considering her inexperience). Before long I got an urgent phone call from a heavy who was to become my editor, Robert Whitehead: Anna had gone home in tears, would I ring her at home and cheer her up?

Bernasek had various adventures in journalism before applying to do a master of public affairs at Harvard's Kennedy School. The reference form asked if, among all the students I'd taught, I'd put her in the top 0.1 per cent, 1 per cent, 2 per cent, 5 per cent . . . I shut my eyes and ticked a box high up. She got in and, after graduating, was headhunted by *Fortune* magazine. It taught me something: the best way for an Aussie journo to crack a job in the Big Apple is to do a masters at a big-name uni and impress your lecturers, who then recommend you to big-name recruiters. Today Bernasek's byline appears in *Newsweek* and the business section of the *New York Times*.

Tom Allard's interview came at the height of my bad-cop period. He'd done political economy at Sydney. I demanded to know if he'd done PE because he was weak at maths. Well, he said, I did do four-unit maths for the HSC. Whoops. I indicated the interview was over, but he didn't leave. In fact, he's the first of my stayers. He worked in the Canberra bureau for many years, was our correspondent in Jakarta and is now a political 'special writer'.

Sean Aylmer, my only boy to become my boss, came from the Reserve Bank with a master of journalism up his sleeve. He's spent his whole journalistic career at Fairfax, going from strength to strength. Now he's too exalted to be my boss. But he's never been too busy—nor too abashed—to find time to make sure I understand my failings. In return he gets my advice whether he asks for it or not.

Toni O'Loughlin had honours in industrial relations from the Uni of New South Wales and came recommended by Professor John Buchanan of the Uni of Sydney. She moved from our Canberra bureau to the *Fin*'s with Laura Tingle as her patron before accompanying her partner, Matt Brown of the ABC, to overseas postings in Jerusalem, Jakarta and back to Jerusalem. There she's been a stringer for various outlets, including *The Guardian*.

Matt Wade was my most mature-age recruit. He'd been well-established in the overseas aid sector and came with a master of journalism. His upbringing on the north shore of Sydney gives him an instinctive understanding of the economic stories that appeal to our readers, as successive editors—and innumerable front-page stories—attest. Since returning from a stint as our South Asian correspondent he's taken a special interest in state economic issues.

John Garnaut, formerly a commercial lawyer, was hired by a *Herald* editor partly because he referred to 'congestion pricing' in answer to a question about problems on the Harbour Bridge. He was hired with one instruction: persuade Gittins to make you one of his boys. But when on our first meeting I confessed I knew little about reporting, he wondered why he was wasting his time. I think I must have had something he found useful. Garnaut's journalism was hard-hitting from the beginning, but he was put out when people started shooting back. He'd wondered why so many journos pulled their punches. I told him now he knew why. References to 'the heat in the kitchen' and growing a thicker skin followed.

Garnaut did well in Canberra, and as our long-lived correspondent in Beijing he put in what I think was a world-class performance. Back in Australia, he has a lot more summits to climb. Garnaut encouraged *The Age* to hire a young Treasury officer, Peter Cai, as its Asian affairs reporter, then asked me to mentor him. So Cai is my first grandboy, so to speak. As a fluent speaker of Mandarin, he's already making his name as a bridge between readers in Australia and readers in China. He'll go a long way, too.

Jessica Irvine is the boy who kept me awake at night most but is now the one of whom I'm proudest. She had honours in PE, but I was most impressed by her being offered a place at Oxford just before her father returned to Canberra from the high commission in London. A lot of people didn't want us to hire her—including a *Herald* heavy trying to prove he could beat me in a corporate arm wrestle—but Irvine's had the last laugh. She taught me you can't talk someone into being hungry. But you don't have to: just drop them into the hugely competitive atmosphere of the Canberra press gallery and wait for them to catch the bug. Once they've had the thrill of a few page-one leads they're away. And once they've mastered the art of writing for page one—as all my boys do, with little help from me—the opportunities keep coming and they quickly establish themselves as someone whose services the trumps would be sorry to lose.

After mastering economics and reporting, Irvine revealed herself to be capable of writing the clearest and most succinct columns, with a wonderfully light touch. An old-school hand told me he used to worry about what the *Herald* would do if I fell under a bus; now he didn't. Readers would stop me in the street to warn me Irvine was after my job. Knowing what my bosses thought of her, she could have had it. But she was young and ambitious, and it wasn't clear how long it would take the old boy to shuffle off to a retirement home. So when News Corp offered to virtually double her salary she took it, becoming not just Australia's first female economics editor but News' first national economics editor, appearing in all their capital city tabloids. Now, however, we've lured her back to the fold.

Jacob Saulwick, grandson of the man who was the *Herald*'s pollster for many years, was shooting for an academic career when he became disillusioned and decided to try journalism. I think I can safely say he's found it a lot more satisfying, as all my boys do. Saulwick has worked in the business section and the Canberra bureau, but is now our highly valued transport reporter, never far from the front page. I tell my boys I run an open prison and they can walk out at any time, with no hard feelings. In any case, my definition of economics is wide enough to encompass transport.

Clancy Yeates was Saulwick's best mate at Fort Street and he, too, has first-class honours in PE from Sydney Uni. Yeates is the first of my boys to return to the business section after his stint in the Canberra gallery. I'm encouraging him to occupy ground I've never had time to master: the intersection of economics and business—that is, using economic concepts to analyse the strategy and performance of listed companies. Never had a boy the trumps speak of more highly.

Gareth Hutchens has a BA honours in English literature and finished his economics degree while working in our business section. He's now taken the well-trodden path to the Canberra gallery. He writes a fine column while filling in for me during my frequent holidays—as all my boys do—and cracked an entry in a book of the best business writing while still a trainee.

Peter Martin, formerly the Canberra economics correspondent for the *Herald* and *The Age*, now the incomparable Tim Colebatch's successor as economics editor of *The Age*, is ex-Treasury, has a deep understanding of economics, a great memory for policy detail and can read official reports much faster than I can. He writes clear, powerful and insightful columns. He's not an official boy, more an honorary one, and is making a first-rate economics editor.

I've long been a great believer in journalistic nepotism. The children of journalists have a realistic view of a journalist's work, they ought to have learnt to think like a journo at the dinner table and for some people the ability to write can be inherited. Once inside the door, they should have a conviction that anything mum or dad could do they can do at least as well. Hiring people at the entry level is about minimising the risk of picking a dud, and someone whose parent was a journo has to be low risk.

Someone with both parents as journos just about comes with a money-back guarantee. You'd think a person with such a pedigree would walk into a job, but not in these straightened times. Of late I've encountered two young female jobseekers with the most illustrious parentage. Remembering my own indebtedness, I've been delighted to help smooth their path with a little arm-twisting.

What I tell 'em

The main thing I do as a mentor is socialise my boys, training them to think like a journo. And write like a journo, not like a student or an academic and definitely not like a bureaucrat. For the first month or so we meet weekly to scrutinise their copy, comparing what they submitted to the subs with what appeared in the paper. You wrote this, the sub changed it to that—why? If a piece didn't get a run, what was wrong with it? Soon enough they imbibe the house style, the preference for short words and short, simple sentences, and a clear, direct approach.

I teach them to become obsessed by the first sentence—the 'intro' in the case of a feature or column, the 'lead' in the case of a news report. In theory, the lead should cover who, what, where and when, leaving how and why for later; in practice, the lead should encapsulate at least the single most interesting and important aspect of the story as briefly and with as much punch as possible. Intros, on the other hand, can be softer, more discursive and alluring. They don't have to spit out the point or even nominate the subject, but *must* entice the reader to keep reading.

You start searching for the best lead from the moment you begin reading or sitting through a press conference, and keep working on it and honing it in the cab back to the office. Get the lead right and the rest of the piece falls into place. The greatest sin is 'burying the lead'—not putting the best bit (often the best angle on the event) first.

The 'inverted pyramid' formula—where the lead summarises who, what, where and so on, and then the facts are listed in descending order of importance—is probably not the best way to go. It can be too staccato and disjointed and, in these days of computerised measurement of story lengths, no stories are cut from the bottom on the stone. The best approach is to summarise the key points in the first few pars, then shift into a more sequential, storytelling approach.

When Gerry Noonan was editor of the *Fin*, a young journo had a great but complex story for the front page. He didn't know where to start and time was ticking away, so Noonan told him to think about how he'd explain the story to his wife when he got home and she asked what he was so pleased about. That would be the best way to explain it to the readers.

The hardest thing for new journos to get a handle on is 'newsworthiness'—what makes one story more worthy of a run than another? The two key ingredients are developments that are either interesting or important—ideally both, though interesting-but-inconsequential always trumps important-but-dull. The most favoured stories always go on the odd-numbered pages, starting with page one, because the reader's eye is believed to fall first on the right-hand page rather than the left-hand.

But a further ingredient is the unusual—which is often the thing that gives a story its interest or importance. I unfailingly repeat the old-school journo's adage that dog bites man isn't news, but man bites dog is. It's hardly surprising that humans take more interest in the out-of-the-ordinary than the ordinary. How else could we process and make sense of the multitude of things going on around us, the vast majority of which don't require our limited attention? When I was an accountant we called it 'exception reporting', and news is no different. It follows that no change—often revealed by phrases such as 'X continued to . . .'—isn't a story.

It's not that simple, however. Newsworthiness is highly subjective and journalists have unspoken rules about what is and isn't. There's no alternative but for the new journo to study the judgements being made by their betters and internalise the profession's prejudices on what makes a good story.

When Peter Bowers was news editor I remember hearing a journo ask him how far he wanted him to push a particular story. Bowers replied, 'I want you to push it as far as you possibly can—but no further.' That was the perfect answer (borrowed from Einstein), even though it's saying everything and nothing. You make stories as interesting and important as you can, without distortion or exaggeration. Just where the line is on that is for you to judge.

I have a two-step approach to my training. Step one: learn the unwritten rules of reporting and judging a story's 'newsworthiness' and follow them without question. Step two doesn't come until you've got what I call 'tenure'—when all the heavies around the office have decided you're a good reporter whose services must be retained. Step two is to break any rule you've decided never made much sense, to experiment with doing things differently and better. To do what most journalists never want to do: innovate.

As part of step one, the old-school in me emphasises the need to always meet deadlines and stick to word lengths. And always deliver the subs 'clean' (error-free) copy. If you get a reputation with the subs for delivering clean copy you'll end up getting a better run and fewer changes to your copy (some of which make it worse rather than better). If you deliver dirty copy, believing you're too important to bother with grammar and spelling, or get a reputation as a 'late filer', the subs will do their damnedest to blacken your reputation with the trumps.

The way to meet deadlines is simple. You make a realistic assessment of how long it will take you to actually write the story, then project back from the deadline. That's the time you call a halt to all your telephoning and gathering of information. One more call might yield the sparkling quote you've been seeking but, sorry, too late. Missed the cut.

When talking to contacts it's vitally important not to be afraid of seeming ignorant by asking silly questions. Why? Because if you conceal your ignorance on the phone in private, you risk revealing it in public in the paper. The contact may not be impressed to be asked elementary questions, but she'll revise her opinion when she sees how clearly and accurately you've explained it in the paper. As the Chinese proverb puts it: one who asks a question is a fool for five minutes; one who does not ask a question remains a fool forever.

The way to develop confidence as a journo is also simple: fake it till you make it. If you act confident for long enough, eventually you'll become genuinely confident. A big part of this is that other people have a surprising tendency to take you at your own apparent assessment of yourself. As an application of this, if you write something you don't think is much good, it's imperative *never* to admit that when you hand it in. Judgements in journalism are highly subjective, and if you put negative thoughts into people's minds they're likely to drive out positive ones. If you don't say anything there's a high chance the others won't notice.

What's more, you're not necessarily a good judge of the quality of your own work. Plenty of times I've submitted stuff I didn't think much of, only to have the readers get excited about it. Once the favourable reaction has come in you go back and read the piece and realise it's not so bad after all. You're always hoping to write what Alan Mitchell calls 'a dago dazzler', but they're surprisingly hard to pick in advance.

Pass me another anecdote

Anyhow, that's the sort of thing we cover in the early tutorials. After that, most of the mentoring happens over lunch. Having boys gives me someone to have lunch with—at the office's expense. The things we talk about are now the contents of this book.

A big topic we discuss is how to handle bosses. On this, I'm my father's son. It's surprising how much people conform to your expectations of them. Keep telling a kid they're clumsy and that's exactly what they'll be. Bosses are the same. If you expect your boss to be honest with you and keep his promises, he'll be reluctant to fall short of your high opinion. But if you believe bosses are usually untrustworthy—as many journos do—you'll gather much evidence to support your thesis.

When you screw up, never wriggle on the hook, but take it on the chin. (And, of course, never mix metaphors.) When a stuff-up comes to the boss's notice, he wants to issue an admonishment and move on. If you make excuses and try to shift the blame, you prolong the agony and lower the boss's opinion of you. Immediately admit your error and the boss is satisfied; unless it's really bad it will be forgotten by the end of the week. Errors are a common occurrence on newspapers.

I encourage my boys not to worry too much about stuffing up. We're not public servants. It's much more important to try new things, press the limits and grow, than to live in fear of admonishment and causing the publication of a correction. You don't get to be a star performer without running risks, and I want all my boys to be stars. No guts, no glory. You learn most from your mistakes and it's surprising how soon stuff-ups are forgotten in the rush to get out another issue.

Every issue of every newspaper ever has been full of errors. Most of them are of little consequence; some do matter. Not all the latter are formally corrected. That depends mainly on how forcefully people complain, which helps explain why some inconsequential errors get corrected. The *Herald* has one senior editor who does little more than respond to complaints, including formal complaints to the Press Council. Newspapers get a lot of complaints and, like most institutions, they're pretty defensive.

I'd be defensive, too, were it not for my experience on the other side of the notebook. More than a few times over the years I've been interviewed and my words reported, so I know how easy it is to be misreported, even by the *Herald*. Maybe the reporter supplied his own answers to background questions he forgot to ask, maybe he misunderstood what I was saying. Once my quotes were full of incomprehensible rhyming errors because the reporter didn't listen carefully enough to her tape.

Thinking about it more generally, it's possible for even the most perceptive reporter not to quite comprehend what someone is saying to them, and a lot of reporters aren't all that perceptive. Just as big a problem are the reporters who knowingly twist what they've been told to make it fit into what they—or their bosses—have decided is a better story. So I don't have a high opinion of the accuracy of reporting.

But, I tell my boys, there are two sides to the story. A lot of complaints aren't justified. A reader will allege your piece was 'factually wrong' when what they really mean is they disagree with your interpretation of the facts, or would themselves have quoted different facts. A piece can be 'wrong' because, in 900 words, you didn't manage to include aspects of the argument the reader considers to be more important.

I think it's common for people to speak frankly to a reporter but then see what they said in the cold light of the following morning and think, 'Gosh, what will the boss say when he reads this?' There's a high chance such people will claim to have been misquoted. Claims to have been taken out of context may well be justified, but may not be. Since reporting is unavoidably selective, it's always possible for an interviewee to tell themselves they were taken out of context because the report failed to include everything they said on the subject. Or 'taken out of context' may really mean being put into a context in the story that the interviewee hadn't expected. (Sometimes the reporter seemed terribly sympathetic on the phone but, on the page, is anything but. That's a journalistic trick dating back long before Truman Capote used it so ruthlessly in *In Cold Blood*. A lot of reporters aren't nice people.)

I tell my boys that if someone accuses them of writing a report 'littered with factual errors' they should always call the person's bluff. Insist on being given chapter and verse of all errors so they can be corrected. In my experience you find there aren't all that many and most are matters of opinion. Sometimes there mightn't be more than one consequential fact that's clearly wrong. Maybe not even one. Readers and interviewees do have a tendency to exaggerate.

On a similar line to faking it till you make it, the way to be treated like a senior is to act like a senior. Be a self-starter rather than waiting around to be given a story to write. Take responsibility, make your own decisions and get on with it. The payoff for being a senior is being able to talk to the trumps direct rather than through intermediaries. But keep acting like a junior and a long time will pass before they start treating you as anything but a junior.

On another topic, I tell my boys there's no politics more important than office politics. I don't advocate game-playing as a substitute for hard work or excellence, but nor do I think you can afford to have a soul above the game-playing going on around you. And there are times when making a certain move is more appropriate than other times.

Since most of us work in big organisations, it's important to understand how organisations work. One conclusion I've come to is that people conform to their roles within the outfit. When their role changes, so do their attitudes. When Paul Kelly was chief of the *Herald*'s bureau in the Canberra gallery, he was full of how the bosses back in Sydney were weak on politics and always making silly judgements about what to put on the front page. But when he was made a trump in Sydney it wasn't long before he was

Media changes on table

Steve Lewis's article, "Cabinet closes on media laws" (*AFR*, December 18), contains a number of inaccuracies.

Mr Lewis claims that on December 17 Cabinet "discussed plans to overhaul media ownership laws"; that in "my progress report to Cabinet" I "provided a snapshot of [my] agenda to introduce changes to both the cross-media ownership and foreign investment rules in the media sector"; and that I "noticed the difficulties facing the Coalition as it tries to secure Senate support for its reforms".

I can only conclude that Mr Lewis has made all this up becuase there was no Cabinet discussion of media ownership laws on December 17.

How Mr Lewis could report on the so-called details of a discussion that never took place is beyond me.

Richard Alston,
Minister for Communications,
Information Technology and the Arts,
Canberra, ACT.

Editor's note: During the two-day Cabinet meeting on December 17 and 18, Cabinet discussed media laws, as reported in the AFR. *The Media law discussion took place on the second day of the meeting in Sydney*

complaining that 'those people in Canberra just don't get it'. (In truth, all Canberra bureaus of all papers always believe head office doesn't understand politics and is always downgrading a story about the latest Canberra kerfuffle for some silly story about the premier resigning.) When John Alexander was moved from boss of the *Herald* to boss of the *Fin* it was just two weeks before, meeting him on the stairs, he told me the *Herald* had 'gone off'.

I tell my boys that, if they want a promotion, they must first 'put out'. I call it the drug-pusher model: you give it away until people get hooked on it, then you demand a price. You shame the boss into lifting your pay to more fairly reflect your contribution. People who don't trust bosses try to do it the other way: once they give me a pay rise I'll work harder. Try that and you'll wait a lot longer.

Young journalists aren't highly paid, but nor are they badly paid. I have no compunction about piling work onto my boys until the point where they become parents. If they're overdue for a pay rise I'll help them get one—though it's a sign of maturation when they get their own. When they get an offer from another employer I'll help them work out how best to exploit it.

This can make my life interesting, of course. Senior journalists are expected to help editors persuade junior journalists they'd be crazy to leave. Sorry, but I won't do that unless I believe it. My first loyalty is to my boys. An editor was outraged when one of my boys got a generous offer and asked him to match it. 'Doesn't he understand how pressed I am on the budget?' I said he was a bright young boy trying to get ahead in journalism. Why should he care about your budget? He's only doing exactly what you'd have done at his age (and, I could have added, would still do given half the chance).

Many editors are too distracted to make sure young journalists know their good work has been noticed. Either that or they're afraid their first word of praise will be met with a demand for a pay rise. But I'm generous with my praise—mainly so I can be candid with my criticism. Young people think the big boss has no idea who they are. I tell them that though he may not recognise them in the lift, in his head is a fat file with their name on it. The entries in the file are what the people you've worked for have told him about you.

Still on office politics, I warn my boys never to let fly in their letter of resignation. There aren't many employers of journos and you never know when you may want to come back. So make sure the last memo on your staff file is one of politeness and gratitude for opportunities provided, smoothing the way to your rehiring.

Particularly when my boys have reached step two and have attained tenure as a valued journo, I tell them they have to protect their reputation for accuracy and honesty—even against the boss, who may be prepared to sacrifice your credibility just to make a splash on the day. If *you* don't protect your reputation, who will? Once Chris Anderson asked me to write a special supplement on how to minimise your tax. I wasn't at all happy with this. One reason I'd left accounting to become a journo was that I didn't want to devote my life to helping the well-off escape their obligations to the community. As an accountant, if I *was* prepared to prostitute myself, I'd want to be paid full commercial rates for my advice, not what a journo got paid. Even so, I did as I was asked. But, as it turned out, Anderson forgot to promote the supplement, so few people noticed it. I breathed a sigh of relief and vowed never again to abandon my principles just for an editor's greater good.

Turning to *party* politics, old-school type that I am, I introduce my boys to the old Canberra rule: if in seeking to explain some development you're faced with a choice between a stuff-up or a conspiracy, go for the stuff-up every time. The older you get the more you realise how common stuff-ups are.

On the soapbox

LBJ was a great one for piss jokes. You know he'd rather have his critics inside the tent pissing out . . . But I like the one that said giving a speech on economics was like pissing down your leg—'it seems hot to you, but not to anyone else'. As a rule, journalists don't make many speeches. When you write for an outlet with a readership of many hundreds of thousands, it's hard to get too enthused about an audience of 1000, let alone 50. So journalists don't give speeches, but I do. I gave my first at my sister's twenty-first when I was eight and have been speechifying ever since. It goes with being an officers' kid in the Sallies.

I do think an appearance in the flesh makes a bigger and more memorable impact on readers than an appearance via the mass media, just as a concert beats a record and attending a play beats watching a TV show. I guess I give maybe 30 speeches a year, which would be more than the editor does. I do it because I'm asked and because I enjoy it.

Towards the end of one year I worked out I'd given 36 speeches, so risked asking our sports columnist Peter FitzSimons how many he'd given. 'About a hundred,' he said, 'or one speech a hundred times.' I do a few repeats, but not many. And it's writing the speech that takes the time, not delivering it. Before I became a journo I used to speak from notes, but years as a print journalist has made me want to get my statements and explanations word perfect. I try to keep my written speech pretty short because I know I'll be adding a lot of ad libs, which are what keeps the speech animated and looking less like it's being read.

Speech-making is by far the most lucrative way of making extra money, far better than writing articles or books. I write books because, for a journo, it's one step closer to immortality than wrapping fish. I used to give speeches for money, but stopped charging ages ago. In theory this was supposed to leave me with more free time, but it left a vacuum to be filled by favours for mates and ego indulgence. When it's someone's 'memorial oration' or I can say 'they asked me, not my competitors', I'm tempted. I'm not tempted when it's a big business entertaining its clients or when I'll be introduced by some ABC personality who *is* charging.

Government departments I rarely say no to. But most of my speeches are to high school economics teachers and regional groups of economics students. The teaching thing again. Some student gatherings I've spoken to every year for more than 30 years. By now

I have premiers and economics professors telling me they used my articles at school. I also accept most invitations to speak to university students.

High school economics teachers are teachers who teach economics, not economists who teach. For decades I've made it my self-appointed duty to help them keep up with the ever-changing fashions in the management of the macro economy. I do it in Sydney and Melbourne and will fly to Adelaide or Brisbane if asked. Most economics editors wouldn't bother, but for some reason I do. High school economics is my favourite cause.

This is the place to acknowledge my debt to Paddy McGuinness—which I'm happy to do now he's dead; our relationship became too rivalrous for me to make any admissions to his face. But in some ways he was a great role model for economics editors. I'm an adherent to the Paddy McGuinness school of public speaking, which holds that there's no point in speaking to an audience unless you say something that makes them sit up, challenges their comfortable assumptions and gives them something *un*comfortable to think about. I've often imagined Paddy telling a bunch of miners that the greenies have a point in the morning, then telling a bunch of environmentalists that the miners have a point in the afternoon. He was that kind of bloke.

And then, of course, there's dress. Paddy, who always dressed in black and whose portrait was entered in the Archibald Prize at least twice, taught me that an ambitious economics editor always uses his clothing to draw attention to himself. Since Paddy was all black, I tried being all white like Tom Wolfe, but was too much of a grub. I settled for 'rumpled casual'. It's partly a reaction against the buttoned-up business look of chartered accounting and also part of an old-schooler's view that journos don't wear suits. But you have to be very old-school still to believe that.

CHAPTER 6
UP THE ECONOMIC LEARNING CURVE

The forecaster is a careful man, he has no gun or pistol,
He walks as gently as he can, because his balls are crystal.

Old poem from a reader

Why did an accountant who'd forgotten most of the economics he was supposed to have learnt at uni, and never really learnt to be a reporter, go from cadet journalist to economics editor in four years? Because he had the immense good fortune to be in the right place at the right time. I joined the *Herald* just as the startling policies of the Whitlam government and the global economic disruption of the first OPEC oil price shock were convincing the nation's editors that the biggest part of politics was economics, that they needed to run a lot more stories about the economy and needed more journalists proficient in economics to do it.

The oil price shock of December 1973 happened to make my first year at the *Herald*, 1974, a watershed in the global economic history of the twentieth century. It proved to be the last year of the almost 30-year postwar Golden Age of strong and steady growth in all the developed countries, with low inflation, full employment, ever-rising living standards and a narrowing gap between rich and poor. The oil shock wrong-footed Western governments and brought to light the hitherto unknown problem of 'stagflation'—simultaneously high unemployment and inflation.

The developed economies entered a period of dysfunction that was to last at least a decade for the major economies and at least two for Australia. Our problems were deepened and lengthened by the inexperienced adventurism of the Whitlam government and the lack of resolve of the Fraser government. Until 1974, the economy pretty much looked after itself. Like governments everywhere, the Whitlam government had no idea the rules of the game had changed. It was justified in claiming part of the economy's problems were outside its control, but its uncomprehending efforts to right 23 years of Coalition wrongs in its first term—in particular, its huge increase in wage costs—made matters much worse. The Fraser government, too, didn't really understand how much things had changed and how much harder it would have to try.

To be fair, it took the world's economists a long time to understand why things had gone wrong and how stability could be restored. The advent of stagflation caused a loss of confidence in traditional Keynesian macro-economic management, which could deal with either high inflation or high unemployment, but not both at the same time. In the search for an alternative, many turned to 'monetarism'—controlling the growth in the supply of money—as promoted by Milton Friedman.

I became an economic journalist when the battle between Keynesians and monetarists was at its height. It turned out that though much of the monetarist criticism of Keynesianism had merit—money did matter, as the monetarists had argued—the rest was mumbo jumbo. Money-supply targeting wasn't the magic answer promised. It didn't even work, and the many governments that adopted it quietly dropped it. Even so, the main instrument for managing the ups and downs of the economy was switched from fiscal policy (the budget) to monetary policy (interest rates).

Another solution to stagflation that economists explored was 'incomes policy'—direct controls over wages, other incomes and prices. Its Australian version came late in the form of the Hawke–Keating government's 'Accord' with the union movement. Even after a big fall in the dollar, it worked well in stabilising the inflation rate—at a still-too-high 8 per cent—and bringing about a significant fall in real wage costs that caused employment to grow strongly and unemployment to fall, until progress was reversed by the recession of the early 1990s. It took until the mid–90s to get inflation down to the 2 or 3 per cent that had pertained during the Golden Age. The unemployment rate will never return to the below 2 per cent level of the postwar era, but by the mid-noughties it did get down to the 5 per cent level economists now define as full employment (hard though that may be to believe).

A related area of dispute at this time was about the underlying causes of unemployment. Because the demand for labour is derived from the demand for goods and services, Keynesians argued the high level of unemployment was explained by the weak growth in the economy, an argument known as 'deficient demand' leading to 'Keynesian unemployment'.

In contrast, more conservative economists—those more influenced by the pre-Keynesian, 'neo-classical' model—argued the demand for labour was weak because wage rates were too high and this discouraged businesses from employing as many workers as they otherwise would. The solution to this 'classical unemployment' was to find a way to lower wage rates in real terms. It wasn't until 1988 that two Reserve Bank economists, Bill Russell and Warren Tease, did a study that, to my mind, satisfactorily resolved this long-running dispute. It found that employment since the mid–1970s had been affected roughly equally by high wage rates and weak demand.

Recessions I've known

Dr Don Stammer, a veteran business economist, says you need to have seen four recessions before you're fully qualified. I thought the global financial crisis of 2008–09 would bring my fourth, but if you don't count that—I count it as a potentially severe recession turned into a mild one by remarkably skilful management—I've seen three big ones. The recession of 1974–75 would by itself have caused the Whitlam government's defeat had there not been more than enough other reasons. The severe recession of the early 1980s brought the Fraser government's reign to an end after just seven years and the severe recession we didn't have to have in the early 1990s—in the sense that all recessions happen by accident rather than design—finally did for the perpetrator of that bravado in 1996, although Paul Keating's execution was delayed three years by the political inexperience of a former economics professor, Dr John Hewson.

It's worth remembering, as only someone like me does, that Keating only ever used that unforgettable line once, withdrew it within a few days and apologised for saying it—all to no avail. He said it because he would much rather have been seen as a knave than a fool, an evil genius rather than a bungler. Similarly, his warning that Australia risked becoming a banana republic was off the cuff and never repeated. It hugely annoyed his cabinet colleagues and licensed everyone from the *New York Times* and *The Economist* down to cast aspersions on our economic management. John Howard's remark about non-core promises is another that was unpremeditated and never repeated. The vast majority of the things politicians say are soon forgotten. The remarks that last long enough to be worth writing on their tombstones are almost invariably ones they'd prefer never to have made.

Feel free to write this on my tombstone: he never fell for the line that economists had finally conquered the business cycle. You only had to live through the Keynesians' humiliation in the world recession of 1974–75 to be permanently cured of such hubris. I soon formed the view that recessions occurred roughly every seven years. I know from the three recessions that have occurred so far 'on my watch'—each of them accurately branded 'the worst recession since the Great Depression'—how terrible recessions are: the fear and pain they cause to small business people, workers who lose their jobs and young people who have the misfortune to be leaving school or university at the time. Whitlam's recession saw the rate of unemployment shoot up from 2 per cent to 6 per cent, Fraser's recession saw it peak at 10 per cent and Keating's at 11 per cent. I know how thoroughly depressed people get for years on end, convinced things will never pick up again. I also know how bitter are the public's recriminations against economists. Recessions may be a 'good story'—in the sense they give people like me plenty to write about—but I hate them.

My notion that recessions occur about every seven years remains pretty true for all the developed economies bar Australia. Even if you count the mild recession of the GFC—which I do—it remains true we haven't had a recession bad enough for ordinary people to notice for 23 years. There are three things to say about this. First, in one sense only it's a pity you have to be so old to know how terrible a severe recession is and hence to be hugely relieved, even grateful, we managed to avoid one in the aftermath of the GFC. Almost seven years later the North Atlantic economies are still embroiled in the Great Recession we escaped.

Second, that we've avoided severe recession for an unprecedented period is thanks more to good management than good luck. Even if you're so ill-informed or partisan as to imagine our escape from the Great Recession is due purely to China and the resources boom, you still have to explain 17 years of uninterrupted growth since the recession of the early 90s, including our exemption from the world recession of the early noughties. We should have been brought low by the Asian crisis of 1997–98, but weren't.

I decided very early in that 17-year period that the ultimate test of good economic management was to keep the recessions as far apart as possible, mainly because recessions put a lot of people out of work for long periods, and the longer you're jobless the harder it gets for you to regain a berth. I could have decided the ultimate test was to keep the inevitable recessions as mild as possible. Either way, our economic managers pass with flying colours. I know Australians find it hard to believe Aussies could be world-class at anything but sport, but it happens to be true of our econocrats.

I know because I watched at close quarters as it happened and I know how they did it. It's certainly true that our economic management was pretty bad for at least the first decade of my time as an observer. But between the late 80s and the early 90s the econocrats started getting their act together. Although most of the seeds were sown under the Hawke–Keating government, the Howard government was the first to enjoy the fruits. The Rudd–Gillard government also enjoyed them—as witness, its avoidance of the Great Recession—though it lacked the wit and internal cohesion to reap the harvest.

The econocrats did it by persuading their successive political masters to subject the conduct of day-to-day economic management to 'frameworks' of rules and targets intended to limit the scope for politically motivated short-termism. The obvious example is the decision—formalised by Peter Costello—to use an inflation target to guide decisions about changes in the official interest rate and to hand control over interest rates to an independent central bank.

The many acts of 'micro-economic reform'—including floating the dollar, deregulating the banks and various other industries, phasing out protection against imports and shifting the locus of wage-fixing to the level of the individual enterprise—also helped. Micro reform failed in its stated objective of permanently lifting the rate at which the economy could grow, but it had an unexpected benefit: by intensifying the competition within industries it made the economy far less inflation-prone and unemployment-prone, thus greatly simplifying the macro-managers' task in keeping the economy on an even keel.

The third thing to say about the 23 years that have passed since our last recession is that it can't last. The business cycle has neither been conquered nor died. We're long overdue for a recession and, rest assured, it will come. When Ian Macfarlane handed over to Glenn Stevens in 2006 after 10 years as governor of the Reserve Bank, both men knew Macfarlane had been lucky to escape having a recession on his watch and that Stevens couldn't be so lucky. He did cop and cope with the utterly frightening events of the GFC, guided the Rudd government in staving off a run on our banks, and slashed interest rates with such alacrity that I heard about it on the BBC while holidaying in France. Phew. But not to worry: there's still a fair chance he'll cop it again before his term expires in September 2016.

Treasurers I've known

In 40 years I've been around for 13 federal treasurers. The Whitlam government's Frank Crean was my first. I was too junior to get to know him, which was a pity. I liked him because he reminded me of my father. I had little to do with Dr Jim Cairns and didn't get to know Bill Hayden until he was in opposition. Once, in a phone interview, he asked if he was speaking too fast for me. It's OK, I said, I'm taping it. This was common practice in the gallery, but illegal if done without permission. Hayden was most upset and said he'd make a complaint to the editor. I sent him an abject apology, also arguing that if I was a bad person I would have been too devious to blurt out what I was doing. To my great relief he let it slide. About that time I had a phone interview with a Country Party shadow minister about super. It went for a while, but didn't seem to make a lot of sense. Only after I'd hung up did I realise I'd been asking about superannuation while he'd been answering about the superphosphate bounty.

After the Fraser government arrived I didn't get to know Rubbery Phil Lynch, but John Howard was a different matter. Later I even accepted an invitation to attend the party at his home in Wollstonecraft celebrating his first election as opposition leader. I've never seen so many Bermuda jackets in one room. I later wrote that I'd parked my dirty Datsun around the corner, something that stuck in his mind, as did my jibe that he represented the interests of 'the typical Wollstonecraft family'.

Keating was an assiduous worker of gallery journalists, who learnt much of his economics from Max Walsh until Treasury took over. So, though I was in Sydney, I got to know him and his staff well. I was seen as too partial to him and his policies, but that was because I invariably agreed with them—rationalism with a human face. To this day I'm unembarrassed that, when I sent him a copy of my first book, I inscribed it 'to God's gift to the economy'. Particularly as prime minister he became notorious for phoning journos to abuse them over something they'd written. For many it was a badge of honour. With me, however, his reproof was always more in sorrow than in anger. Our greatest treasurer, with daylight second.

When Keating decamped to the backbench after failing to topple Bob Hawke at his first attempt, his successor, John Kerin, did a more-Keating-than-Keating impression. His one most unKeating-like act was to demonstrate that the budget could be delivered satisfactorily without any need for a lockup. His subsequent fate, however, made it a unique occurrence—or lack of occurrence. With a degree in agricultural economics, Kerin was far better qualified than most treasurers, so I thought it terribly unjust when the TV news bulletins hounded him from office by repeatedly playing a clip of him forgetting that GOS stood for gross operating surplus. None of his righteous accusers would have known that. As for that gallery smartarse question—what's the dollar figure for GDP?—many highly competent economists wouldn't carry the figure in their head—as I don't—because it's trivia.

John Dawkins was competent but tetchy. Ralph (pronounced the Victorian way to rhyme with Elf) Willis was well qualified academically, but terribly reserved. Once when his staff had a story they wanted him to give me they arranged that I would fly to Melbourne, follow him around most of the day, then fly to Canberra with him on a VIP jet so he'd have time to talk to me. We talked all right, but he wouldn't cough up the story. He was too decent and too competent to deserve to end his career in the ignominy of using a document in the 1996 election campaign that proved to be fake.

Peter Costello had two counts against me: I was from Sydney and, like virtually all journos, I was biased against him politically. It's true I criticised him on more issues than I supported him. But though I backed him vigorously on some unpopular measures, it would never have crossed his mind that my criticism arose from our differing values, not from partisanship. Early in his term someone on his staff suggested I fly to Canberra and have dinner with him so we could get to know each other. It wasn't a success. Unlike most politicians he didn't have the wit to nod noncommittally while I gave him free advice, just kept telling me dirty jokes.

He cured me of having a lot to do with the treasurer's office, helping me realise something that would never have occurred to him: since there's no shortage of expert economic advice, he needed me more than I needed him. Once, his press sec decided to give me the treatment regularly dished out to gallery reporters who'd incurred his displeasure by inviting all economic journalists to some function except me. I couldn't believe he could be so incompetent. Gallery reporters had no choice but to cop such treatment in silence, but as a columnist in Sydney I had nothing to lose and everything to gain by making it public. Normally I resist the temptation to go for cheap cheers, but this time I opted for a little self-publicity.

I kept it up for two weeks until the call came through from Costello. 'I'm sorry to shock you, Ross, but I didn't actually read the column you say I took offence at.' Etcetera. It was as close to a conciliatory call as Costello could get, so I too was conciliatory. People kept telling me Costello was bright but lazy, but a treasurer who didn't read my columns? I believed him. What it proved was something I suspect happens a lot: his press sec had taken offence on his behalf. It was probably the press sec who'd finally decided to ask the boss to call off the Gittins dog.

Costello's greatest achievements were his carriage of the goods and services tax and his reform of the prudential supervision of the financial system, which kept our banks out of trouble in the GFC. I hope I'm big enough to acknowledge these and other achievements, but the notion that he's up there with Keating as a reformer is partisan propaganda.

Wayne Swan fell well short of either of them. In opposition he put a lot of effort into getting to know me and I grew to like him. A couple of times as treasurer he gave me heads-ups before big announcements which helped me work out my position. But the truth is I feel a bit guilty about Swan. I let my liking for the man stop me from writing what I thought: that he was too weak to be treasurer. He wasn't brave enough on the reform front nor tough enough in controlling government spending and he couldn't sell ice-creams on a hot day at the beach. He was particularly poor on the mining tax, though it's true Treasury let him down with some serious revenue and political miscalculations. He wasn't tough enough with Treasury, either.

When he was succeeded by Chris Bowen my first thought was regret that I'd neglected to take up opportunities to get to know Bowen better. But thinking about my problem with Swan I decided

I was better off not getting to like these guys and so being freer to judge them on their merits. I know Joe Hockey well enough to know he's a likable guy—and to expect him to see more easily than Costello that, with me, he'll win some and lose some—so that's close enough.

The best of 13 treasurers

1. **Paul Keating**. By a country mile. He instigated the sweeping reforms that transformed the economy and laid the groundwork for better day-to-day management of it. He made the economy less inflation-prone and more flexible, thus able to reduce unemployment faster.
2. **Peter Costello**. Greatest achievement was to free the Reserve Bank to change interest rates as it saw necessary, meaning the economy is now managed more by econocrats than politicians. He also ensured our banks were tightly supervised while the Americans were letting theirs create so much havoc.
3. **Wayne Swan**. Despite his failings, he deserves a spot on the treasurers' honour board purely for his surprisingly deft handling of stimulus spending and human confidence in the wake of the global financial crisis, ensuring we suffered only the mildest of recessions.

Econocrats I've known

In the Fraser and Hawke years, prime ministers and treasurers each had their in-house economists, often professors doing a stint in government. These guys had as part of their job descriptions responding to approaches from very senior journalists, particularly economics editors. I found them good value, much more informative than their bosses, who invariably spoke to me in question-time platitudes. They were best at explaining and justifying some new policy measure. When they'd say, 'Of course, we couldn't say this, but . . .' I knew I was getting good oil.

I met Dr John Hewson when he was working for Phil Lynch and got to know him a lot better during Howard's long treasurership. In the days when the Reserve Bank was under the thumb of Treasury, the governor and the secretary to the Treasury would agree on a line and stick to it when they went in to see the treasurer. Hewson saw his job as trying to drive a wedge between them so as to widen the choices being given to his boss.

While Hewson was working for Lynch he sat in on a meeting with one of my old lecturers, Professor Warren Hogan, by then at Sydney Uni. As they talked, Lynch slipped Hewson a note: 'Who the hell is Pigoo?' Arthur Pigou was the Cambridge don who identified 'negative externalities'—costs imposed on other people by a transaction between me and you—and proposed a 'Pigouvian tax' such as a tax on pollution to correct this market failure.

Once Hewson and I agreed to have lunch at a city restaurant. I waited at least three quarters of an hour for him, then decided to leave. As I left I found him waiting outside for me. As a boy from Newcastle, my heart went out to him. My Mosman-girl wife had soon trained me to meet her inside the venue not outside. This poor Baptist schmuck didn't know middle-class ways. Only much later did I learn he was notoriously late for appointments. He'd arrived late, then waited for me to come out so his tardiness could be passed off as a misunderstanding. He was that kind of bloke.

Hewson was always telling me how hopeless the politicians were. So when, some years later, he ask me to contribute to the telephone book of endorsements he was putting together as part of his bid to enter Parliament, I was happy to comply. I would never do such a thing today. I told the Liberal preselectors for the seat of Wentworth he was an able economist and they'd be mugs not to accept his offer. That was true enough, but my real motive was: OK, smarty, let's see *you* have a go.

Fraser's economist for much of his time was Professor John Rose, of the Melbourne Business School. Rose and Hewson did much to persuade Howard and Fraser to commission the landmark Campbell report on financial deregulation. Despite Fraser's scepticism, they'd made some progress in removing regulations controlling bank interest rates, and in reforming the way government bonds were sold, before Fraser lost office. Hewson deserves much of the credit for financial deregulation and also for the move to central bank independence and inflation targeting.

Labor had been critical of financial deregulation while in opposition, but when Keating became treasurer he changed all that. He got the banker Vic Martin to do a quickie report which, in effect, sanctified the Campbell recommendations for implementation by a Labor government. Perhaps because Treasury secretary John Stone was so bombastic—you could be honest and do it his way, or utterly unprincipled and do it some other way—Howard had a pretty adversarial relationship with his department. So I was a bit worried when Keating filled his office with Treasury advisers. 'Don't worry, Ross,' he said, '*they* will be working for *me*.'

Well, yes, I suppose they did—sort of. Keating was young and vigorous, with a lot of political skill and a burning desire to make his mark. But coming from the New South Wales Labor Right, what he lacked was a world view, a comprehensive and internally consistent cause to fight for. Treasury provided him with the intellectual framework of economic rationalism and educated him in its implications. In return, he went out and won battles for the cause. Treasury loved Keating and gave him great loyalty because he could win debates in cabinet, unlike Howard, who was always being stymied by Fraser.

Keating was also highly effective at selling the rationalist message to the media and the public. It took me far too long to realise, however, that the reasons he gave for pursuing certain policies were those he believed would appeal most to the electorate, not necessarily those that were the econocrats' true reasons for wanting the reform. He made much fuss about cutting the current account deficit by increasing exports and reducing imports but, though Treasury may have shared his concerns about the current account to some extent, its real priority was to eliminate the *budget* deficit. Similarly, Keating preached that micro-economic reform was aimed at making Australian businesses more internationally competitive so as to increase exports. Its true goal was to increase the domestic competitive pressure on our businesses, making them more efficient and thus causing faster economic growth.

None of my econocrat contacts would ever spill the beans to me, letting on that the boss's arguments were arguments of convenience, not the real deal. For insights like that I was on my own. It took a lot of effort by two professors from the Australian National University—John Pitchford and Peter Forsyth—to convince economists and economic journalists that all was not as it appeared.

Keating's other—much greater—failing was his predilection for meddling in takeover proposals in particular industries, especially the media. All governments fail to keep their legitimate role in media regulation separate from their party's political interests and their relationships with particular proprietors. But when Murdoch and Fairfax were circling the old sprawling Herald and Weekly Times group as it was breaking up and sinking under the waves, Keating had personal scores to settle. Murdoch emerged with a tabloid paper in almost every state capital and more than 60 per cent of the nation's metropolitan daily circulation. Fairfax emerged with next to nothing.

Keating was quite frank in telling you about his role in such commercial battles. I remember the contempt in his voice as he told me how Max Suich and Fred Brenchley were hamstrung in the negotiations because their chairman, James Fairfax, had chosen that time to be 'on holidays with his boyfriend in Antarctica'. Keating was out to punish Fairfax because of things we'd written about him. The fact is that governments of all colours ended up hating Fairfax because they couldn't do deals with us. Our chairman or chief executive couldn't promise support because the high degree of autonomy enjoyed by the editors of our papers and even their columnists—something owed mainly to James Fairfax's tolerance—meant they couldn't deliver.

For much of his time as treasurer, Keating's economist was Professor Barry Hughes, Welshman turned South Australian. Hughes was a well-known labour economist (note the 'u') and I'd had dealings with him before he took the job. On our first contact in his new role he gave me a warning: 'I promise I'll only ever tell you the truth, Ross, but I don't promise to tell you the whole truth.' I realised he meant he'd give me the arguments *for* the government's policy but, unlike an academic, wouldn't mention the arguments against. I thought that was fair enough. I preferred to talk to technocrats, and was too proud to talk to press secretaries, but always knew what I was getting was just a better class of bulldust.

Hughes taught me a lot of economics—and a little politics. At the new Hawke government's economic summit in 1983 it laid out the policy choices as three 'scenarios', options A, B and C. The government's preferred policy was option B. It had been attacked by Coalition-leaning business people, but then some Labor-leaning academics—one or two of whom had been hoping to get Hughes' job with Keating—criticised it for not going far enough. I thought this pretty poor, but Hughes was unperturbed. When you wanted to be seen as reasonable, he explained, it helped to be criticised by both extremes. Ah, so that's why B was the right answer.

At Labor's tax summit two years later, option C was the right answer. It contained proposals to broaden the income-tax base by taxing fringe benefits and capital gains, as well as introduce a 'broad-based consumption tax' to replace wholesale sales tax. But despite Keating's close links with the boss of the ACTU, Bill Kelty—rightly seen as an extra, invisible member of the cabinet—the unions were implacably opposed to the consumption tax, as was almost the whole of Labor, bar Keating.

The Business Council delegates wanted the consumption tax, but opposed option C because of its new taxes on capital gains and fringe benefits. Their opposition killed the last hope for option C. They ended up with those new income taxes, but no consumption tax. If there's a way to play your cards wrong, be sure the Business Council will find it. Little has changed over the years. Never has so much policy effort been expended to so little public benefit.

One day during the tax summit Hughes and I decided to go into town for lunch. He knew some photocopier salesman who'd give us a lift. We pushed through the consumption-tax protestors outside Parliament House and jumped into the car, which to my horror was a Porsche. We roared away to greatly invigorated cries of 'Tax the rich, not the poor'!

I got to know other people on Keating's staff. His initial tax specialist was Greg Smith who, after the tax summit, went on to a successful career in Treasury. He was replaced by a young chap with a still-shiny PhD called Ken Henry. Henry taught me a lot of tax economics.

Prime Minister Hawke's first in-house economist was Professor

Ross Garnaut, who did a lot to push for floating the dollar against the implacable opposition of John Stone. After Garnaut came Steve Sedgwick (who has since headed various federal departments) and Rod Sims, now chairman of the ACCC. I learnt from all of them.

Stone was the first Treasury secretary I had a lot to do with. He had an eye for young talent and for a time took me under his wing. I had lunch with him on the day of the Hilton bombing when he was in Sydney as part of Fraser's entourage at the Commonwealth regional heads of government meeting. Another time I had dinner with him at the Macquarie Inn the night before a meeting of the Reserve Bank board, of which he was an ex-officio member. When a different waiter came to clear our table between courses, Stone was at pains to tell him the small stain on the tablecloth had been made by his predecessor, not Stone. He was that kind of bloke.

Fraser thrived on manufactured crises and was a micro-manager who wanted to second-guess all his ministers. He thus built up a huge economic division within the Department of Prime Minister and Cabinet (PM&C), initially headed by a former Treasury officer, Ian Castles, then by another Treasury type, Eddie Visbord. Indeed, the economic division was staffed by a host of highly capable economists in exile from the dissent-intolerant Stone: Dr Mike Keating, Dr Vince Fitzgerald, Dr Ed Shann, Steve Sedgwick, John Spasojevic (Spazzo) and more. Most of them went on to head government departments.

And I got to know them all. Every so often Alan Mitchell and I would go to Canberra for the day and do the rounds of treasurer's economist, PM's economist and PM&C. Visbord would always bring in his top people to join the discussion. Once, I asked a question, he gave me his answer and then asked if his boys had anything to add. 'Well, as you know, Eddie,' Mike Keating began,

'I've never agreed with you on that,' and on he went. I have nothing but admiration for a boss big enough to take that in his stride.

It's always surprised me that econocrats rarely admit to having read anything you've written. But one day Visbord broke his rule, telling me how much he'd enjoyed one of my pieces arguing that the budget should be brought forward from August—well into the new financial year—to May, well before the start of the year to which it applied. 'In fact,' he said, 'I liked it so much I drew it to the prime minister's attention.' I forbore from reminding him why he liked the piece so much: it was a faithful rendering of all the arguments he'd given me when I rang to ask what he thought of the idea. It was actually one of David Bowman's 'editor's specials' about which I had no strong opinion. Looks prescient today, though.

Although both men were rationalists, Stone's Treasury was hawkish whereas Visbord's PM&C was dovish. I felt a lot more comfortable with Visbord's underlying values, so soon gravitated into the PM&C orbit. Visbord was always surprisingly forthcoming whenever I'd ring to ask for the thinking behind the latest policy move.

It took me quite a while to realise I was taking sides in an unending battle between Treasury and Treasury-in-exile. Politics in Canberra is fought on more levels than most people realise. The battle between the two departments was fought in cabinet, of course, and in inter-departmental committees, but also in the media via journalistic proxies. I hadn't quite realised I was chief public proponent of the dovish view and was being briefed accordingly. Since it *was* the less extreme view, however, it causes me no embarrassment to admit it at this late stage.

When Stone took early retirement not all that long after the arrival of the Hawke government, Keating had to select a new secretary of the department. I wrote a column advocating the appointment of Dr Chris Higgins, who was back from exile at the OECD in Paris. Higgins was widely acknowledged as the most technically accomplished of all the Treasury heavies. Earlier he'd teamed up with Dr Chris Caton in developing Treasury's early econometric models. (Caton had been my first Treasury contact. When no one would bother talking to the unknown Gittins, he did. Today, Caton is among the best of the business economists. He's far too capable ever to need my support but, should he ever need it, he'll get it without hesitation.)

But Keating gave the job to Bernie Fraser, a more balanced, less ideological man than Stone. Fraser abandoned Treasury's longstanding disapproval of the Arbitration Commission and its centralised wage-fixing system and was actively supportive of the Accord. Speaking to my contacts at PM&C, however, I discovered they'd become terribly worried about wages and the risk of a breakout.

Huh? At the moment Treasury had gone from hawk to dove on industrial relations, PM&C had gone the other way. Oh—now I get it. At that time PM&C's economic division justified its bureaucratic existence by offering an alternative view to Treasury. So when Treasury's position changed on something, PM&C felt it had no choice but to do the opposite. More evidence that people adjust their views and behaviour to fit the needs of their institution and their role in that institution.

Unlike Malcolm Fraser, however, Hawke had no desire always to be armed with the alternative position to that of his ministers and their departments. He was more chairman of the board, intervening in a minister's portfolio only when it became clear the minister had stuffed up. PM&C's economic division's role became less adversarial and, in any case, my underlying values—my Sally upbringing, if you like—were now a better fit with Treasury's.

Ten reforms that transformed Australia

1. **Floating the dollar**. Letting the market set the value of the Aussie dollar after December 1983 allowed it to fluctuate between US48 cents and US$1.10 so far, making it an absorber of shocks from the rest of the world. This has made the economy more stable and stopped the resources boom causing an inflation blowout.
2. **Deregulating the banks**. Introducing foreign banks and allowing banks to set their own interest rates made it much easier to get a loan and increased competition between banks and other lenders, but led to excessive lending to businesses and caused the deep recession of the early 1990s.
3. **New taxes on capital gains and fringe benefits**. In October 1985 Paul Keating announced new taxes, but cut the top income-tax rate from 60 per cent to 49 per cent. He also abolished negative gearing, but reversed this under pressure from estate agents.
4. **Removing import protection**. In May 1988 Keating announced the virtual phasing out of the import duties and quotas imposed on most manufactured goods. Predicted demise of manufacturing industry did not materialise.
5. **Privatising government businesses**. Sale of the Commonwealth Bank began in 1991 and Qantas in 1992. The Howard government sold Telstra in three tranches from 1997. State governments sold their banks, insurance companies and some power producers and distributors.
6. **Enterprise bargaining**. In 1993 the Keating government ended centralised wage-fixing through a 'national wage case' and introduced collective bargaining at the enterprise level. In 2005, Work Choices sought to promote individual contracts by reducing worker protections, to further encumber unions and end reliance on industrial rewards. The Rudd government reversed the most extreme parts of Work Choices, but left much of it in force.
7. **National competition policy**. In 1995 Keating sought to encourage deregulation and privatisation by state governments and tighten Trade Practices Act's restrictions on anti-competitive behaviour. Premiers tended to drag their feet.
8. **Central bank independence**. In 1996 Peter Costello allowed the Reserve Bank to make its decisions independent of the elected government,

endorsing its target of holding inflation between 2 per cent and 3 per cent, on average. The Reserve has raised interest rates more than a politician would—including during the 2007 election campaign—but this has kept inflation under tighter control than when politicians were in charge.

9. **Goods and services tax**. The start of the GST in 2000 came 25 years after it had been proposed by a major inquiry. It replaced wholesale sales tax and various unconstitutional or inefficient state taxes. Much death and destruction were predicted; little eventuated. But now the GST is showing signs of wear and needs renovation.
10. **Taxes on mining and carbon**. Wayne Swan planned to raise huge sums from taxing miners' high profits and use the proceeds to give tax cuts and concessions to business and individual savers. He also used a tax to impose a price on carbon dioxide emissions. Both reforms were badly mishandled and Tony Abbott has reversed them.

Power shifts to the Reserve

Another change was a big shift in economic power from Treasury to the Reserve Bank. This came in a couple of steps. The first was the developed world's post-monetarist consensus that the best instrument for managing the economy from day to day was no longer fiscal policy but rather monetary policy.

The second was financial deregulation, which occurred around the developed world in the late 1970s and early 80s. When monetary policy was conducted by 'direct controls' over banks' reserves, interest rates and lending, decisions to change the settings of the controls were made in Canberra by the government, acting on the advice of Treasury. But when the banks were deregulated and those controls removed, decisions about the appropriate level of interest rates to encourage or discourage demand were implemented by means of purchases or sales of government bonds. These 'market operations' were best decided and executed on location in Sydney by the Reserve. Similarly, when the dollar's value was fixed, decisions to devalue or revalue it were made in Canberra by the government on Treasury advice. Once the dollar was floated in December 1983, any efforts to influence its ups and downs had to be undertaken in the nation's financial capital, Sydney, by the Reserve.

The third step in the transfer of primary responsibility for management of the macro economy from Treasury to the Reserve came in the mid–90s with the move to inflation targeting by a central bank acting independently of the elected government.

It's a little-remarked fact that the attitudes economists and commentators take on macro management policy choices are strangely influenced by the city they live in. The further they live from Sydney the more critical of the Reserve they tend to be. As a Sydneysider, I had good links with the Reserve even in the Whitlam and Fraser years when it was treated as a virtual outpost of Treasury. After financial deregulation, and particularly after it gained its independence, the Reserve has taken its media relations very seriously as part of its efforts to ensure policy reasoning is well understood by the financial markets, business and the public. It's put a lot of effort into raising the level of understanding of monetary issues, and economic journalists are the purveyors of its messages.

Central bankers I've known

I've known well all the Reserve's governors and deputy governors since the days of Sir Harry Knight in the second half of the 1970s. But the Reserve has long had a special port of call for economics editors. In the old days it was the head of the research department, but these days that job goes by the fancier name of assistant governor (economic). This job is effectively the third most important in the Reserve after the governor and his deputy. Its occupant has a staff of 80 economists—almost as many as Treasury—and is the person who presents and defends the staff's recommendation to the monthly board meeting on whether the official interest rate should be moved or left unchanged, even though the 'staff's' view is determined by the governor. It's a position often occupied by people on their way to the very top.

I was too late on the scene to have much contact with the legendary Aussie Holmes, mentor to generations of central bankers. I did try to take him to lunch once, but he insisted on paying. I asked him if he was a monetarist, but he replied he was too old to be one. I puzzled over that for a few years, but I think I know what he meant: he'd long known that if you put interest rates up far enough this would weaken the economy and get inflation down, but he was too experienced to believe there was any magic that made this process anything less than brutal.

Once I was hurrying down a corridor at the Reserve's headquarters in Martin Place looking for someone's office. As I looked into one room there was the soon-to-retire Holmes at his desk, sucking an unlit pipe with spittle running down its stem. 'Ah Ross,' he said, 'come in, come in. Sit down, sit down.' Sorry, Aussie, I said, I can't stop I'm late for a committee meeting. A committee meeting? That's a choice I've regretted for years.

Holmes once observed that every economist needed to be equipped with 'a sense of the relative magnitudes'. He meant you needed to acquire a feel for what was big enough to be worth worrying about and what wasn't. He was right. I hope it's a standard I've attained and have imparted to my boys.

Being my father's son, when someone I respect tells me something, I'm inclined to believe them. But journos get told a lot of things by people with axes to grind, and thus need to be pretty sceptical. So I've made a rule: you can lie to me, but you can only lie to me once. Early in the Hawke government's term the papers were accusing it of having interfered in some decision of the Reserve's. I rang one of Holmes' successors and he assured me there was no truth to the story, so I wrote a column giving a detailed refutation of these silly claims.

The same week I ran into a young fellow who'd just resigned from the Reserve, who told me I'd been deceived and that the gent in question had even been laughing about it around the office. But I didn't much like the kid, so I didn't believe him. One of the gent's successors, however, went out of his way to tell me I had indeed been lied to. Though the events in question would have long been forgotten by most people, I immediately wrote a column confessing I'd been wrong and making it clear I'd been misled. I've had no further dealings with the gent from that day to this.

Governor Bob Johnston was much more a banker than an economist. Someone who later became very senior told me Johnston was always quoting my columns approvingly and demanding to know why all the high-flying economists working for him couldn't send him memos as clear and persuasive as my columns. Eventually, the high-flyers got wise. Whenever they had a proposition they wanted to sell the boss they'd first explain it to me, I'd write a column and Johnston would read it and quote it back to them approvingly. Hard to credit, I know. But the chap who told me was *very* senior and he told me twice.

When Johnston retired as governor in 1989 there was much media speculation about who Keating would appoint in his place. The Reserve's internal candidate was John Phillips, the deputy governor, but there was talk Keating might appoint the secretary to the Treasury, Bernie Fraser, or even one of his deputies, David Morgan. I wrote a column championing Phillips and describing Morgan as the 'joke candidate'.

This drew an angry phone call from Morgan, who accused me of destroying his chances. I found it terribly hard to believe anything I said could influence Keating's choice. But I can imagine what happened: Keating had always intended appointing Fraser but, in breaking the bad news to Morgan, used me as his excuse: 'Sorry, David, but now Gittins has poured shoot on you I couldn't possibly give it to you.' Morgan had phoned me before he'd figured that out. But he got the last laugh: he left Treasury not long after and soon became chief executive of Westpac.

As chief executive it would have given him immense gratification to recommend the appointment of his old boss, and recently retired Treasury secretary, Ted Evans, as chairman of Westpac's board. Sometime later Evans told me the experience in banking had changed a lot of his views. I would love to have had further and better particulars—I suspect it was an admission of Treasury fallibility coming from a most authoritative source—but then, most of the advice Evans had given me over the years was too cryptic for my simple mind.

That episode cured me of playing favourites in the appointment of senior econocrats. When the search was on for a successor to Fraser as Treasury secretary, I told Chris Higgins this time I'd do him a favour and *not* promote his cause. He got the job.

Ten biggest economic changes in my time

1. Parents' changed view that girls are just as entitled to an education as boys, leading to huge increase in women's participation in the paid workforce.

2. Dramatic increase in 'educational attainment', with much higher proportions of young people completing Year 12 and going on to university, and many doing double degrees. Girls now better educated than boys.
3. Outlawing of anti-competitive practices by business, including price-fixing and cartels. In the mid–1960s I used to audit a cartel that fixed the prices of ceramic pipes and tiles in northern New South Wales.
4. A revolution in banking, with banks willing to offer large home loans to almost all comers, passbooks replaced by internet statements, use of plastic rather than cash for purchases, wages and pensions paid by direct credit to bank accounts rather than by cash or cheque, and ATMs meaning people rarely visit their bank branch.
5. Much more intense competition in many industries following widespread deregulation, privatisation and removal of protection against competition from imports. Governments used to control the prices of bread, eggs and petrol.
6. A return to low inflation, low interest rates and the disappearance of economists' incessant complaints about excessive wage growth. Not to mention frequent disruptive strikes.
7. The rise of self-service in service stations and travel bookings, but also takeaways and pre-prepared meals, microwave ovens, dishwashers, home air conditioning, nannies and home cleaners.
8. Mobile phones that greatly changed our contact with family and friends, then smart phones that are coming to control our lives.
9. The rise of the internet, which is changing the way we shop, bank, pay bills, discover the news, play games, listen to music and read books.
10. The significant increase in the inequality of income and wealth, with those at the very top gaining a greatly disproportionate share of the growth in income, while rates of home ownership among the young and middle-aged fall.

Bernie, our best governor

Much as I like and respect Bernie Fraser's successors—Ian Macfarlane and Glenn Stevens—I believe he was the best governor of my time. It was he who set the template for the modern, independent, open central bank conducting its own communications with the world. Alan Greenspan, chairman of the US Federal Reserve, once said that 'if I seem unduly clear to you, you must have misunderstood what I said'. He was only half joking. In the old days central banks took a pride in being opaque and mysterious. Fraser put an end to that conceit.

As a mate of Keating's, Fraser was ideally placed to begin the assertion of the Reserve's independent judgement. In the run-up to the 1996 election, some in the money market were convinced Fraser would lower interest rates to assist his mate. In the event, he used his mateship to get away with not cutting rates, since that wouldn't have been appropriate to the economy's needs.

I believe it was Fraser who, reacting to the noise being made by Hewson about the latest fashion for independent central banks and inflation targeting, decided he'd better get in first with his own, acceptable version. His staff determined that the inflation rate had averaged 2 or 3 per cent during the Golden Age so, while the more ideologically correct New Zealanders set themselves a rigid target of zero to 2 per cent, Fraser set the more relaxed target of 2 to 3 per cent, adding the rider that it needed to be achieved only 'on average over the medium term'.

I attended a private lunch at the Reserve where one of the world's foremost macro-economists, Professor Stan Fischer, then deputy managing director of the International Monetary Fund, congratulated us on our inflation target and added that, now it had been implemented so successfully, we should move to a more rigorous target. What did 'on average over the medium term' actually mean? I said we all knew precisely what it meant.

After the lunch Macfarlane's able and independent-thinking

deputy, Dr Steve Grenville, took Fischer aside and straightened him out. We Aussies won that debate, with the Kiwis and others with lower, 'sharp-edged' targets discovering they couldn't be attained and moving to something more like ours. Another demonstration of Bernie Fraser's superior 'feel' for managing the economy successfully.

It remains true, however, that—as he once publicly confessed—had his only concern been to get the economy moving as quickly as possible after the recession of the early 1990s, he could have cut interest rates much harder and faster than he did. Fraser was no manic inflation-fighter; he did care about people having jobs. But I think he decided that, with Australia's era of high inflation now having run for almost 20 years, it was past time to act decisively to return to lasting low inflation. We'd had a severe recession, and it was important we emerged from all the pain with something valuable to show for it—even if this involved accepting more pain.

So Fraser kept the deflationary pressure on for longer, beat inflation out of the system and, with the help of his new targeting regime, kept the actual inflation rate low enough for long enough to lower the inflationary expectations of businesses and unions, thereby making the return to low inflation to some degree self-reinforcing. The fact that inflation has remained low and the next severe recession has so far been delayed for 23 years is owed, to a fair degree, to Fraser's toughness and good judgement. No bunch of politicians—conservative or Labor—could have exercised the courage and self-control needed to achieve that record.

My experience watching the bad, indifferent and good management of our economy over the past 40 years has left me sure of one thing: Malcolm Fraser may have lacked the resolve to live up to it, but his slogan 'Fight Inflation First,' is dead right. Part of the policy debate between Keynesians and their opponents rested on the belief that Keynesians cared most about unemployment because they worried about people at the bottom, whereas conservatives cared most about inflation because it diminished the wealth of the rich. In one of his earliest speeches as governor, Bernie Fraser demolished that neat dichotomy by pointing out inflation actually hurt the poor more than the rich because the poor were unable to afford the expert advice needed to protect themselves from—even benefit from—the effects of inflation. Negatively geared investment in property or shares is a classic instance of benefiting from inflation.

If you force me to choose which is the greater evil, inflation or unemployment, there's no shadow of doubt in my mind: unemployment wins. I'm sure Bernie Fraser, his successors and most econocrats would agree with me. But the choice we have to make—and the relationship between those two evils—is more subtle than that. To me, if you care about achieving low unemployment in anything but the short term, you start by fixing inflation and keep it fixed, so you can then grow the economy at a steady but healthy rate and thus grind down unemployment and keep it low for as long as possible. That describes how we've managed our economy over the past 20 years. In the preceding 20 years governments pursuing the alternative strategy of fighting unemployment first would rev up the economy after every recession, soon bringing inflation back up and thus sowing the seeds of the next bust.

My five worst predictions

1. Expecting the severe recession of the early 1990s to be a 'soft landing'.
2. Doubting the move from centralised wage-fixing to enterprise bargaining in the early 90s would be an improvement.
3. Saying the US authorities were right to allow Lehman Brothers to fail in September 2008.

4. Expecting Australia to be caught up in the subsequent Great Recession.
5. Failing to foresee the adverse social effects of micro-economic reform.

Advantages of long teeth

By now you may have detected a pattern: I've been round so long I know most of the top econocrats well because I had extensive dealings with them when they were in middle-level jobs and responsible for contact with journalists. Indeed, many of them have spent hours on the phone making up for the deficiencies in my university education. This huge investment of time on their part is a tribute to their dedication in ensuring the public is well-informed about the objectives of policy and the reasoning behind it.

This is how I got to know senior Treasury people such as Ken Henry, Dr Martin Parkinson, Mike Callaghan and others I probably shouldn't mention, as well as Reserve Bank people such as Macfarlane, Stevens, Dr Phil Lowe, Dr Malcolm Edey, Dr Guy Debelle and many more.

When I took a self-organised sabbatical in California in 1990, Macfarlane suggested I drive up the coast and visit one of his bright young fellows who was on secondment to the Reserve Bank of San Francisco. Since I've long believed it's much easier to get to know promising econocrats while they're on overseas postings, I did. He was Glenn Stevens and I'm glad I took the trouble.

Economics is a remarkably inexact science—if you could call it that, which I wouldn't. Economists rarely see recessions coming, even something as monumental as the GFC. Sometimes it even takes them months or years to understand precisely why a major recession came about. As we've seen, this was certainly the case with the world recession precipitated by the first OPEC oil shock. In Australia this was also the case with the recession of the early 90s, which Treasury wrongly predicted would be just a 'soft landing' because, unlike the two previous recessions, it hadn't been precipitated by tight monetary policy (high interest rates) in response to a wages breakout. Interest rates were high enough, of course—mortgage rates hit 17 per cent at one point—but inflation had stabilised at about 8 per cent.

It was Macfarlane, newly promoted to deputy governor, who was the first to twig to the unusual nature of the slump. It was a 'balance sheet' recession, coming from the financial side of the economy rather than the 'real' side of production and consumption. In a probably inevitable overreaction to their new-found freedom following financial deregulation, the banks had lent far too much, particularly to business, in the process fuelling a commercial property boom.

When ever-higher interest rates eventually caused the financial bubble to pop, the banks were left with huge bad debts and many businesses were left with liabilities that now exceeded the much reduced value of the properties they had borrowed so heavily to buy. The resulting recession would be deep and prolonged as businesses sought to 'repair their balance sheets'—get on top of their debts—by postponing expansion plans, slashing their wage bills and otherwise cutting costs. The banks themselves would avoid doing much new lending while they wrote off their bad debts and got on top of their own balance sheets.

At the time, Macfarlane's analysis was a great eye-opener to me. But it left me in good stead to understand the peculiar nature of the later Great Recession. It too was precipitated by the bursting of a credit-fuelled US property bubble—this time residential rather than commercial—which would necessitate years of grinding balance-sheet repair by households and governments.

Looking back over the 20 years of the Reserve's management of the macro economy since the advent of inflation targeting, I conclude that though its performance hasn't been perfect, nor has it got anything badly wrong. Overall, it's been surprisingly skilful. Throughout that time, however, there's never been any shortage of people willing to second-guess the central bankers, arguing interest rates are too low or, more commonly, too high.

My life as a commentator may have been more comfortable had I joined in the second-guessing. Perpetually being 'agin the guv'ment' rarely gets you into too much trouble. But my strongest emotion over the years has been: thank God they're making the tricky decisions, not me. So I've largely contented myself with making sure my readers are as well informed as I can make them on what the people running the economy think they're doing and why they're doing it. Same goes for Treasury with its usually more micro-economic policy positions. If that leaves me open to criticism for not being sufficiently critical, I'll wear it.

CHAPTER 7
A RINGSIDE SEAT IN POLITICS

The first rule of being a political junkie is to always remember that you are a very weird person, and most people are not like you.

Ezra Klein

In September 2004 one of my economic heroes, Robert Frank of Cornell University, whose text had introduced me to behavioural economics, was visiting Sydney as a guest speaker at the Australian Conference of Economists, the academic economists' annual bunfight. I seized the chance to take him to dinner. Would he see me at the conference? Gosh no, we're in the middle of a federal election campaign, I said.

Frank was nonplussed—a top economic journalist not attending the annual economists' conference? Well, it must be different in America, but in Australia an economics editor would no more miss covering an election campaign than they'd be away for the budget. Indeed, I'd had to cut short a holiday in Britain because John Howard had called the election two weeks earlier than expected. As I've said, in Australia economic journalism is a specialisation within political journalism.

I've always put my economic columns in the context of government policy and politics. Truth be told, my interest in politics long predates my discovery that economics was more than just a boring stumbling block to getting myself qualified as an accountant. And one of my favourite themes is what I call 'the politics of economics' and Treasury people call 'the presentational aspects'—all the human factors that help or hinder the implementation of good economic policies.

In this I try to avoid being too naive—no policy will be textbook-pure by the time it becomes a legislated reality—while also avoiding the boys-will-be-boys line of commentators who fancy themselves as hardboiled realists. There are always more than enough pressures for politicians to avoid taking a risk; my job is to use my puny weight to urge them to greatness and help keep expectations high, not make excuses for their lack of courage. In any case, having seen the politically impossible happen so many times in the days of Hawke and Keating, I know what courage can achieve.

For many years the Australian Business Economists group asked me to do the political forecast at their annual forecasting conference and I used to enjoy trying my hand at pure political commentary, though it always had an economic tinge. I flatter myself that, by now, I know a bit about the topic. The *Herald* has no dividing line between what's economic and what's political and I regularly see our political commentators straying into areas I think I know more about than they do. So, particularly as I've got older and closer to the finishing line, I've written columns that were more political than economic whenever the fancy has taken me.

Campaigns I've covered

As a journo I've covered the past 16 federal elections. I remember them all, to the extent that I use them to recall the timing of more important events in my life. My daughter, Katie, for instance, was born not long before the start of Bob Hawke's Long March to his first re-election in December 1984, a much closer-run thing than he expected. I took a month off to help my wife cope with a second young child. At the time I thought this made me a pretty good husband; with hindsight I should have taken a lot longer, but I was anxious to get back to work for the campaign.

My first election, of May 1974, was also John Howard's first as an MP. Outlasted you, John. But it came only a few months after I joined the *Herald* as a cadet, so my main role was as a kind of penciller on the night of the election. I thus witnessed the amazingly laborious, cumbersome way we had to cover the result, a world away from the slick digital performances we see today on every TV channel. Tally boards were arranged right around the newsroom, with the names of electorates and their candidates already written on them. Reporters at the official tally room would phone the office with a fresh count for an electorate, which a team of reporters would write down on slips for other reporters to chalk up on our tally boards. This would continue into the night while the editor, and the senior political correspondent charged with writing the page-one story, would move around the boards trying to work out what was happening.

It being a Saturday night, this was a nerve-wracking business. Early editions of *The Sun-Herald* bound for the country would start leaving the building not long after polling closed. Reports and headlines had to be written and rewritten as the night—and the count—progressed. The successive editions would all be read the next morning when radio was broadcasting the most up-to-date results. What if the winner wasn't apparent early in the night? What if the lead switched over the course of the evening?

It was in Malcolm Fraser's first re-election campaign in late 1977 that David Bowman got me to write a column, 'The Plain Truth', examining the two sides' claims and counter-claims. I'd pick a subject for each column—inflation, unemployment, taxation—and head it up with two seemingly diametrically opposed quotes. I focused mainly on sorting out the facts of the matter, identifying the key choice available to voters without pronouncing one way or the other. It was under Bowman that I formulated my views about how sensible editors—and columnists—should conduct themselves during election campaigns, times when partisan sympathies were at their seasonal high. You should aim to get through the campaign while losing as few readers from either camp as possible.

I kept that column up for a number of subsequent campaigns, but it became ever harder as politics became more 'scientific', with advertising and marketing people encouraging the pollies to be less cerebral and factual and more emotive and reliant on slick slogans. This meant fewer newspaper ads and more TV ads. And the claim- and conflict-laden election policy speeches came later and later in the campaign. These days, the 'campaign launch' comes no earlier than week four of the five-week campaign. Why? Because the launch is when the burden of paying for the leaders' travel shifts from the taxpayer to party coffers.

Politicians learn from their own mistakes, but more from those of their opponents. I've seen election practices change over the years accordingly. Long before I arrived they learnt from a mistake of Bob Menzies' to keep House and Senate elections aligned because separate 'half Senate' elections would be used by voters as a giant by-election to reprove a government without removing it.

This meant that, when double-dissolution elections became fashionable in the 1970s, we got a lot more early elections, with full-term elections becoming almost the exception to the rule. Howard put an end to this trend, claiming this was because voters disapproved of being obliged to vote earlier than necessary. But I knew arguing over the rights and wrongs of an early election petered out in the first week of the campaign, giving way to more substantive and forward-looking issues.

I think Howard always went full term because he was getting older, and campaigns took a lot out of him. Of course, as the years have gone by campaigns have become less physically exhausting. Leaders don't rush around addressing public meetings, but limit themselves to visits to radio stations and just a few mall walks or factory visits each day, aimed mainly at producing colour and movement for that evening's TV newscasts. This means their public day can be over by late afternoon.

Hawke's surprisingly poor showing after the 1984 Long March taught leaders to stick to the minimum statutory-length campaign of five weeks. And it, combined with Nick Greiner's near loss in New South Wales in 1991, probably helped convince politicians that being seen as a shoo-in only encourages people who would otherwise have supported you to indulge in a protest vote. These days, all leaders claim to be the underdog no matter how far ahead they are in the opinion polls.

Jeff Kennett's shock loss in Victoria in 1999 would have reinforced that attitude. It's also a reminder that not all election outcomes are well predicted by the polls. In 1998 Kim Beazley came a lot closer to making Howard a one-term prime minister than anyone expected. And, though there was a lot of wisdom after the event, Mark Latham didn't do nearly as well against Howard in 2004 as many were expecting.

And then there was Dr John Hewson's loss of the unlosable election in 1993. The truth of the rule that oppositions don't win elections, governments lose them was demonstrated yet again by Julia Gillard's loss to the unpopular Tony Abbott in 2013. But there are exceptions to the wisest rules and, in Hewson's case, the government didn't win, the opposition lost. His problem was political inexperience and a professional economist's excessive reforming zeal, in equal parts.

I remember—as the man himself in his hubris soon forgot—that not even Paul Keating thought he'd win. He was obviously a more skilful political performer than Hewson, but I also remember he won partly under false pretences. Hewson was promising huge income-tax cuts in return for his 15 per cent goods and services tax. Keating claimed to be able to roughly match the tax cuts, but without any GST. In the event he couldn't afford it. He reneged on the second tranche of his 'L-A-W' tax cuts and, in the first budget after the election, whacked up all the rates of the wholesale sales tax.

Hewson's shock loss reinforced the folly of overconfidence. I'd learnt the corollary of that from Malcolm Fraser, who was heavily into overkill. No matter how well placed he seemed to be, he'd keep piling on the electoral bribes—although his 'fistful of dollars' tax cut at the 1977 election was partially reversed by his new treasurer, Howard, in the post-election budget.

The breaking of election promises has a long history—a history that seemed to be forgotten in all the confected outrage that accompanied Gillard's broken promise on a carbon tax. There was a new doctrine in Canberra that the electorate had become much more unforgiving of broken promises, but I remain to be convinced. Kevin Rudd began his term insisting every promise would be kept, but ended up breaking plenty. Now Abbott's done the same. The hard truth is that, first, sometimes promises are overtaken by forces beyond your control and, second, politicians who genuinely intended to keep their promises would be far more cautious in the promises they made and would add more caveats. Any pollie who promises 'no surprises, no excuses' isn't fair dinkum. All that remains is to see how forgiving the voters are by the time the next election rolls around.

But probably the greatest—and most regrettable—lesson learnt from the Hewson debacle concerns policies. What defeated him was the public's fear of a GST, but it didn't help that this was only part of his phonebook-sized economic reform plan, Fightback!, dubbed by some wit 'the longest suicide note in history'. Howard learnt that lesson and at the following election, in 1996, eschewed policy detail so as to make himself the smallest target possible. This 'small target' strategy was copied by Rudd in 2007 and Abbott in 2013, suggesting it's become de rigueur for oppositions.

Gallery journalists begin demanding that oppositions release their policies long before elections are due, but their demands are ignored. The pollies know that were they to oblige, the gallery would take almost no interest in the document. Voters would arrive at the election campaign none the wiser. These days, policies are held for release almost daily during the campaign. This gives opposition leaders something important to do during the campaign, but also means the policies come too thick and fast to be adequately reported and analysed—even assuming the media were interested in doing so, which they aren't. In these days of infotainment and politics as sport, there isn't much journo enthusiasm for chat about policies.

Finally, I suspect Hewson's experience with Fightback! has produced a new view—certainly, not one that ever occurred to Whitlam in 1972—that reform is best promoted from government, not opposition. Howard made it to government in 1996 promising 'never ever' to introduce a GST, but went to the 1998 campaign with a detailed proposal for just such a tax. (Incidentally, I've never had any sympathy for the contention that this behaviour amounted to a broken promise, as opposed to a change of policy from one election to the next.)

Now Abbott is using the same approach, promising that any plans for major industrial relations change or tax reform would be taken to his *next* election campaign. We've yet to see, of course, just how much braver he'll be by then. If he isn't, his promise of 'next time' will be revealed as merely a device to get the business lobbies off his back in 2013.

I've long been, and remain, a firm believer that any government presiding over a recession will be shown the door and that governments are rarely turfed out for any other reason. But the evidence for this 'economic theory of politics' has become hairier than it was. There was an uptick in unemployment before the McMahon government lost office in 1972. The 1974–75 recession would have been sufficient to see the demise of the Whitlam government had the governor-general not intervened in 1975. There's little doubt the recession of the early 1980s led to the premature demise of the Fraser government in 1983 and, following the recession of the early 90s, the intervention of Hewson and his GST merely delayed the defeat of the Keating government by one election.

After that, however, the record gets murky. The Howard government—which, admittedly, did survive to the ripe old age of almost 12 years—was tossed out even while the economy was in the throes of the resources boom Mark I. And then, despite our avoidance of the Great Recession—which, for these purposes only, you can attribute either to good luck or good management—the Rudd–Gillard–Rudd government was first censured in 2010 and then unceremoniously dispensed with in 2013.

The latter puzzle is perhaps explained by the conjunction with a separate political law: 'disunity is death.' That one's always been true, and its truth is reaffirmed by both Gillard's failure to win a majority in 2010 and Rudd's failure to benefit from his destabilising of Gillard that began even during the 2010 campaign.

It may be the oldest and least doubted political truism, but that didn't stop Labor forgetting it for more than three years. This is thanks to the political genius of Sussex Street—the New South Wales Labor Right—which, before it decided to sort Labor's problems at the federal level, thought engineering the Carr–Iemma–Rees–Keneally government would secure Labor's future in New South Wales.

It takes no more than 48 hours following a federal election in which government changes hands for the denizens of Parliament House to agree on the reasons for the change and for their view to be set in concrete. After about six months the political scientists at the Australian National University issue a carefully researched and more authoritative explanation, but by then it's far too late to shake the conventional wisdom.

Both sides of politics have agreed that Labor's latest failure is explained by the never-ending infighting between the Gillard and Rudd forces. True, as far as it goes. But Labor will do itself a great disservice if that's the only lesson it learns. Labor needs to compare its most recent performance with that of the Hawke–Keating government. When I do that I conclude Labor has lost its race memory of how to govern effectively. And I put that down to its continuing devolution into a party of apparatchiks—professional politicians following a career path from union researcher or ministerial staffer to cabinet minister—devoid of core values. When you lack deep commitment to progressive policies, you don't work as hard to convince the world of the rightness of your proposals, you drop policies you'd said were vital, and the punters' sixth sense tells them you're in it more for personal advancement than the public good, and they aren't impressed.

PMs I've known

Journos in the Canberra press gallery take great pride in the closeness of their contact with politicians, the more senior the better. Intimacy with ministers has never been a high priority of mine. I've known a few well enough to have them tell me things worth knowing, but I've always preferred to deal with technocrats. Similarly, I haven't put a lot of effort into getting in with ministerial staffers.

But though I don't cultivate the bigwigs, I do have some contact with them, including when they come to the *Herald* office for lunch. And if you've been around for a while as a commentator, no pollie would fail to greet you as a long-lost friend just because they couldn't remember having met you before.

My brushes with prime ministerial fame began in the old parliament house in 1975 when I was hovering in the doorway of a committee room. Someone with a deep voice said 'Excuse me' and squeezed his great frame past.

Once I was in the tiny office of the prime minister's economist, who was gently taking issue with a column I'd written that morning, when the door opened and a tall man with an egg stain on his tie leaned in. 'I hope you've sorted him out,' the man said.

'Yes, Malcolm, I'm doing it now.'

I got invited to some Parliament House reception early in Hawke's term and experienced his legendary charm at full strength. He assiduously worked the room and, when it was my turn, put his hand on my leg and gave me every ounce of his attention as he asked about my life. The feeling that he and I were special friends lasted at least a week.

Keating began cultivating our relationship before he became treasurer, even asking my advice on how he should set up his office. Whenever I was visiting his staff he'd usually find time for a chat. On one of my visits to Canberra with *Herald* colleague Alan Mitchell, Hawke's economist said he—the adviser—would meet with us if he could, but might be too busy because cabinet was meeting that day. We arrived at Hawke's suite in the old parliament house and the economist took us into the PM's anteroom, passing the door of the cabinet room, but apologised for being snowed under and unable to talk. That's OK, mate, perfectly understandable; see you next time. As we were walking back out, the cabinet room door flew open. It was Treasurer Keating. He greeted us with glad cries, took us back to the anteroom and talked for at least half an hour before returning to the cabinet meeting. He was that kind of bloke.

Next time you're asked which famous person, living or dead, you'd like to have dinner with, pick Keating. No one can tell more interesting stories than he, even if he *is* the hero of every one of them. But my contact with Keating and his office ceased from the time he became prime minister, and that wasn't only because he had bigger fish to fry.

Keating was always fully invested in his sales pitch, even when circumstances required him to change what he was selling quite abruptly. When his long crusade for a broad-based consumption tax was so roundly rejected at the tax summit in 1985, it took him only about a fortnight to begin campaigning against consumption taxes. Anyone who remained convinced by his former arguments—as I did—was morally suspect.

And when, despite all his own doubts, he won the unwinnable election in 1993, he identified with Labor's True Believers and took all his unworthy self-doubt and projected it onto the press gallery and journos generally, including me. Some part of Keating's success to that point was owed to his long years of cultivating the media. Some part of his defeat at the next election was owed to his semiconscious decision to preserve his self-image by making journos his enemy.

I had no contact with Graham Richardson when he was in parliament and a minister in the Hawke and Keating governments. But in his subsequent career as a Packer lobbyist and radio personality he interviewed me a few times and seemed embarrassed that I hadn't been paid an appearance fee (not that any other station paid for casual appearances). So a couple of times he took me to lunch.

I found them most educational, but resolved not to do it again when he took me to an Italian restaurant in Leichhardt. While I waited for Richo, the proprietor quizzed me and asked for my business card, then didn't charge Richo for the meal. I had visions of being phoned in the early hours and made an offer I couldn't refuse because I owed the guy.

One lunch came not long after Kerry Packer had been sniffing around Fairfax and stories were circulating that he had a hit list of journos he intended to get rid of. 'I want to assure you, Ross, there's no hit list,' Richo told me. 'And what's more, your name's not on it.' When you remember it was a Fairfax paper that had christened Packer 'the Goanna', it isn't hard to work out the one journo who wouldn't have survived a Packer takeover.

Few of Howard's admirers would see him as a man of great charisma or charm. But he had his moments and, as a politician, was possessed of many valuable traits. For instance, he not only remembered people's names, he remembered their spouses' names as well. Soon after he became prime minister I flew to Canberra to interview him with the *Herald*'s Peter Bowers. 'Your son goes to a private school,' he said, 'which one is it?' Trinity Grammar. 'Oh, that's right. How's he getting on?' That night I casually remarked to Sandy, 'The prime minister inquired after you today.' Can you imagine how big it made me feel to be able to say that to my son? Howard was that kind of bloke.

People who've had a lot of close contact with prime ministers tell me no one attains the top job without being ruthlessly ambitious and self-seeking. After all, politics is terribly competitive—both within parties and between them—and there are a lot of bodies to be climbed over. Kim Beazley—the only pollie I've heard of who enjoyed being opposition leader—just didn't have the killer instinct. But all the rest have, including Howard and even the saintly Julia. It's just a question of what other, more likeable qualities you have or, for the truly cynical, how well you can hide your bastardry.

Howard was someone who wouldn't have kissed his granny goodnight without the political implications of the act flashing across his mind as he lent across. He always reminded me of the joke that if you can fake sincerity you've got it made. But I never caught him with his guard down in private, saying something super cynical. I did, however, have two experiences that convinced me he wasn't as innocent as he seemed.

On the day when, for just a few hours, the Canberra denizens were convinced I had a big leak on the contents of Keating's draft white paper on tax reform, Howard said something utterly offensive about my relationship with Keating. When sometime later I told him I hadn't appreciated it, he professed to be surprised and sorry I'd taken offence.

Another time someone leaked to me a document I knew the Labor government would find quite embarrassing. This was in Howard's first go as opposition leader. In an effort to maximise the splash my story made, I gave him a copy of the document in advance, so he'd be ready for it. But I told him I didn't want him to give copies to the gallery; if they wanted to confirm the story they'd have to interview me. Howard kept our deal—by giving the document to his deputy to distribute to the gallery.

I got to know Howard long before he was prime minister, when he was a natural fan of the *Herald*. After his ascension his allegiance switched to the *Telegraph*. On one of the times he came to lunch at the *Herald* he was monstered by David Marr and others over the republic, but I came to his defence. He was so surprised he mentioned it in his autobiography.

It was no surprise to me that Peter Costello never became prime minister. He was a good barrister, could always speak well and master his brief, but lacked some of the most basic political skills. Politics 101 teaches that, in any democracy, power is diffused—spread thinly between a lot of people and interest groups. The secret to political success is to make sufficient compromises to always be able to put together a big enough coalition of interest groups.

Most pollies understand that instinctively. Costello never did. He thought he had all the power and you had none. When bank economists made comments about economic management he objected to, he wasn't above phoning their bosses, complaining bitterly and making vague threats.

When the GST was introduced it had the predictable amount of administrative bugs in it, but Costello stuck to his dig and declined to make adjustments. Howard, anxious to keep annoyance of the public to a minimum, had to intervene with his own modifications. I've long suspected that when the Democrats in the Senate forced him to exclude fresh food from the tax, Howard wouldn't have lost much sleep over it.

It was common practice for the Democrats to oppose the odd unpopular budget measure. Someone involved in one such episode, involving a rise in the pharmaceutical benefits scheme co-payment, gave me a detailed account of what happened. Costello summoned them to his office and read them a lecture on the vital importance of the measure and the irresponsibility of their behaviour. Needless to say, they were unmoved.

So Howard had to intervene. He invited them round to his office for a cup of tea and a chat, then began by saying he understood perfectly why they were objecting to the measure. If he were in their shoes he'd do the same. But if they couldn't agree to increase the charge by the full $6, couldn't they give him something? How about $1? My informant said his greatest desire became to get out of Howard's office before they'd given him almost everything. As his survival for almost 12 years attests, Howard was a modest, ordinary man with considerable political skills. And he moved a long way up the learning curve between his first go as opposition leader and his second.

When Rudd was campaigning for office he came to lunch at the *Herald* and we were all introduced. 'Call me Kevin,' he said to me. Early in his prime ministership he resolved to meet once a month with all business and economics heavies from Fairfax (and separately with News Corp, presumably) and delegated his finance minister, Lindsay Tanner, who we all knew well, to line it up. I was very doubtful how long it would last. It didn't happen once.

I think it was in the weeks before the Rudd government's second budget that Tanner advised us to expect a heads-up call from Rudd. Nothing happened. We were in Mitchell's car heading to Canberra on the morning of the budget lockup when his mobile rang. I guessed it must be Rudd he was talking to. Mitchell finished with 'Oh, in that case I'll put him on' and handed the phone to me. Rudd didn't have anything much to say, certainly nothing that wasn't already obvious. I tried out on him some of the lines I was thinking of using in my comment on the budget next morning, but he didn't really engage with them. It reinforced all my prejudices against talking to pollies rather than technocrats.

I was waiting in the foyer of the Commonwealth parliamentary offices in Phillip Street, Sydney once when Gillard—still a shadow minister in those days—walked across it. She made to come over and introduce herself, but thought better of it. Sorry, I met her once or twice as prime minister but never got to know her. But I do know she was far more engaging in the flesh than she was on telly. Politicians who lack the mysterious ability to project their personalities through TV screens and into living rooms aren't likely to get far.

Abbott I first got to know when he was a minister in the Howard government. It was about the time he'd been campaigning in defence of the monarchy and I expected him to be a bit rabid. Instead I found him charming. On the occasions when he's been jogging through the corridors of Parliament House and almost knocked me over he's always nodded a greeting.

What they do in Canberra

There's a highly rationalist strand of economic theory known as 'public choice' which holds, among other things, that politicians and bureaucrats always act in their own interest rather than the public's interest, and that, whatever its original motivations, all government regulation of industry ends up being 'captured' by the industry and turned to the industry's advantage in, say, reducing competition within the industry (to the incumbents' advantage), increasing protection or in persuading the government to subsidise industry costs. The regulated have a huge incentive to *get* to the regulators so as to modify the regulation in ways the industry finds more congenial, or to advantage the existing players against new entrants or rival industries.

I don't accept for a moment the accusation that *all* regulation of industry is subverted. But I do believe there's more than a grain of truth to the accusation: there *is* considerable scope for regulatory capture. And I've long suspected that the way our bureaucracy is organised—where the department of agriculture looks after the farmers, the industry department looks after the manufacturers, the environment department looks after the greenies, the resources and energy department looks after the miners and the tourism department looks after the tourist industry—could have been purpose-built for regulatory capture.

In the various industries' battle for their share of industry assistance, in the inter-departmental battle for influence and resources, each industry has its own special champion, those whose *true* role is supposed to be to keep the industry acting within the bounds of the wider public interest. Is the bureaucracy divided up this way just to gain the benefits of specialisation, or is each department's real role to keep their particular industry happy and not making trouble for the elected government?

Of course, the two government agencies whose motivations and behaviour I've watched most closely are Treasury and the Reserve Bank. Being—like Prime Minister & Cabinet and the Finance department—'co-ordinating departments', Treasury and the Reserve have no particular industries they regard as 'clients'. For instance, though the Reserve has daily dealings with the banks and the financial markets, I've never suspected its decisions about the level of interest rates were influenced by anything other than what it believed to be in the best interests of the wider economy over the medium term.

In other words, Treasury and the Reserve *are* on about macro management or 'stabilisation policy'—trying to smooth the economy's path through the ups and downs of the business cycle. But since they each wield different macro instruments, there is some specialisation between them. The question I ask is: what would they die in a ditch over? They care about lots of things, but what do they care about most?

In the Reserve's case, the answer is inflation. Its attitude is, if we don't accept ultimate responsibility for keeping inflation under control, who will? It also regards its instrument—monetary policy, or the manipulation of interest rates—as the best one to use to keep inflation in check. All this is implicit in its single target of keeping the rate of inflation between 2 and 3 per cent on average over the medium term. When it first adopted that solitary target 20 years ago, some took this to mean achieving low unemployment was not something it cared much about. Fortunately, our experience since then has dispelled such fears. The best way to think of its objective is 'non-inflationary growth'. Even so, it does mean that, when forced to choose, fighting inflation will always come first.

So what does Treasury care most deeply about? What does it see as its ultimate responsibility, the responsibility others are less likely to care so much about? This took me longer to realise, but treasuries—state as much as federal—care most about the budget and getting it back to surplus just as soon as the state of the business cycle permits. As the recent troubles of governments in America and Europe attest, left to their own devices politicians are capable of running budget deficits year after year, in bad times and good, for decades until finally their lack of self-control gets them into serious difficulties, invariably at the most inopportune times.

That our governments' records have been so much more disciplined is testimony to our treasuries' obsession with keeping budgets in balance 'over the cycle' and thereby avoiding the build-up of excessive levels of public debt. It's testimony also to our treasuries' greater success in persuading their political masters to curb their natural instinct to spend more than they raise in taxes.

Bearing in mind the wide discrepancy between the politicians' willingness to increase taxes to cover their increased spending, much of Treasury's effort goes into urging politicians to restrain their spending and into developing devices to help the co-ordinating, 'purse-string' ministers keep the other 'spending ministers' in line. In this, Fraser's attempt in the mid–1970s to punish Treasury by splitting a finance department off from it—with Treasury responsible for revenue and Finance responsible for spending—had the unexpected effect of doubling Treasury's influence at the cabinet table. It *could* have meant Treasury lost interest in the spending side of the budget, but it certainly hasn't.

When Costello introduced the reforming Charter of Budget Honesty early in the Howard government's term, he included—no doubt at Treasury's suggestion—a requirement for Treasury to produce an 'intergenerational report' every five years to assess the fiscal sustainability of present government policies over the next 40 years. The first of these reports in 2002 found that (given a quite restrictive assumption about the growth in tax revenue) the present comfortable budget surpluses would soon give way to ever-growing budget deficits thanks to the ageing of the population and, more particularly, the public's ever-growing demand for access to medical science's ever more expensive advances in health care.

The following two reports have used the same assumptions to tell essentially the same story. From the first report it became clear to this (not unsympathetic) Treasury watcher that the report was being used by the treasurer as a kind of waddy to wave over the heads of the spending ministers. See the problems we face down the track? See how much worse it would be if I were to stop beating off your grandiose schemes? It was such a handy implement the state treasuries lost little time in producing their own inter-generational reports, each telling a story remarkably similar to federal Treasury's.

But the state treasuries' favourite disciplinary device is the state governments' triple-A credit rating, ratings that emerged early in the Hawke–Keating government's budgetary reforms when it ceased the practice of borrowing on the states' behalf. No innovation could have been more effective in disciplining the states' propensity to borrow, probably to the extent that it helps explain those governments' inadequate spending on infrastructure.

State governments of both colours live in fear of the political censure that might follow a downgrading of their credit rating, not the modest increase in their borrowing costs it would also bring. And state treasurers exploit this fear indefatigably. When occasionally state governments do suffer a downgrading, they work untiringly to get their top rating restored.

When the Queensland government was downgraded just a few weeks before an election, but Labor was comfortably re-elected in 2007 under the new leadership of Anna Bligh, I thought the disciplinary power of credit rating may have been punctured. But I spoke too soon. No sooner had Bligh been installed than she embarked on a huge unforeshadowed program of privatisations aimed at restoring the credit rating ASAP. It was so unpopular with the public and her Labor supporters it became the greatest single reason for her ignominious defeat at the next election. And ratings-motivated privatisation proposals were part of the reason for the New South Wales Labor government's many changes of leadership before its own ignominious defeat in 2011.

I half agree with the academic economists who think too much attention is paid to credit ratings and that state governments could borrow for infrastructure investment a lot more heavily than they do without this creating an economic (as opposed to political) problem. I also suspect the rating agencies draw their lines in the sand more conservatively for governments than they do for businesses.

When you remember the big American rating agencies' disgraceful contribution to the subprime debt debacle—where they sold paying customers triple-A ratings for the mortgage-backed securities they were issuing, only to have those securities ultimately revealed as 'toxic assets'—you wonder why they give governments such a hard time. I finally decided they do it because they view the state treasuries as their clients, and know full well the treasuries want them to take a hard line.

But having conceded all that, I don't criticise treasuries and their treasurers for the way they use credit ratings to beat back spending ministers' insatiable demands for more spending on this worthy cause and that. What the academic critics forget is that their theories provide no clear dividing line between what level of borrowing is safe and what isn't. In the real world of government, treasurers have to draw an unavoidably arbitrary line and then enforce it. If they use the bogeyman of credit ratings to keep their governments out of trouble, I'm not disposed to criticise.

As I watched Keating move from treasurer to prime minister, with only a brief intermission, and then Howard do the same—admittedly, with 13 years of opposition in between—I detected echoes of the championing of special interests as well as further evidence for my notion that people change their behaviour and attitudes to fit with their changing role in the organisation.

As treasurer, both men devoted all their energy towards doing what treasurers are supposed to do: getting the budget back to surplus and delivering economic reform for that (small) part of the electorate that wants to see reform. (A cabinet minister once told me Rudd viewed economic rationalists as just another interest group, to be thrown the occasional bone as other groups were.)

As prime minister, however, both men saw their ultimate responsibility as political rather than economic. It was down to them to ensure the totality of their government's actions added up to political survival, and this might well mean subordinating budget purity and economic reform to other non-economic priorities. Apart from that, I sometimes wondered whether Howard's treatment of his treasurer was subconsciously modelled on the way Fraser had treated him by blocking most of his reform proposals.

How politics has changed

The departmentalisation of government and the changing of behaviour in line with the individual's changing role are nothing new. But

I *have* noticed big changes in the way politics is carried on in my time as a ringside observer. As I've noted, I've seen politics become a whole-of-life profession with an entry level of young people barely out of uni becoming ministerial staffers (or, in Labor's case, low-level union functionaries) and working their way up the hierarchy.

This has been truer of Labor than the Liberals, but the Libs are rapidly catching up. Ministers have always had staff members, but it was the Whitlam government that started the almost inexorable growth in their numbers. Federal trends are invariably followed at state level and, these days, Labor or Liberal staffers tend to migrate around the country when their party loses office in one state and gains office in another, or in Canberra. One effect of this is that staffers tend to be more knowledgeable about what governments do to stay in office than about what oppositions do to gain office.

The advent of apparatchiks has made the new political class more pragmatic and expedient and less idealistic and principled. Take that progression to its logical extreme and you're left with the New South Wales Labor Right, which will throw a long-espoused reform overboard at the first sign of electoral resistance. That the Sussex Street solution has been so pervasive at the federal level is an indication of how spiritually hollowed out Labor has become throughout the land.

One thing that's gone by the board is loyalty. Back in the 1960s, Labor stuck with Arthur Calwell through three losing election campaigns. Can you see that happening today? After all the infighting and failed leadership challenges, combined with the fact that almost all of them hated Rudd's guts, I was convinced Labor wouldn't dump Gillard in the months before the 2013 election. But no. In the end loyalty to her and hatred of him came a poor second to most of caucus members' hope that maybe the unspeakable Rudd might save their own seat. For their part, the Libs would be no better. Loyalty is a luxury careerist politicians can no longer afford.

As intensified personal ambition has heightened competition between the parties, unwritten rules that certain subjects were off-limits to the political contest have gone by the board. The obvious example is immigration, Asian immigration in particular, and boat people. For many years, both sides knew there was an ugly, xenophobic side of the Australian character and tacitly agreed not to do or say anything that would give it air. Howard was part of the breakdown of that taboo, but perhaps a bigger cause was the arrival of radio shock jocks who didn't care what demons they unleashed.

As politics has become more of a job for life it's also become more of a science and less of an art, as parties have made more use of sample-based polling and the techniques of marketing, including sophisticated advertising and focus groups. There was a time when politicians relied on their own contact with voters and their gut feelings to assess how their policies and performance were being received by the electorate. These days, their polling and reports of focus group discussions leave them in no doubt about what voters are thinking on all topics.

Or, at least, leave them imagining there's no doubt. In truth, even quantitative polling can be misunderstood—that's what they think now, but how will they feel when they've got used to the idea or other things have transpired?—and qualitative research from focus groups is so subjective it's notorious for the bum steers it can give. Even so, it does seem the parties get very similar messages from their rival efforts.

When focus groups were introduced, the rationale was that they would inform the parties on how to frame the policies they wanted to pursue in ways that made them more attractive to voters. But when you are—or imagine yourself to be—fully informed on what the punters like and dislike, the temptation to let those preferences determine what policies you pursue must be almost irresistible. Similarly, why think up your own slogans when you can merely feed back to the electorate the lines that arose and drew a favourable reaction in your focus groups?

What this seemingly less amateur and more scientific approach to politicking overlooks is the often paradoxical quality of human nature. Tell me only what I want to hear and I begin to wonder whether I can trust you. What exactly do you believe? Keep it wishy-washy and I wonder if you really believe anything. Only ever tell me nice stuff and I wonder whether you're tough enough for the job. Become a slave of focus group approval and you risk forgetting that, though I don't like the sound of your plan, I could be persuaded it's what the country needs. In the old days, a politician like Fraser won elections because he was seen as the stern father the times called for, not because he was popular.

Another drawback of the more calculated approach to politics is governments' ever-increasing superficiality. If, as all politicians believe, 'the perception is the reality', why not focus on perceptions and appearances and let reality slide? If the trains aren't running on time or people are waiting too long for elective surgery, why not measure these things in ways that are more favourable? If the media are carrying on about rising crime, why not implement the solutions the public imagines will fix the problem—longer sentences, more cops on the beat—rather than doing research to find out what actually works?

Why not favour responses to problems that are flashy or emotionally gratifying rather than boring but effective? Why waste scarce resources on repairs and maintenance or renovation when you can build something new and be seen cutting the ribbon and making great progress? When shock jocks highlight the terrible treatment the system meted out to Mrs A or the neglect of Mr B, why not drop everything and square away Mrs A and Mr B rather than trying to correct the systemic failures of which they're mere examples?

When the number of problems or worthy causes far exceeds the revenue you've got to spend, why concentrate on those where your spending is likely to be most effective rather than slinging an inadequate sum to as many as possible and so mollify as many potential critics as possible? When money is short, why give much to people such as the unemployed or single mothers for whom there's so little public sympathy? When the public takes an irrational set against outsiders such as boat people, why not gratify their prejudices rather than defend the needy?

When people convince themselves they're struggling to keep up with the cost of living but the objective indicators say wages are rising faster than prices, why try to set them straight when it's so much easier to pretend to be sympathetic? In short, why not reinforce prejudices and misperceptions rather than educate? Why not follow the voters rather than lead them? 'There go the people. I must follow them for I am their leader.' When memories and political terms are so short and punters so ungrateful, why not be short-sighted and risk-averse?

In case you haven't noticed, all those temptations are reinforced by the media. It's the media that are overly preoccupied with and impressed by the new rather than the old, by the flashy and the emotionally gratifying, by what's on the surface rather than what's underneath, by the immediate rather than the prospective, by the irrational rather than the rational, by the sympathy-rousing case study rather than the systemic failure.

Politics has changed over the years, but so too have the media. And they've both changed in ways that are mutually supportive. The two institutions have become more symbiotic. In his book *Sideshow: Dumbing down democracy*, Lindsay Tanner powerfully describes the trends I've sketched. But, perhaps because he didn't want to be seen as dumping on the Rudd government he had been part of, or the Gillard government he had declined to be part of, he explained the retrograde process almost wholly in terms of the politicians' need to adapt to media's changing demands if the pollies were to get their messages through to the electorate.

There's no doubt that the speeding up of the 24-hour news cycle is essentially the product of the media's ever-shortening attention span as part of the intensifying competition between the media's ever-proliferating mediums, including the advent of 24-hour news radio and TV channels. But, as I've tried to demonstrate, a lot of the dumbing down has been initiated by the politicians and their party machines for their own reasons. There is plenty of blame to be shared between the two institutions.

The view from the gallery's gallery

After spending just 15 months in the Canberra press gallery in the mid–1970s, I retreated to Sydney to write about economics and politics from afar. From that day to this I've been something of an intermediary and interpreter between head office and our bureau in the gallery, able to see things from both points of view. I have to say there's no more defensive part of the media than the gallery. Those guys know exactly what's what and no critic no longer on location knows anything much. But, from where I sit, not all I see is beyond criticism.

Before I get into that, however, let me clarify a few things and defend the gallery against some unwarranted criticism. Historically, Liberal politicians such as Costello and their supporters suspected the gallery of pro-Labor partisanship in their reporting. These suspicions were unjustified. Though it's true most gallery journalists, like journalists generally, are Labor-leaning in their private sympathies—and that journalism is quite heavily unionised—I can't imagine a journo in possession of a story embarrassing to Labor failing to write it or push for it to get the best run possible. The journalistic ethos combined with the competitive spirit put a good story way ahead of private sympathies.

Of course, in more recent times the behaviour of the Murdoch press means it's more common for people to suspect the gallery of anti-Labor bias. But this incontrovertible bias—affecting which stories are selected, which are given prominence and the way headlines are written and lead sentences rewritten—comes from editors back at head office, not from gallery journos. While I guess it's likely that Liberal-leaning reporters and conservative columnists gravitate to the now much more overt crop of Liberal-learning papers, I'm confident the great majority of Murdoch reporters simply accommodate or passively tolerate their editors' preferences because they need a job and alternative employers are scarce.

The broader point is that reporters generally and gallery reporters in particular—as opposed to long-established commentators like me—don't have as much control over their work as their critics usually assume. They don't write their own headlines, they don't control the length and prominence given to their stories, and they soon adapt to writing in the style and about the subjects their bosses are looking for. If you want to criticise the trend to 'race calling'—politics as sport—do so by all means. Just don't blame the gallery. As an economist would put it, reporters respond to the incentives they face. If they ever had reason to believe the best run went to deep and meaningful analyses of policies, that's just what they'd produce.

The last thing to say in the gallery's defence is that, contrary to repeated allegations, it rarely imagines stories about leadership unrest. It's standard tactics for incumbents and their supporters to allege such reports are unfounded, but this is usually just a tactic aimed at countering the tactic of their opponents in keeping their destabilisation anonymous. It's true, of course, that publicity probably adds to the momentum of leadership challenges, but the question of whether we'd be better off if the media told us less about what was going on is a much bigger issue. In the meantime, remember that now the Rudd–Gillard–Rudd government has been put out of its misery, both sides readily admit that destabilisation was virtually continuous during more than half of Labor's six years in office.

So what valid criticisms can be made of the gallery's performance? The great occupational hazard of all journalism is the temptation to take on the values and biases of your contacts and become an unpaid apologist for their vested interests. In my case, I'm sure some would accuse me of being too close to Treasury or the Reserve Bank, but these days I draw a distinction between making sure my readers are fully informed about what the economy's managers say about what they're doing and why they're do it, and endorsing their attitudes. As my readers would know, I've become increasingly sceptical about the push for endless economic growth, the unquestioning support for high levels of immigration, the narrow definition of what constitutes micro-economic reform and the dubious arguments used to urge more of it, as well as the inadequate attention paid to continuing environmental degradation.

In the gallery's case, their temptation is to take on the values of the politicians and political staffers they spend so much time with. Years of observation have convinced me that, like the pollies themselves, the gallery admires political success over policy virtue. Try but fail to introduce some controversial reform and you're a mug rather than a tryer. Some politician who embarrasses his side by blurting out the unvarnished truth on some matter deserves derision, not praise for telling the public something it didn't realise. Isn't the gallery supposed to be revealing the truth?

The gallery's related failing is its obsession with itself. It's intensely competitive, more so than the rest of journalism, probably because the range of bureaus makes comparison so easy. But this means gallery members are almost wholly preoccupied with impressing each other, playing the daily comp according to the long-accepted rules and avoiding doing anything that might draw censure from their peers.

This imparts a sameness to the gallery's performance. The gallery tends to hunt as a pack, with unwritten rules intended to stop you embarrassing the rest of us by getting ahead of the pack. When you get a story the rest of us missed, our strongest emotion is to avoid the ignominy of having head office demand we follow you up on day two. Much better for the rest of us to convince ourselves—and head office—there was something wrong with your story. It either wasn't true or wasn't new.

A year or two ago some journos who specialised in using freedom-of-information requests to get stories complained bitterly when a number of departments, obliged to make information available to the applicant, started making the documents available at the same time to all comers. This was most unfair; disgracefully manipulative, they objected. Why would anyone bother searching for revelations if they couldn't have the results exclusively?

The trouble with the gallery's intensely inward focus is whom it forgets: the reader. Gallery journos conduct their daily contest primarily for their own satisfaction. They compete because competition is fun; they don't compete to see who's best at serving the reader back in Sydney or Melbourne. Would the reader back home value more detail about some new impost the government has decided on rather than a blow-by-blow account of the fight in caucus that preceded the decision? 'Who cares?' Will the reader know about the content of my rival's scoop this morning if I don't swallow my pride and write a follow-up? 'What's that got to do with anything?' Is there some different way I could do my job that would be of greater value to the reader? 'How's that going to help me in the comp?'

The gallery has unwritten rules about subjects that are off-limits. People rarely write about the government's ever-more-blatant efforts to manage the media—'no one's interested in that navel-gazing stuff'—mainly because there's so much scope for the government's minders to retaliate and little likelihood of your competitors supporting you rather than seeking to exploit your vulnerability. This, of course, makes it easy for the spin doctors to manipulate the gallery by playing people off against each other. Stories about the pollies' private peccadilloes are usually off-limits. This is no bad thing, but the main reason for it is the journos' fear of provoking retaliation in Coward's Castle. More generally—but with the notable exception of the *Fin*'s Laura Tingle—the gallery tends not to write about what happens under the bonnet. They don't tell tales out of school.

When I was in the gallery many moons ago, it was common for journalists to have regular dealings with senior bureaucrats, who were usually happy to provide background information to press people they thought genuinely committed to accuracy. Since then, governments of both colours—but particularly the Coalition—have vigorously discouraged contact between journalists and public servants, insisting that all press queries be referred to the minister's office. And both the Howard and Abbott governments began their terms by sacking a few department heads to ensure a sufficiently fearful atmosphere.

These days many gallery journos would have little contact with the public service—apart from that most anodyne race, departmental PR people. A leak made to look like it comes from Treasury will almost always have come from the treasurer's office, perhaps via the prime minister's press office, which undertakes most of the official leaking, particularly at budget time.

Sometimes I think the gallery behaves like an oppressed minority. Most of the time it knuckles under, but when occasionally it sees the chance to riot with impunity it starts looting shops. That's what the pollies mean when they say the gallery is either at your feet or at your throat. For as long as a prime minister is winning, the gallery will be almost obsequious. But when the journos judge you to be on the slippery slope, they toughen their reporting in a way that makes you more likely to keep sliding than to claw your way back.

And when they see you clearly faltering as the finishing line approaches, they put in the boot. I noticed this when, in the last week of the 1983 election campaign that everyone knew Fraser would lose, Peter Bowers questioned him in a way that was utterly disrespectful. I remembered that when I heard Laurie Oakes treating Gillard the same way in 2013, just before Rudd finally got the numbers.

Some years ago the gallery's electronic media gained an advantage over the press. A print journo can ask you the same question

10 times until they gain an admission, then ignore the previous nine goes. In a live radio or TV interview, a journo can't ask the same question more than twice for fear of taxing the listeners' patience. What's more, any perceived impoliteness on the interviewer's part could well elicit sympathy for the pollie and a reaction against the journo. Ministers have come increasingly to prefer live interviews that, by their nature, can't be edited.

More recently, however, the spin doctors' art has evolved in a way that favours the press. You've got some announcement you want to make splash. The announcement may be in a speech you're delivering tomorrow. So you 'drop' the story to key newspapers for publication tomorrow morning. They'll run it on the front page because it's kind of exclusive and because if they don't they'll be left out of the next drop.

The electronic journos are well trained and can tell a drop when they see one. Early the next morning they put in a quick call to a press sec to confirm the facts, then run hard with the story. They probably give it a better run because it's been all over the front page that morning. Does anyone object that this a manipulative, even underhand way for a government to behave? Does anyone ever refuse to play ball? 'Don't be silly.'

The trouble with this game is that, by feeding the gallery's most senior press reporters on a steady stream of no-effort pseudo exclusives, the media managers make them dependent on maintaining the government's goodwill and complicit in their own manipulation.

Although the media's proud claim is to be keeping the political bastards honest—and, to be sure, we'd be very much worse off without their inevitably imperfect efforts—it remains true that the relationship between government and gallery is to some extent symbiotic. For instance, it suits the pollies to leave the public with an exaggerated impression of the significance of budget measures by quoting their value 'over four years'. It suits the journos to exaggerate the significance of their stories by quoting the value of measures 'over four years'.

If you're in the business, it's not hard to deduce that—with the honourable exception of a few journos so prominently placed in the electronic firmament they can't be avoided—gallery radio and TV journalists are house-trained: they know how far they may go in their questioning and never cross the line.

Although prime ministers, treasurers and finance ministers repeatedly insist they couldn't possibly speculate about budget measures, implying it's an improper question to have asked, the gallery never contrasts this sanctimony with the ever-rising tide of budget leaks, almost all of which are deliberate and from ministerial offices rather than unauthorised and from the bureaucracy.

Regrettably, powerful journalists gain enough from the government's media management to keep them compliant and reluctant to let the public know what goes on.

CHAPTER 8
HOW TO BE A COLUMNIST

A newspaper columnist is a person obliged to find significance three times a week in events of absolutely no significance.

John Kenneth Galbraith

Note to ABC broadcasters: just as the 'n' in column is silent, so is the 'n' in colum-nist.

My guess is that when most people dream of becoming a journalist, they imagine being a columnist, not a reporter. I do know that when politicians and econocrats imagine a subsequent career as a journo, it's column writing they have in mind. I didn't have columnising in mind when I joined the *Herald* in 1974, but in just three years David Bowman had given me a little column in the business section on Mondays when, with the share market having been closed for the weekend, the business writers didn't have a lot to say.

About two years later Bowman gave me a Wednesday column on the op-ed page and I handed the business page column on to my understudy in Canberra. That lasted for not much more than a year, when I took it over again. And then in June 1983 I took over a column in the business section on Saturdays, which had been started by my mate Alan Mitchell. So, for more than 30 years I've written those three columns each week, on the same days and in the same parts of the paper. I'm not bored yet, mainly because the economy keeps changing and I keep learning more about how it works.

It would be wrong to give you the impression it's easy to get a guernsey as a columnist. It isn't. Very few journos are given the opportunity. I was shunted towards column writing because I wasn't much good at anything else, certainly not reporting. But if you're undeterred and would like to know how I do it, I'm happy to reveal my trade secrets.

The right frame of mind

All newspapers and most of the mainstream news media are profit-making businesses. Since my education had veered into the commercial stream before I was out of high school, this has never bothered me. I've never seen myself as an artist painting pictures for my own benefit, but always as a craftsman aiming to make something the customer will find of interest and value. But that doesn't mean you can't produce something that's truthful and of high quality, something you're proud of, that gives value for money. There's plenty of journalism that falls short of these ideals, of course, but it comes from people who aren't trying hard enough.

Columns come under the heading of 'opinion and analysis'. You can err in one direction or the other. You can write a tub-thumping column that expresses your opinion with lots of emotion, righteousness, name-calling and condemnation of anyone who disagrees.

All those people who share your opinion will love it—'someone had to say it!'—and a fair proportion of those who disagree will enjoy being reminded of how stupid you are and how right they've always been.

We imagine people read for enlightenment but, in truth, most of us read for reinforcement. People tend to read those columnists they know they'll agree with, but even when we read stuff we disagree with it almost always reinforces our existing views. This is why I've never believed my efforts do much to change the world—but I've never let that discourage me. Like my father before me, I do my duty and leave the rest to providence.

I've written the odd tub-thumper in my day, but mostly I err in the direction of analysis. I spell out the argument and say why I accept this point but not that one. I try to back up my argument with facts and be honest in the way I present them. People I meet often say, 'I read your columns—don't always agree with them.' That's fine by me. If I've rehearsed enough of the argument to remind you of why you've never agreed with the position I'm putting, I've done my job and earnt my money. But I've been around for long enough to know most readers share Harry Truman's disdain for two-handed economists so, except maybe during election campaigns, I always come down on one side or the other. There is an element of showmanship in column writing, and if you don't realise that you're not likely to last long.

A couple of years ago the *Herald* ran an ad campaign I think was intended as a dig at the Murdoch press. A handful of senior journos were asked to repeat a bunch of statements written by the ad agency and its people would pick the clips they preferred. I was sorry I didn't decline to declaim 'The *Herald* has no agenda' and relieved when they didn't use me saying it. If they meant the *Herald*

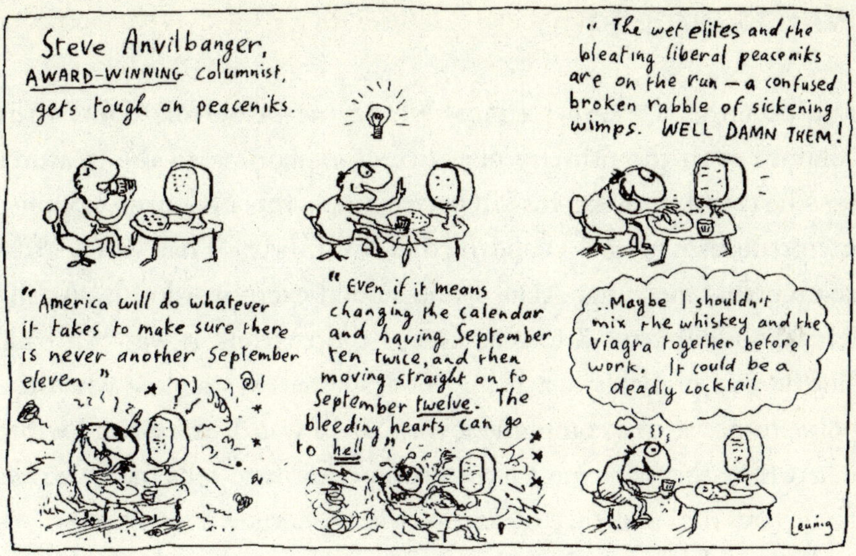

doesn't twist its reporting of news to reflect its policy preferences or favourite party, that's fine. And true.

But the truth is that, as a columnist, I do have an agenda. All economics editors have policies they advocate and others they oppose. An economic commentator who didn't anchor their critique in a clear and consistent view about how the economy works and how it could work better—the positive and the normative, as economists say—wouldn't be worth much.

For much of my time as a columnist this has meant that the range of opinion offered by the nation's economics editors hasn't been very wide. But as I've become more sceptical about the mainstream model, the gap has grown. What matters more, however, is the ethical standard: your opinions about what's good policy and what's bad shouldn't be influenced either by your own hip pocket or partisan sympathy. I often disclose to the reader how my own finances would be affected by the policy I'm advocating.

Who to write for

I suspect the economics editors who came before me wrote their columns with the primary objective of explaining to the treasurer how he could be doing his job better. I remember a journo stopping my predecessor Alan Wood in the pub to say, 'That was a great column this morning, Alan, I understood every word of it.' As she left, Woody muttered to me, 'Gee, I didn't think it was *that* bad.' But he was probably just being modest: that was a time when the polite response to a compliment was, 'Aw, I was drunk when I wrote it.' At the other extreme I have a competitor who tells me he writes for 'an internal audience of one'—otherwise known as his boss.

Who do I write for? No question: the reader. Always have, always will. To be specific, I write for the well-educated person who, though lacking economic qualifications, knows the economy is important and wants to be informed about it as painlessly as possible. As for the internal audience, I appeal over the boss's head to the customers. I was reinforced in this approach by thinking about the most successful talkback king of my early career, John Laws. I knew the politicians didn't have a high opinion of the depth of Laws' political understanding, but his audience was so big they wouldn't have considered declining an invitation to appear on his show. If I had a big enough audience, whether or not the boss liked my choice of topics for my column wouldn't matter.

But when I say I write for the reader, let's be clear: I don't write what the reader wants to hear. The way I think of it is, the reader gets to set the question—I write on those issues I believe are of most interest to the reader—but I choose the answer. I meet the reader where the reader happens to be, then gently lead them to a better, more informed place. But, just as we didn't know we wanted mobile phones until they were invented, I also often write about things I believe will interest readers once I've drawn them to their attention.

Of course, the deeper reason I write for the reader is that I'm a frustrated teacher. Similarly, I favour analysis over opinion because I'm a teacher, not a preacher. From the very first feature I wrote for the *Herald*, my instinct was to find out how something worked—tax indexation it was, actually—then explain it to the reader. And though this was completely instinctive, it fitted perfectly with my need to relearn the economics I'd found so uninteresting at uni. As well, it wasn't long before I started getting feedback from readers and colleagues that told me I was onto something.

There are a lot of things I wouldn't mind being written on my tombstone, but I know what *will* be: he was the only economist we could understand. People have been saying that to me for most of the past 40 years. And for all of that time I've been thinking: if that's what you want, that's what you'll get. I've been honing my ability to explain economics simply but accurately for all that time, and in chapter 9 I do my best to explain how I explain.

I flatter myself I've become a champion of 'explanatory journalism'. It's not something that turns on other journalists—a bit like their disdain for 'news you can use'—but if what I get paid is anything to go by, it's a skill in great demand but short supply. And why shouldn't it be in great demand? The world is chock-full of 'breaking news', far more than anyone can absorb, but what's harder to find is someone you can trust to tell you what it all proves. I've long wanted to be that person—in the field of economics, at least—and I've long believed it will be satisfying the public's 'search for meaning' in an ever more complex and confusing world that will provide most of the future for quality journalism when newspapers are no more.

But in my case the question of who to write for can be answered at a more detailed level. My impression is that most columnists who write more than one column a week produce essentially the same kind of column for essentially the same audience. Not me. I doubt if many readers are conscious of it, but the three columns I write each week are aimed at different audiences.

My Monday column on the business page is, in a sense, the most indulgent: it's intended to compete directly with the other economics editors and is aimed at economists, business people and people with a serious interest in 'the politics of economics'. My Wednesday column on the op-ed page—which, because of its greater prominence, I regard as my showpiece—is aimed at the broadest audience and is written about those issues I judge to be of the widest interest. Of late I've usually written about issues that have attracted a lot of attention in the media, but for many years I gave most attention to 'home economics'. That is, issues so much a part of daily life that many readers wouldn't have defined them as part of the subject matter of economics, and many economic writers would have regarded them as beneath their dignity. The mechanics of bill-paying, the cost of kids, whether it's smart to pay HECS fees up-front, retiring early versus retiring late, and that sort of thing.

But it's my Saturday column in the business section I'm proudest of because I regard it as unique in Australian journalism. It's teaching thinly disguised as current affairs, aimed at 'students of all ages'. A lot of actual students read it, but it's also intended for business people, chief executives' wives, politicians, political staffers and bureaucrats—all the people who, while lacking a degree in economics, do have a need for a better grasp of the subject. I often take some economic event that's happened during the week and try to expose and explain the theory that lies behind it. I'm a great believer in the importance of theory (even when it's wrong) and I'd love to be thought of as the journalist who imports the most theory into the pages of a newspaper. In my Wednesday column I usually carefully avoid using economic jargon, but on Saturdays I use as much of it as possible, always explaining what it means. Why? So that when my readers see other people using the technical terms they'll know what they mean and won't be bamboozled. That's the service my Saturday readers are paying for.

And there's one more twist to my horses-for-courses approach to column writing. Over Christmas and on long weekends I have visions of people sitting back and reading the paper at the beach or their weekender, so I try to avoid the standard economic fare and write about something a bit offbeat and more entertaining. This is where my interest in behavioural economics—the application of psychology to economics—comes in handy. And, though my primary attraction to behavioural economics is its more credible account of how the economy works, I know how interesting readers find its puzzles and experiments.

There's one more thing to say about who I write for: people on both sides of the political fence. I long ago decided I didn't want to halve the potential size of my fan club by writing just for one side or the other. It's true my opinions are based on a discernible set of moral values, but nothing annoys me more than people who want to consign me to one party-political box or the other. I try always to be on the lookout for topics that will confound their preconceptions.

Where ideas come from

A lot of my friends tell me they don't know how I'm able to keep coming up with ideas for my columns. And it's true that a lot of pollies who couldn't wait to be invited to write for a paper soon discover they really only had half a dozen things they were burning to say.

To be truthful, however, this isn't hard for a professional columnist. It's an easily acquired skill. All you do is grow a pair of antennas which continuously search your environment for potential topics as you go through the week. If you can't remember the ideas that cross your mind, you write them down. I never read the paper at home without a writing pad beside me to note down the thoughts that occur as I read. If I hear something interesting or annoying on the radio, I make a note. If, lying in bed, a good line comes into my head, I've trained myself to sit up and write it on the pad I keep on the bedside table. Then all I have to do next morning is decipher what I wrote in the dark.

It's very common for me to think of ideas for other columns while I'm busy writing one. I always stop and make a note. Of course, I often end up with notes for far more columns than I need. But that's OK, I pick the best—or rather, I pick the ones that still excite me. That's the test: can you get excited enough about the topic to be able to convey some of that excitement to the reader?

It's common for exam questions in the HSC to provide students with 'stimulus material' to inform their answers. I'm just as reliant on stimulus material as any student. I read the papers much more thoroughly when I find myself stuck in an aluminium tube for an hour or two, flying to Canberra or Melbourne. I rarely get off a plane without a sheaf of notes written on boarding passes or any bit of paper I find in my pocket. When I sit down to read a government report or academic paper, I don't just make notes, I write down any thoughts or potential first paragraphs that pop into my head as I read.

I find, however, that if all I do is react to the things other journos or local economists are saying, the debate can get a bit incestuous: the usual suspects chasing the same ideas around and around. So whereas in the early days I used to read economic textbooks in my spare time, these days I read the latest books by big-name overseas economists and psychologists. I rarely find my competitors get onto those books earlier than I do—not that it would worry me if they did.

I've become notorious around the office for sneaking off on Tuesday arvos to go to the movies, usually more than one. What people don't know is that between movies I indulge in my favourite read of the week, *The Economist*. It keeps me up with the latest interesting ideas from academic economists (there aren't many) and, in any case, I often find myself furiously scribbling down notes for columns, that speech I've got to give, or the next book I'm not getting on with.

Do I ever have times when I just can't come up with a topic? When I get 'the dries', as writers call it? No, never. Writers get the dries, but journos never do. Why not? Because we can't afford to. Dries are about deadlines. In all my time as a columnist I can think of just two or three occasions, long ago, when I couldn't come up with a topic; when I worked through a towering mullock heap of government reports and things I'd put aside as potential column material, looking for a nugget, and just couldn't find anything I could get excited about—Nah . . . nah . . . nah.

The trick is that each of those rare occasions happened on a Friday and related to a column for Monday. I couldn't settle on a topic because I knew I had most of the weekend to come up with one. Since then I've made it a rule to at least get the back of my Monday column broken before going to bed on Friday nights. Fortunately, not much happens in the economy over the weekend—or not much that can't be accommodated by changing, adding or deleting a par or two. Even when you'll be writing on Monday about an election result on Saturday night, most election results are quite predictable and, if you've been paying attention during the campaign, you'll have thought of plenty of things that will need saying on the Monday after.

My experience as an editorial writer left me with the leader-writer's great faith in 'a form of words'. This is the unshakeable belief that, no matter how much the ground has shifted since you wrote your leader, there is a simple form of words that will get you out of trouble and remove the need to scrap it and start again. The test is your ability to find the sentence that will save the day.

It gets back to deadlines. Journos face immovable deadlines and know they have no choice but to meet them. They may feel rising anxiety, even occasional panic, as the deadline approaches, but they never feel uninspired because they know they'll be in big trouble if they do. Professional writers and academics can get the dries—sometimes for weeks or months on end—because the deadlines they face aren't immovable. Publishers impose deadlines, but know there's not much they can do to enforce them. Self-imposed deadlines are infinitely movable.

Journos know the best deadlines are externally imposed. You often hear journos complaining about deadlines—and if you want to test their power, try phoning a journo on deadline and listen to the monosyllabic barks you get in reply—but the truth is deadlines are part of the great attraction of working in journalism, particularly daily journalism. The point is, once you've met your deadline you're free. Whereas many people work on projects that may last for months, daily journalists go home each night with a clear desk (metaphorically, never literally) and return next morning wondering what new topic the new day will bring.

Journos know there's much truth in Parkinson's Law that work expands to fill the time available. They also know—well, I do—that the amount of time you've put into something isn't a reliable guide to its quality, so they learn not to start on a piece until the deadline is close. It's actually a way of exploiting your adrenaline rush.

I confess, however, that I've been meeting deadlines for so long that I can't get anxious no matter how close it is to deadline before I've thought of a topic. Knowing you have no choice means you know you'll come up with something, even if it isn't your most inspired choice or all that long since you wrote on the topic. This may be why my former boss Eric Beecher's rule was that you judge columnists not by their best columns but their worst. Or by how many duds they have. Youngsters don't seem to know the meaning of the word 'potboiler' but I've written a few. It's about batting averages: it's not possible to have a perfect score, but you keep the average as high as you can.

One thing I've learnt as I've got more experienced is that it's not how much you know that matters, it's how much you get into the paper. A lot of economic commentators put a lot of work into keeping on top of economic developments all over the world. In my case, I spend a lot of time reading the latest books on economics and psychology. *Fine.* But I don't see much point in acquiring knowledge that you don't pass on to the reader. Only when I retire will I have to settle for the joy of knowledge for its own sake.

Timeliness versus importance

Usually during an election campaign I think of far more things to say than I'll have opportunities to say them. And, of course, there's an immovable deadline by which they have to be said. So I often map out a timetable of what I'll say on this day and that up to election day, just so I don't lose the chance to say the things I'm most keen to get said.

Such plans can be overtaken by events, of course, but, even so, it may shock some journalists that I could be so premeditated. For many, the role of columnists is to follow the news: you comment on what's in the news and pick your topics from what's been in the news, allowing as little time to elapse as possible and feeling pretty guilty if you're commenting on something that happened as long ago as last week.

Sorry, but that's not how I play the game. I'm not prepared to say something superficial about a topic just because it happened yesterday. Perhaps it's just that, like my father, I'm too slow in the uptake to be that quick off the mark, but I'd rather take my time, let some development sink in, make a few inquiries, think of something worthwhile to say, and even wait until the dust is starting to settle. I'm in the how and why department, and that takes longer than the who, what, where and when.

Set-piece events such as the budget or a change in interest rates are different, but I don't see columnists as slaves to the front page. I've never wanted to be part of the day-one overkill, which provides readers with far more stories on a development than they'd ever have the time or interest to read, and is primarily intended to impress other editors and journos.

If the momentous event isn't momentous enough to be worth writing about over the following seven days or more, it's not worthy of comment in the first place. I'm in the business of telling my readers what the front-page excitements add up to do, what's worth worrying about and what isn't, and that's a job better done after a little time has elapsed. Rather than be first with a comment, I'd prefer to go last. Forgive me, but when I'm last out of the blocks I tell myself that's OK because I'll also be the best. (I did warn you about journalists' egos.)

As part of my office-politics policy of never pushing my luck too far—or my economic training to avoid extremes and seek the best trade-off between conflicting objectives—I'm happy to make my choice of column topics as timely as I can, provided the price isn't too high. But the truth is I value interest a lot more highly than timeliness. I want to write on topics that I and my readers find sufficiently interesting, and if I can do well on that count I'm not worried about other journalists finding my choice of topics 'off the pace'. (See the earlier reference to John Laws.)

I'm not prepared to be a victim of the perceived need for 'a peg'—a reference to a very recent event to justify the subject of the column hanging from it. This is a quite passive approach to column writing; I prefer a more active stance. A fellow columnist once complained how hard it was to find subjects significant enough to write about during the summer holidays silly season. 'Mate,' I said, 'you've got it the wrong way round. You should be pleased when there's nothing that demands to be written about because that allows you to ride your hobbyhorses.' I've never subscribed to the notion that my choice of topics should follow 'the news agenda'. If other people can put items on the agenda, why can't I?

In the economic year there are events that matter a lot and others that don't matter much. But in the ever faster flowing stream of the 24-hour news cycle, events that matter a lot tend to float away before they've been adequately digested. Not with me they don't. There aren't many events in the economic calendar more important than the May federal budget, but it lasts a maximum of a fortnight on the news pages. I'm usually still gnawing at the budget bones a month later. And a big tax-reform package could take me longer.

The truth is, the ultimate requirement of a columnist is neither to be timely with your choice of topics nor to write always about the important, but simply to be interesting. And the ultimate judge of that is the reader.

Still doing it my way

It's fashionable for politicians and chief executives to give speeches extolling the virtues of 'innovation', but no one in journalism makes such speeches. When you regard being judged a winner in the comp against your rivals as the main way you get your jollies, you stick religiously to the rules to avoid accusations of cheating. When your goal is to serve the reader, however, it's not hard to imagine the job could be done in ways the reader finds more useful or just more attractive.

Early in my career as a columnist I put a lot of thought and experiment into doing the job differently to my elders and betters. I wrote a few heavily satirical pieces, even though my boss Guy Harriott warned me there was nothing in journalism more dangerous than irony. He was right, of course; there are always readers who take you literally. My solution is to lay it on so thick only the most obtuse could miss my drift. It's a long time since I wrote a whole piece saying just the opposite of what I meant, but I still throw in the odd inverted jibe.

There's no room for subtlety in journalism; we're not writing great literature. The reader gives what you've written a quick squiz, often while watching telly at the same time. I'm a naturally blunt, some would say insensitive, person. Certainly, what little I know about diplomacy I've learnt the hard way. But while I've found my bluntness a social liability, it's been a professional asset. There was a time when one of my mottos was 'moderate views, immoderately expressed'.

It may be a hangover from the doctrine of the universal journalist, but the longstanding tradition of writing news reports very much in the third person was also part of the way columns were written when I arrived on the scene. I had a competitor who took it so far he would refer to himself as 'this space', but he may just have been taking a dig at me.

I decided early on to write in the first person, to put myself and my doings into the column. This may be just a sign of an overinflated ego, but I do remember being inspired by Channel 9's veteran Sydney newsreader Brian Henderson, who had risen to national fame as host of *Bandstand* on Saturday nights. Nine was promoting its evening news bulletin with the slogan 'Brian told me', running ads showing Henderson walking through the station's newsroom, looking over the shoulder of typing reporters, nodding, and walking on.

I happened to know newsreaders get zero say over the stories they're given to read out. But that wasn't the point. It was obvious Nine thought attaching Hendo's personality to their ordinary old news bulletin would win it more viewers. It was only what any marketing type would tell you to do. But if Nine saw an advantage in personifying their news bulletin, why shouldn't I personify my economic column?

So I did. I wrote about my wife (until she banned me from mentioning her), my young kids, my home life and my financial affairs. My first column after an absence would always be a composition on What I Did on My Holidays. Once I even wrote about the trouble I had persuading the taxman to charge me enough tax and revealed the total amount of income tax I'd paid since I joined the workforce. (Only an accountant would keep such a record. It was a frightening amount because it seemed so huge to me, but also so puny to a politician, who could waste that much in an afternoon.)

I don't put as much personal stuff in my (Wednesday) column as I used to, partly because its length has been slowly cut from 1500 to 900 words as, in the *Herald*'s assessment, readers' attention spans have shortened. The effect of personalising my columns has been to leave many readers feeling they know me. When strangers greet me in the street as 'Ross', I've learnt to reciprocate as though we're old friends.

But I didn't understand the power of putting yourself in the column until my boy Jessica Irvine started doing it with her columns. In almost no time she had lifted herself above all the *Herald*'s vaguely familiar bylines to be someone our readers knew and loved. Why so few columnists are prepared to get personal I can only explain in terms of the power of group norms.

My other innovation was to abandon the excessive formality of the way quality newspapers express themselves and move to a much more relaxed, conversational tone. Why people who wouldn't dream of wearing a suit and tie to a dinner party, or even to the opera, still write in such a formal, starched-collar way is beyond me. What do they think it achieves?

I try to write the way I speak, using all the contractions of everyday speech. I don't do it just to be eccentric (though that would be a good enough reason) but because conversational speech is what readers feel most comfortable with and are able to absorb most easily. Once my niece Sonia, who had to study a lot of my columns when she was doing HSC economics, told me she could hear me speaking as she read. That was possibly the best compliment I've had.

But I don't just write in a conversational style. I try to make my columns a conversation between myself and the reader by interposing the questions and reservations a reader might have about what I'm saying. Again, why more columnists don't do the same I don't know.

A menu of formulas

There are many different ways you can structure a column—different formulas you can use, if you like—and I've tried a few, though some have become favourites. For a long time I called the one I used most the *War Cry* formula, after the stories in the Sally newspaper my father sold in pubs every weekend. They used to start off chatting about some quite interesting topic but then, about a quarter of the way in, abruptly switch to the spiritual hard sell. I still often begin a column with a thick layer of chocolate covering a much less palatable lesson on the economics of something. The only hard part is coming up with the one-sentence segue that joins the chocolate to the brussel sprouts.

I've always liked to write a column challenging the conventional wisdom about something. For this I usually use the set-it-up/knock-it-down formula. I describe the conventional view as fully and persuasively as I can and then, just when I've got everyone nodding in agreement, I insert the magic segue: 'There's just one small problem with all this: it's nonsense.' Remember seeing that one before?

Very occasionally a scoop comes my way. If so, I want to include it in my column in the normal way, for much the same reason people used to hide sixpences in Christmas puddings. But in such cases I'll usually open the column with a 'hard lead'—a succinct, no-nonsense, news report-like statement of my new and surprising information—and then relax into storytelling mode. It's worth remembering that, for reasons I explain in chapter 10, stories are the most natural, enticing format for readers, so the more you can make the most technical explanation sound like a story—mainly by the order in which you arrange your points—the better you'll do.

When Wall Street and other share markets around the world crashed in October 1987, the biggest crash since the Great Crash of 1929, Max Walsh wrote a comment predicting it would produce another depression, while I wrote we'd get a world recession, but no worse. The world wasn't coming to an end. Walsh's pessimism was run on page one; my relative optimism was pushed inside. Turned out I was quite wrong; we didn't even get a recession.

I'm a natural optimist, Walsh a natural pessimist. That was just one of Walsh's many dire predictions, most of which are yet to come to pass. You could conclude he was a hopeless forecaster, or you could conclude—as I did—that he was playing a different game to me, using a different formula. I cared about my long-term record, Walsh didn't. His idea of a win was to write the column that had everyone talking about it at morning tea that day. By that measure, he was an inveterate winner. I call it the Doing-a-Max formula.

Sometimes the best formula is the simplest: write a simple explanation and backgrounder on the big economic story of the week. Another approach, for use particularly by those who feel obliged to have a 'news peg' for every column, is the filing cabinet (mental or literal): you spend your life seeking out particularly pertinent articles and reports on particular generic topics—say, the economic benefit to a city from staging the Olympics or a Formula One race, or the economic effects of natural disasters—and file them away for use the next time an appropriate peg floats past. If you don't want to go to that much trouble, you need to put together a short-list of the contact details of academic economists who specialise in 'special-event economics', 'disaster economics' and so forth.

As I'll say more about in chapter 11, I'm becoming increasingly uncomfortable with the conventional view that 'investigative journalism' is something done by journos assigned to the paper's 'investigations team'. There's a crying need for more of the columns written by economics writers to take the form of an investigation. Some government claims to have a study showing that a certain policy reform will increase GDP by $X billion over 20 years. Some lobby group claims to have proof that the loss of the motor industry would wipe $21.5 billion off GDP. OK, let's investigate the claim and see if it stands up.

Next comes something that's partly a style of column and partly a source of columns. I call it the half-eaten pie formula. Econocrats and ministers are always giving speeches about the economy, and government agencies are always issuing reports on economic questions. The Canberra press gallery checks every speech and report to see if there's a story in it.

But time is limited and space in the paper is limited and some days a good economic story is squeezed out by a much more momentous yarn. So it's surprisingly common for the secretary to the Treasury to give a thoughtful and informative speech on some new policy challenge, but for this to be ignored because something he said seemed to be a dig at the government. Eye-opening speeches by central bankers can be brushed aside because an answer they gave in question time hinted that another rate cut is coming. A couple of controversial recommendations can dominate news reports of government inquiries, squeezing out the committee's reasons for believing such measures are needed.

So I see a big part of my role as coming along behind the gallery like a bag lady, scrounging in its garbage tins for food that's still edible. I don't accept the attitude that if some econocrat or pollie proposes something I disagree with I'll tear it apart and won't tell my readers *why* they're making the proposal. Nor do I accept that if I *don't* disagree with a proposal, I won't bother mentioning it at all.

In other words, I see myself as a kind of auxiliary economics correspondent, using my greater length, greater discretion about what goes in my column, and more expansive definition of timeliness to make sure the reader gets told all the economic news they need to be told. What the economic trumps think is happening in the economy, why they think it's happening, what they think needs to be done about it and why they favour policy A over policy B.

So a formula I use frequently for my column is just the extended and annotated news report: here's my summary of what the Reserve Bank governor said in an important speech he gave last week. It will be a mixture of direct quotes and paraphrasing (which allows me to avoid or explain stuff that's too jargon-ridden) as well as background explanation.

I may liven things up with a few tart interjections and I'll make sure I get my own opinion in there somewhere. But what I won't do is fail to ensure my readers get a fair account of what the bloke's trying to say. The better written the speech is, the less work I'll have to put into my account of it. Some people regard this style of column as lazy or improper—a column should be the columnist's original work, not someone else's—but I don't care.

I guess this is more a trick than a formula, but it works well: be the first to say the obvious. It's a fact of human nature that the obvious isn't obvious until someone has said it, and then lots of people have repeated it. For columnists it's the corollary that matters: it isn't obvious until you've said it. And provided you're the first, you'll be seen as perceptive, not a pedlar of the commonplace.

A related trick is to say the unsayable. I don't mean breaking taboos against the sexist or racist, I mean telling tales out of school. There are plenty of things the insiders think shouldn't be passed on to outsiders—aka readers—and you're just the right person to defy unwritten rules.

The last of my favourite formulas is the beat-down. Someone gets terribly excited about something on the front page: it's not only unprecedented but will change the world forever. You write a piece a few days later saying that, seen in context, it's not such a big deal. This was an old favourite of the *Herald*'s Alan Ramsey. When I do it I always exercise a little diplomacy and I haven't had a complaint from any of the bosses I've worked for. I suspect they regard my piece as insurance: if someone accuses them of exaggeration, they point to my column. Sometimes I think nirvana for an editor is having a lot of energetic, inexperienced young journos who get excited about things they've never seen before, plus a couple of ageing journos prone to saying, 'Aw, I've seen it all before and it doesn't amount to a hill of beans.' On the front page, the kids march it up to the top of the hill and, up the back, some old fogy marches it down again. Maybe I should call it the grumpy-old-man formula.

How to keep it up

I've written on the past 40 federal budgets, never missing one, 16 federal election campaigns, more tax reform packages than you can poke a stick at, and more changes in the official interest rate than you could count. (Actually, there have been 68 changes since the start of 1990, 27 ups and 41 downs; the Reserve keeps a list.) How could anyone maintain their enthusiasm for yet another run round the track? Well, it hasn't been a problem so far. Why not? A big part of it is my good fortune in leaving uni not knowing most of the economics I was supposed to have learnt. I've been on a journey of discovery for 40 years and I keep finding new and interesting stuff.

I don't get tired of saying the same thing each year because I don't say the same thing. My understanding of the topic has deepened and my views have changed as I've read more and lived more. My views have slowly become less conventional and more radical. I've become more sceptical of the received wisdom, more humble about what economists know and don't know—including how hopeless they are at predicting the future—and conscious of the need for economics to be more 'fit for humans'.

My readers always assume I'm an economist; the top econocrats I deal with never do—as I discovered when the new Treasury secretary, Dr Ken Henry, made that clear in a footnote to one of his speeches. He did me the greatest favour with that revelation; I found it hugely liberating. For years I'd been uncertain about how to describe myself professionally. I said I was an accountant pretending to be an economist, but after a couple of decades that wasn't true either. A journo pretending to be an accountant pretending to be an economist.

A lot of economic journalists strive for acceptance by the real economists as one of their number (though those with a full economics degree and a stint in Treasury don't have to worry). If that had been my semiconscious ambition, Henry blew it away. He didn't start my changing perception of my role as an economics editor, but he certainly pushed it past the point of no return. If there was no way I'd be admitted to the economists' union, I didn't have to live by union rules, did I?

From now on I'd correct anyone who assumed I was an economist. No, I'm a journalist who writes about economics. Since I've been doing this for so long I probably know a fair bit about the topic, but that's all. Were some authority to force me to choose between the two—no contest. As an occupation, journo does me proud.

So whereas early in my time I took my role to be convincing the *Herald*'s readers of the wisdom of economic rationalism—which

I'm sure all my predecessors saw as their role—for a long time now I've seen my role as providing our readers with a critique of economics, economists and economic policies. I'm the theatre critic for economics. This, of course, is a much better fit with my ethical compass, Serve the Reader.

Viewing yourself as a critic does reduce the likelihood of getting bored with the topic. But another saving grace of economics is that it's a broad church, it covers a vast territory. The mainstays are macro-economics (stabilising the economy to limit inflation and unemployment) and micro-economics (studying particular industries and how markets work), but just about every part of life and work has an economic dimension.

So if I decided defence or town planning were more interesting than economics, I could just start writing about the economics of defence or the economics of town planning. There's a lot I could write about the economics of sport if only I was interested in sport. As it is, *people* interest me, so I can and do write about economic psychology and economic sociology. Economics covers such a big territory that, when you feel a district has run out of interest, you just pack up your humpy and walk somewhere else.

It's true, however, that when I was younger I did worry a lot about burning out. When the kids were little my wife, Claudia, told me she wanted me home by seven o'clock each night. As a columnist this wasn't hard to comply with and I got into the habit of reading to the kids before bedtime, which we all enjoyed and I remember with great fondness. Quality time. Spending evenings at home became easier with the advent of the personal computer. And when I got my own office in the backyard above the carport, it became possible for me to work the longest hours without much offence. I could attend every meal and was available whenever needed. Another way I was unconsciously shaping my life to make it more like my father's.

Because they work on public holidays, journos get more annual leave than most people, so Claudia said the primary responsibility for looking after the kids during school holidays would be mine. Fine. The most important element of my anti-burnout plan was to take all my leave every year. I'd take a lot of short breaks through the year during school holidays, plus a longer break at Christmas. And I'd always go away; none of my leave would be spent at home.

As the years have gone by I've found ways of wangling more leave and adding a bit of long-service leave on the top. By now I take a huge amount of leave each year, so much so that I use it as a kind of early retirement. It allows us to get on with spending my retirement savings on overseas travel before I'm too old to want to bother. It means I need be in no hurry to retire.

And as a strategy to prevent burnout, it seems to have worked. My job is terribly routinised. When I wake up each morning I need only ascertain the day of the week to know exactly what I'll be doing that day. I always look forward to going on hols, but I'm always just as keen to get home and get back into it. If your life is a rut, just take a break from the rut as often as you can.

Of course, there's whether *I'm* feeling browned off with my column and there's whether the *reader* is. There are tricks to being a long-term columnist without the boss getting the message the readers' interest is wearing thin. My opinions have evolved, but they don't change radically from one year to the next and some issues come around yearly if not more often.

A big saver is the 'first law of journalism': readers have short memories. And they've no doubt shortened since someone first said that. I long ago realised that people can read what you've written about something, feel they fully understand what you're saying, but have forgotten it within a few weeks.

A good trick is to keep changing the subject, never writing on the same topic twice in a row unless it's clearly a 'crisis' that's on everyone's mind. This is the convention in column writing, but I learnt it the hard way. The 'terms of trade'—the prices we receive for our exports relative to the prices we pay for our imports—is a long-established economic concept, but in more than a decade as an economic journalist no economist had mentioned it to me until sometime in 1985 when, in a conversation with an econocrat, he advanced it as the obvious, but hitherto unrecognised, explanation for why our floating dollar had suddenly sunk to become the Pacific Peso.

I realised this was a 'new departure' in the economic 'narrative'. It was an unfamiliar concept that was about to become a big deal. I realised, too, that I'd stumbled on it just a week or so before it became commonplace. It was a kind of scoop and I should give it a big bang so people would attach my name to this 'new' idea. More dutifully, it was my job to make sure my readers were full bottle on this great technical insight. So I hatched a plan I was inordinately proud of: I'd run my new discovery through my full column cycle.

On Wednesday I'd explain it simply for the mums and dads. On Saturday I'd reveal its theoretical underpinnings to the students of all ages. And on the Monday I'd discuss the appropriate policy response from the government. Brilliant. I remained inordinately proud until I bumped into the editor, Eric Beecher, in the corridor: 'I see you've written the same column three times in a row, Ross.' If someone as smart as Beecher thought that, I could be sure the readers would, too.

Another trick to maintain reader interest is the 'change of pace'. If you've been writing on serious topics, throw in a light one. If you've been writing for a few weeks on problems managing the national economy, throw in one about managing your bank account. If you've been dwelling on Australian problems, write about the international scene. If you've been criticising the government's performance, piece after piece, find something nice to say about 'em.

If disunity is death for politicians, death for columnists is predictability. When people start saying 'I used to read Jock's column, but now when I see his topic I know what he's going to say', you know Jock's days are numbered. Continuously changing the subject and always looking for the change of pace are good tricks to reduce predictability. So is not riding your hobbyhorses too often.

But the greatest predictability problem comes when the reader thinks they've got you unequivocally tabbed in the Right box or the Left box. Of course, some columnists don't mind that, so for them it's just a matter of adequately gratifying the sympathies of the side they've chosen to champion. But, though it's changed a bit with the advent of Murdoch's Fair and Balanced substitute for journalism, most staff columnists—as opposed to contributors—don't want to be pigeonholed in that way. I know I don't.

So how do you stop yourself being pigeonholed? Well, if your opinions are derived from partisan loyalties, it ain't possible. And even if they derive from a consistent set of values, it's still not easy. Whether your values emphasise individual freedom or social responsibility, it won't be hard for the compulsive categorisers to detect that they fit more easily with the professed values of one side rather than the other. But politics being what it is, it's common for parties to pursue policies that are inconsistent with their professed values.

So that's your first chance to confuse and confound the compulsive box-assigners. Stick to your principles and never fail to call out the side that professes to uphold a principle but lets it slide in particular cases for reasons of expediency. Similarly, don't be slow to support the side that, contrary to its stated values, does something consistent with yours. If, for instance, you were a libertarian, fond of delivering diatribes against the Nanny State, you wouldn't attack the Rudd government for failing to adequately regulate the installers of pink batts, as I saw one Murdoch tub-thumper do.

The other defence against the categorisers is to ensure your views and values are sufficiently complex, or 'nuanced', as it's fashionable to say. The box-consigners almost always have an overly simplified view of Right and Left—that's what makes them so sure they've got you pegged. But the world is an ever more complicated place and most if not all issues involve striking a balance between conflicting values. So if, like me, you can usually see both sides of the story, it shouldn't be too hard to have views on particular topics that are hard to categorise, or that don't fit the expected stereotype.

And don't forget . . .

It's obvious, but it bears repeating: if you're writing an analytical column, your aim is to cut through all the superfluous or secondary factors and isolate the key choice to be made or key imponderable to be grappled with. What facts are pertinent to the matter in contention and what aren't? For instance, there's no point worrying about an advantage or disadvantage that's common to both alternatives—though that simple truth may need to be pointed out to the reader.

Although economics is very much a Canberra-based subject, the *Herald*'s approach—unlike some newspapers'—has always been to have its economics editor based at head office in Sydney rather than in the Canberra press gallery. This has suited me; I've wanted to view economics from the geographic perspective of our readers, not that of the people who think they run the economy.

In the old days I used to go to Canberra with Alan Mitchell on the occasional Wednesday, the day my column appeared. Once, after the 1982 budget, I dashed off a column criticising the Fraser government for engaging in a lot of new spending when it had been struggling for years to get on top of the budget deficit, picking up an argument from the leader of the Liberal Dries, John Hyde.

We bowled into our first appointment at the prime minister's department and met with a very frosty reception. At our meeting with Fraser's economist it was more of the same. The bollocking didn't bother me, it was their argument: 'We could see demand was falling away, so we applied a bit of stimulus—why wouldn't we?' Whoops. Why not indeed? I'd got caught criticising for the sake of criticising in a way that was inconsistent with my views about economic management.

The deeper lesson, however, was that when I dashed off an attack on the government, it hadn't once crossed my mind that I'd be fronting those people the very same morning. And this was a good thing. If I worked in Parliament House, I'd be conscious of the pollies looking over my shoulder as I wrote every column—and then meeting me in the corridor—which would surely inhibit my willingness to say what I thought.

So, back in a state capital is the best place for economics editors. Only in recent days as I've observed the performance of *The Age*'s capable Canberra-based economics editor, Peter Martin, have I realised the counter-argument: being in the gallery can't help but leave you with an encyclopaedic knowledge of details of new policy measures and the debate about their pros and cons.

Columnists get it easier than reporters in one important respect: contacts speak to you a lot more freely. So whereas these days most reporters in the gallery have few contacts in the bureaucracy, I've been able to maintain mine, mainly because I'm never looking for someone to quote in a news story.

I tell public servants I'm in the plagiarism business. Explain to me some economic concept or how a policy's intended to work and your expertise becomes my expertise. Tell me your opinion about X and, if it fits with my other views and values, it becomes my opinion. Unlike academics—some of whom would like a citation for telling you the time of day—econocrats like being plagiarised. I'd prefer to make more use of academic economists but, assuming they're not away at an overseas conference when you need them, they often don't keep up with the news and—being academics—don't want to comment before seeing it for themselves.

One of the journos invited to make a guest appearance at Frank Moorhouse's adult education course on journalism in 1972 was Kevon Kemp, by then the wine writer for the *National Times*. When someone asked him if he had much trouble thinking of what to say, he said, 'When you've been writing as long as I have, the words just pour out your fingertips.'

I'd say it took 25 or 30 years of staring at the page and then the screen, but at last I began to experience it. These days, the words flow from my fingers, too. Even earlier I discovered I no longer needed to plan my columns as carefully as I had been. Just gather your thoughts, start writing and it all falls into place. Old age has to have *some* compensations.

Finally, an indiscreet disclosure. All bravado notwithstanding, the dirty little secret is that no experienced political or economic columnist goes into a set-piece event such as the annual budget lockup with an open mind, waiting to see what the government will serve up and how the muse will strike. If you do, you run two risks: first, that you won't have time to detect the government's unacknowledged game plan or to come up with a memorable line. And, second, that you're open to being misled by the spin-masters, including their 'cherry'—the nice measure they've taken care *not* to leak in advance, hoping it will attract all the gallery's attention because it's the only bit that's 'new'. A favourable initial reaction to the budget is thereby assured.

If you've been paying attention, you don't need the budget to tell you what stance of policy the state of the economy requires the budget to adopt. And these days so much of the budget's contents have been leaked—including the approximate size of the budget balance—that there's not much you don't know in advance.

In my preparation for the budget I put myself into a kind of trance, trying to project myself into the mind of the reader when she hears the news. What will most interest her? What will most worry her? What's she likely to think about this development and that one? What misunderstandings may she have fallen into? What mysteries will she most want or need explained? Will she conclude the budget overall is good or bad? And what other side of the coin will she need drawn to her attention?

When I come out of my trance, I write a first draft accordingly. Sometimes in the lockup it needs a lot of rewriting, but mostly it doesn't and I've rarely had to scrap it and start again. And when I see all the sparkling prose that appears the next morning, I know I wasn't the only boy scout in the room.

CHAPTER 9
GITTINS' GUIDE TO ECONOMIC JOURNALISM

If economics religion be
As we must surely hope
John Maynard Keynes was Jesus Christ
And Ross Gittins is the Pope

Letter to the editor from Tim Austin, economics student

As far as journalism is concerned, economics is the great contradiction. On the one hand, there's no subject more likely to get you a guernsey on the front page. On the other, there's no subject more likely to confuse, irritate or simply bore the reader rigid. That's the ecstasy and the agony of economic journalism.

The first rule of journalism is that people are interested in people—*stories* about people, to be precise. What people aren't much interested in is abstract concepts. Guess what? Economics is about abstractions analysed in a completely impersonal way. Economics is as far as you can get from storytelling.

So how do you take a subject with so much potential for boredom and make it interesting? Well, I know what I do: pull every trick in the book.

How to make it interesting

The veteran business economist Dr Don Stammer used to say that if, God forbid, economists were ever forced to join a union, it would have to be Actors Equity. As it happens, when the Australian Journalists Association became the Media, Entertainment and Arts Alliance in the early 1990s as part of the push to reduce the number of unions, Actors Equity was the main union we amalgamated with. The other was the Theatrical and Amusement Employees' Association, representing people who work in fairgrounds.

So I'm not too proud to see myself as part of the entertainment industry. And though I don't much like the term 'infotainment', I don't have the same problem with 'edutainment'. I suppose you could say we're a spoilt generation, but the plain fact is that unless you make a serious topic reasonably entertaining, you won't get much of an audience. And making a serious topic entertaining doesn't have to mean dumbing it down—not if you're trying hard enough. Dumbing down is the *easy* way, not the only way.

Similarly, every public performance needs to involve a degree of showmanship: making the difficult look easy, making sure the audience can't see the wires and generally keeping the mechanism beneath the bonnet. John Kenneth Galbraith once boasted that sometimes it took him only four drafts to achieve the air of spontaneity he was seeking. Someone who worked with Graham Kennedy, famed for his outrageous ad libs, told me Kennedy's motto was Rehearse, Rehearse, Rehearse.

The easiest way to make a dull piece interesting is to beat it up—to exaggerate the significance of the news you've got to impart. But beat-ups are a sign of lack of imagination and lack of effort. I try to make economic pieces interesting by injecting a touch of lightness:

a joke, a pun, a dig, a sarcastic aside, an unexpected colloquialism. Economic writing is usually pretty formal, so that's another reason I write in a conversational tone.

I try to personalise economics by writing in the first person and putting myself and my doings in the column. I try to personalise policy measures by never attributing them to 'the government' but always to 'Tony Abbott' or 'Joe Hockey'. This is a distortion, I know. It reinforces the drift to presidential-style politics—which the party marketing machines themselves encourage—and feeds the illusion politicians are superhuman, with one man or woman capable of doing the work of hundreds. But in the interests of making economics seem human—which it is, it's about 'the ordinary business of life'—it's a distortion I'll live with.

It's always better to start a column or feature with an anecdote rather than an observation—since anecdotes are usually about people—but the obvious answer to the economic writer's problem is, unfortunately, one from which they instinctively recoil: build your analysis around a case study.

Econocrats are always dinning it into economic journalists not to base judgements about the state of the economy on anecdotal evidence rather than economy-wide statistical indicators. But the media are largely devoted to the provision of anecdotal evidence because anecdotes are just stories about people, and stories about the experiences of people (including themselves) are what our readers understand, identify with and are motivated by.

The answer? Do it the other way round. That is, ascertain what the macro indicators are telling us about the state of the economy and then find stories about individuals which illustrate the stats. The same approach can be used for both news reports or features and columns. Trouble is, it's labour intensive and it requires roughly the opposite set of skills to those usually possessed by more cerebrally inclined economic journalists. I've never managed to persuade any of my boys to specialise in this brand of economic journalism—which would be a guaranteed hit with editors and readers—nor seen any of our rivals show us how it's done.

Apart from personalisation, another simple trick in making economic concepts more palatable is always to illustrate them with the most concrete examples you can think of. The less exotic and more commonplace your examples, the better. As well, nothing makes an example more real, more easy for the reader to identify with their own lives than to quote brand names. People warm to brand names they recognise; that's why businesses use them and, in fact, put so much effort into ensuring they do evoke feelings of confidence and identification.

How to make it understandable

Every editor I've met believes that if you can't explain something simply, you don't really understand it. I'm glad they believe that, but I don't. Universities are full of people who understand things intuitively, but can't pass on their understanding to other people. Indeed, I think the reason so many people can't understand maths is that it's so commonly taught badly. And it's badly taught because so many maths teachers are people who just 'got it' from the beginning and can't understand why other people don't get it.

If my experience is a guide, the people who are best at explaining economics are those who remember the misconceptions they had to overcome before *they* understood it. I do believe the corollary, however: by the time you've worked out how to explain some tricky concept to the reader, you understand it a lot better yourself. You should also have discovered the weaknesses in your own explanation. The sad truth is we don't so much help people understand economics as leave them with the impression they understand it. But I shouldn't have revealed that trade secret. Forget I said it.

Returning to the script, readers have a lot of trouble understanding what economists say about economics so the primary role of economic journalists is to make economics understandable, to find the dividing line between simple and simplistic. I think of the economic institutions—Treasury, the Reserve Bank, the Productivity Commission, the Bureau of Stats, the universities—as the wholesalers of economic information and economic journos as the retailers of that information. Our job is to take it in bulk, then break it down and repackage it for household consumption. This may be less true for those on the *Financial Review*, but most of their readers lack economic qualifications and even economists don't enjoy having to wade through literary porridge. It shouldn't need saying that there's no place in economic journalism for people trying to impress the reader with the profundity of their own understanding by being obscure and using long and unfamiliar words.

Economists' word and spelling list

- targeting, targeted
- budgeting, budgeted
- benefiting, benefited
- forgo = to go without; forego = to go before
- autarky = self-sufficiency; autarchy = self-sufficiency (English spelling)
- discrete = separate; discreet = circumspect
- complement = to make up a whole; compliment = to praise
- supplement = to add to
- extrapolation = to assume existing trend will continue
- interpolate = to assume how two points are joined

- mercantilism = belief that exports are good and imports are bad
- altruism; philanthropy
- empirical = evidence from observation, not theory
- fungibility = ability to be interchanged (one dollar is the same as any other)
- seigniorage = difference (profit) between face value of currency and its cost of production
- simulation = modelling the effect of a possible economic change
- nominal = not adjusted for inflation
- expect = to expect; anticipate = to *act* on your expectations (especially in markets)

All technical terms—the current account deficit, the terms of trade, gross operating surplus and all the rest—need to be defined. The well-equipped economic journalist maintains a carefully honed list of mini-definitions that can be slipped into the text of a news report without being intrusive. But while in such circumstances brevity is a virtue, in others it can be a vice.

One of the simplest of tricks can make a surprising difference. Economists speak in shorthand for professional convenience—the 'money supply', for instance—but to non-economists the addition of just one two-letter word can produce a flash of comprehension: the 'supply of money'. Not impressed? Try this one: 'lower output growth volatility' is more readily comprehended if turned into 'lower volatility in the growth of output'. Moral: dropping two- and three-letter words is false economy.

Economists' economical definition of the terms of trade is 'the ratio of export to import prices', but my somewhat longer definition is much more meaningful: 'the prices we receive for our exports compared with the prices we pay for our imports'. Sometimes economists behave like German speakers, piling on prefixes and suffixes to make one long, puzzling word. I don't even like failing to hyphenate macro-economic.

It's said to be bad form to include a word in the definition of that word's meaning, but I do it all the time. Economics uses a lot of words whose common meaning is not what economists mean by the word. People think they know what 'efficient' means, for instance, but economists attach a quite different meaning to the word. Similarly, I'll happily use tautology for emphasis or clarity. I define the labour force as all those 'in work or actively seeking it'. Why the seemingly superfluous 'actively'? How can you inactively seek something? (That, by the way, is how you detect tautology.) 'Actively' helps because lots of people who don't have jobs would like to work and would take one if it were offered, but only those busy seeking a job are counted as unemployed and thus part of the labour force.

It's important to ensure references to a 'rate cut' are preceded by an initial reference to a 'cut in the *interest* rate' and to be clear whether the reference is to a cut in the 'official' interest rate—strictly, the overnight cash rate—or to market interest rates generally. The reader is easily confused by references to 'the deficit' or 'the debt', so it's important to make it very clear whether you're talking about the budget deficit or the current account deficit, the public debt (still known confusingly by many oldies as the national debt) or the foreign debt. Governments and economies (which are by no means the same thing) usually owe money as well as being owed sums by others, so levels of debt can be quoted as gross or net. The smaller net figure is usually the more meaningful but, either way, conscientious journos will always make clear to which they're referring.

Economists are notorious for using metaphors to explain economic concepts. The economy is forever slowing down, overheating, running off the rails or going off the boil. There's no point feeling bad about the resort to metaphors—economic understanding would be much lower without them—though it would be nice to come up with a few new ones occasionally. You do need to watch out for and try to avoid mixed metaphors, of course.

Most-used clichés in press releases (in order of frequency)

- leading
- innovative
- unique
- pleased to announce
- substantial
- optimise
- leverage
- award-winning
- world-class
- next generation
- milestone
- outcomes
- state of the art
- scenario
- sophisticated
- meaningful
- value-added
- prestigious
- cutting-edge
- going forward

Source: *The Australian*, 13 August 2010

But I've been known to mix metaphors knowingly—once I had three in one sentence—and get away with it merely by adding 'to mix a few metaphors'. I've also been known to assert that just as poets have licence, so economists deserve a special licence to mix. As I've said, my old editor Vic Carroll used to remind me it was illegitimate to argue by analogy, which is no doubt true, but cognitive psychology has found that analogies are how humans learn.

That is, by comparing new phenomena with something already familiar to us. So metaphors and similes are ubiquitous.

The first and most important rule in explaining some complicated proposition is: don't skip steps in the argument. Every time you skip a step you lose someone. The corollary is: never be afraid to state the obvious. Some people live in fear of offending the reader's intelligence, but I never do, for two reasons. First, people like reading things they know and agree with because they find it reinforcing (and, as we've seen, reinforcement of our existing beliefs is one of our main motives for reading). When you know what you're saying is obvious, all you have to do is excuse yourself by adding 'of course' or 'naturally' or 'as we know'. But the second reason for stating the obvious is more important: you can't spell out an argument without doing so. You mount an argument by proceeding from the known to the unknown, from the agreed to the contentious.

And then there's another consideration: how do you know what's obvious to you is obvious to the reader? Much of the time you don't. Psychologists have a concept called the curse of knowledge: the assumption that if you know something, everyone else knows it too. It's rife among economic journalists, particularly those who know they didn't learn as much economics at uni as they should have. I've seen journos who started the day knowing squat about a concept and ended it convinced it was something everyone knew. Perhaps it's the teacher in me that's protected me from this journalistic failing. Or perhaps it's my tendency to agree with that old-school journalists' hero H.L. Menken: 'No one ever went broke underestimating the intelligence of the American people.'

Another vital element in making economics understandable is: get your points in the right order. This is often the hard part. You need an order that flows logically and smoothly so you carry the reader with you and give them a clear and enjoyable ride. When you do research or preparatory reading for a piece, you make lots of notes, but that's just the start. On a separate piece of paper you note down all the points you want to make and then number them in that logical, flowing order. This process should also help you see which of your points are subsidiary or tangential, and thus prime candidates for being dropped for lack of space. As you write up your points you'll probably realise you need to modify the order to improve the flow.

The tyro thinks the goal is to fit in as many points as possible; the experienced writer knows it's better to limit yourself to the most central and persuasive arguments so you can do justice to them and provide the reader with a smoother ride. It's probably this realisation, combined with the regulation 10,000 hours of practice, that these days allows me to write a column of 800 to 1000 words without first painstakingly numbering my points. (This book's been a bit more demanding, of course.) It would be nice to believe it's the person who puts the most sweat into preparing and writing a column who writes the best column—or, at least, the column that draws the most appreciation from the readers—but, in truth, expertise and experience count for more than hard graft.

Sometimes little things count for a lot. Another trick to making economics understandable is to signal changes of direction in the piece so the reader never gets lost. Numbering points helps readers know where one point finishes and the next begins. If you begin by outlining arguments about the supply side of a question, you slip in a signal as you switch to outlining arguments on the demand side: 'Turning to the demand side, . . .' When you jump to a quite different aspect of the topic: 'As for B, it shouldn't be a problem provided . . .' Remember, this is technical writing, not great literature. So clarity always trumps elegance.

How to prepare

I've remarked already (note the way I excused myself for repeating a point, something clarity often requires) that journos don't do research, they phone people who know. In the long-gone days before the closure of the *Herald*'s afternoon stablemate, *The Sun*, one of its business journos asked me what the inflation rate was. I said I couldn't remember offhand, but it wouldn't be hard to check. The *Herald* library's file of CPI releases was on the shelf on the left, just inside the door, about the second shelf from the top.

Later I asked how he'd got on. 'Oh, it's OK, mate, I rang the Bureau of Statistics in Canberra and they told me.' Picking up the phone was a lot easier than walking 50 metres to the library. When my boy Greg Bright left our bureau in Canberra to work briefly as press sec to Treasurer Howard, he was disillusioned to discover most of his job consisted of doing elementary legwork for lazy junior journos.

Well, they may not do research, but economic journalists have to be a bit more resourceful than that. They need to know where to find all the official indicators on the bureau of stats' website and where to find a lot of other statistical information on the Reserve Bank's website, know their way around the voluminous federal budget papers—as well as the archives of old budget papers on Treasury's website—and be able to locate the various statistical indicators produced by the private sector, mainly the banks.

One of the basic roles of the Canberra economics correspondents is to report the steady stream of economic indicators published almost daily by the stats bureau. This involves having in your head a lot of technical understanding of seasonal adjustment, trend, chain volume measures, deflators, the three different measures of GDP and such like, as well as a lot of background information about just what particular indicators actually measure and their quirks and traps for young players. If you can't look up, calculate and evaluate your own stats, you're not qualified as an economic journalist.

But, of course, economic journos do spend a lot of time on the phone questioning statisticians, econocrats, political staffers, business economists and academics. When you start out, you might ring half a dozen economists for their thoughts on some development, or more if you've got time. As you get more experienced, however, you tend to reduce the number of calls you make, having sussed out the economists who are happy to give you the time, seem more competent, give the best quotes—and, for commentators, have values that sit well with your own. You need to develop a sixth sense about who's well respected and who you can trust to give you straight advice.

But though you reduce the number of people you speak to regularly, you make sure you've got contacts on both sides of the bureaucratic and political fences, of course. And, as a commentator, I like to rely mainly on experts in each of the specialised areas of economics. You can find economic rationalists happy to use their pocket models to pontificate on every dimension of the economy, but I prefer to talk to labour economists about the labour market, health economists about health care, and so forth. Within macro-economics, the monetary policy guys may have an interesting perspective on fiscal policy, and vice versa, but for the most part I talk to central bankers about monetary policy and Treasury types about fiscal policy.

In all contact with sources, the best pose to adopt is to keep your mouth shut and your ears open: it's what they can tell you, not what you can tell them. But this is advice I find very hard to practice. After almost 40 years of expressing strong opinions on every subject even vaguely related to economics—and a few quite unrelated—I rarely resist the temptation to give all and sundry the benefit of my views. Sad, but true.

Special responsibilities

If economic journalists have added to their academic qualifications a lot of specific expertise, they have to do better by the reader than he-said/she-said journalism. The American Nobel laureate turned economic columnist Paul Krugman once wrote that if George W. Bush said the Earth was flat, the mainstream media would have stories with the headline: 'Shape of Earth—Views Differ.' Then they'd quote some Democrats saying that it was round.

This is a hangover from the American media's lingering love affair with the doctrine of the universal journalist, who knows nuttin' about nuttin' except getting an accurate quote and making sure their report is 'balanced'. But Australian economic journalists put their expertise at the service of the reader, making it clear whose views are in line with the received wisdom and whose aren't. They should at least be able to quote an independent authority coming down on one side or the other, but not one of each.

It follows that, unlike unqualified reporters interested only in a sensationalist story, economic journalists shouldn't pass on to readers without qualification the results of allegedly 'independent modelling' procured by campaigning vested interests. All such modelling is built on assumptions, some of which are standard and some specially selected to ensure the modelling produces the results the client was hoping for. And even the standard assumptions adopted by models of this type do much to predetermine the results they generate.

The journo should ask the modeller—as opposed to the sponsor and purchaser of the modelling—to outline the key assumptions used and the modelling's main limitations, then report these to the reader. Failing this, it shouldn't be too hard to identify the most dubious assumptions and report these to the reader. If all else fails, merely quoting the legal disclaimer at the front of the modeller's report—which usually warns everyone but the client not to rely on its findings—should provide the reader with sufficient warning. Should the interest group not be willing to make the modeller's report available, the journo should proceed with extreme caution.

When I was a young journo, bosses only ever had one question to ask about any economic development of consequence: what's it mean to the man in the street? I don't think they say that these days, and not only because its wording is politically incorrect. Substitute 'person' for 'man' and it's still exactly the right question to be asked of, and answered by, any economic journo on a general newspaper or news outlet, whether they're writing a news report or a comment. So, no matter how expert we are, let's not consider ourselves too grand to stick with the basics.

John Kenneth Galbraith is supposed to have said that economists make forecasts not because they know, but because they are asked. Good point. And something every economic journalist has to come to terms with. Unless you have the memory of a gnat, it doesn't take long to realise economists are spectacularly bad at forecasting, getting far more of their predictions wrong than right.

In something seemingly as simple as business economists' forecasts of this month's rate of unemployment, they often predict an increase when none occurs and not infrequently even get the direction wrong. The hard part of forecasting is picking the turning points—when months of up turn to down, or vice versa—and this is where economists are at their worst. This is not because of any lack of effort or care on their part, but simply because their theories aren't remotely capable of coping with the many variables involved.

Since everybody knows economists are bad at forecasting, I puzzled for ages over why, as Galbraith says, people keep asking for more. Friends and acquaintances planning an overseas trip often ask me what I think will happen to the value of the dollar. I don't know, I say, not even the governor of the Reserve Bank knows; no one knows. 'Yes, I know that, Ross,' they reply, 'but what do you reckon?'

I kept puzzling over it until someone put me onto the book *Dance With Chance*, by Spyros Makridakis, Robin Hogath and Anil Gaba. Psychologists have long understood that humans are suckers for the 'illusion of control'—we have a strong desire to control our future and delude ourselves this is more possible than it is. To control our future we must first know what will happen and, as part of our illusion, we overestimate humans' ability to make accurate predictions. All this is so deep within us that repeated experience of failed predictions doesn't deter us from asking for more.

So economists make predictions because they're asked to. And it's a safe bet people will go on asking them. The conscientious economic journalist won't be too pure to meet this basic human need, but he or she *will* avoid implying that the future can be known or that forecasts are anything more than educated guesses. Treasury and the Reserve Bank monitor the accuracy of their forecasts and regularly make public the disillusioning results of that monitoring. We shouldn't be too busy banging on about the latest forecasts to draw those results to our readers' attention. It really is ironic that the makers of those forecasts are far more aware of their limited usefulness than the punters who take them at face value.

How to use numbers

Numbers—I prefer the old-fashioned 'figures', but never 'data'—are the special stock-in-trade of economic journos, so we need to be especially mindful and skilled in their use. The first rule of numerical journalism is simple, but hard to obey: use as few figures as possible, and try hard to keep them out of the lead. It's easy to get carried away with all the wonderful superlatives and other comparisons to be made, but most readers find numbers off-putting and are easily confused by them, so it's always the best policy to pick a few of the most spectacular and informative and leave the rest.

I always round numbers when I can. It's often possible to avoid quoting decimal places and, even for very small values, almost never necessary to go beyond one decimal place. Rounding makes figures easier to mentally absorb as well as easier to remember. A related rule is never to use a percentage when you can use a vulgar fraction. Fractions are much easier to absorb than percentages—they save the reader from making the mental translation that, for instance, 67 per cent is two-thirds—and have the further advantage of being words rather than numbers. Readers cast their eye over articles before they starting reading them, and if their eye spots too many figures—or too many acronyms and initials, for that matter—they're more likely to pass on to another article.

Particularly when I'm writing comment and analysis, I round figures up or down to turn them into fractions—'just over a quarter' or 'almost half'—and thus aid both comprehension and readability. A further advantage of rounding is that it avoids spurious accuracy—of which the economic realm abounds. Almost all economic indicators are estimates—often derived from sample surveys—as are amounts produced by economic models, something many readers don't realise. Ethical economic journalists don't allow figures to look or sound more precise than they are. Aristotle is said to have observed that the mark of a trained mind is not to expect more precision than the subject matter permits. It's worth noting that, according to research by the German psychologist Gerd Gigerenzer, the formulation people find easiest to comprehend is the 'two people in five' approach.

A hierarchy of degree

- none
- few
- some
- many
- most (more than half)
- almost all
- all

Similarly, competent economic journalists are aware of how easily readers are misled by 'base effects' and honest journalists avoid using base effects to impress the uninitiated. Part-time employment, for instance, constitutes only a bit over a quarter of total employment, even though its proportion is growing. It's therefore easy at times to state correctly that part-time employment is growing, say, two or three times faster than full-time employment and give people a quite exaggerated impression of the rate at which employment is becoming part-time. One way to avoid misleading base effects is to quote the change in the *shares* of full-time and part-time jobs over the period. Another way is to quote the percentage of the *increase* in employment accounted for by part-time jobs. The numerate can often catch doctors playing the base-effect game. The next time one tells you that committing some sin doubles your chance of contracting some terrible disease, you should ask: from what to what? It could be from one chance in 1000 to two.

One area where my old-school proclivities show is my insistence that every figure be adequately labelled. The quoting of figures is commonly dogged by the psychologists' curse of knowledge—if I know what it means, doesn't everybody? No, they don't. Good journos inoculate themselves against the curse of knowledge. I once caught a top econocrat writing that compulsory superannuation contributions would be phased up from 9 per cent to 12 per cent. Nine per cent of what? He didn't say. Economic journos can't afford to be so sloppy. It's particularly important to signal whether figures are 'flows' (an amount that accumulates *over a period*) or 'stocks' (a total that's true *on a particular day*, but not necessarily the day before or the day after). If it means anything to you, all the figures in a profit and loss statement are flows, whereas all the figures in a balance sheet are stocks. A better example: I can tell you the increase in foreign investment in Australia during a period (the flow) or I can tell you the total value of all the foreign investment that has occurred over the years on the last day of the latest period (the stock). Obviously, it helps for me to make clear to you which one I'm quoting.

Similarly, there are three main ways to calculate the annual increase in some economic indicator. I can compare the latest quarter with the same quarter of the previous year. I can compare the whole of the past year with the whole of the previous year. Or I can take the latest quarterly increase and compound it (roughly, multiply it by four). The three may give quite different answers; only in the rare case of the indicator growing at an unchanged rate quarter after quarter will they give identical answers. The Reserve Bank tends to do it the first way, Treasury does it the second way and the Americans do it the third way. The point is, a competent economic journalist not only knows all about the different methods (and doesn't compare figures calculated in different ways) but also is careful to label the figure she quotes in a way that allows at least the initiated to know which method is being used. The Australian convention is for the first, 'year-ended' method to be labelled: the economy grew by X per cent 'through the year' or 'over the course of the year'. The second, 'year-average' method is labelled: the economy grew by Y per cent 'for the year as a whole'. The third, compound method is labelled: the economy grew during the quarter at the 'annualised rate' of Z per cent. Annual*ised* means '*made* annual'.

Another thing I'm a stickler for is saying 'percentage points' rather that 'per cent' when that's what I mean. I once reminded my boss that an increase in an interest rate from 5 per cent to 6 per cent could be described as an increase of 1 percentage point or 20 per cent. He threw me out of his office. But it gets back to the curse of knowledge: the numeracy of readers differs so widely that it's just not good enough for journos to assume the reader will know what they mean.

A variable may rise *to* 5 per cent or *by* 5 per cent. Because economists are so obsessed by growth, usually it's by. And if it is, I always say so. But the world is full of subs who think that dropping the 'by' from 'the economy grew by 5 per cent' saves a word without any loss of meaning. Perhaps if subs were more numerate it would occur to them that a two-letter word is a cheap price to pay to make certain sure.

It's often difficult for people who are comfortable with figures to appreciate how many people—including those highly educated in other fields—struggle with figures. Not everyone realises, for instance, that to say that something has declined in relative terms is not necessarily to imply it's declined in absolute terms. I'm forever reminding people that the manufacturing industry's declining *share* of total employment from 25 per cent to 8 per cent is explained much more by the faster growth of other (service) industries than by a fall in the number of workers employed in manufacturing.

Aussie Holmes, great guru of the nation's old-school central bankers, used to say economists need to be equipped with 'a sense of the relative magnitudes'—a feel for what's big enough to be worth worrying about and what isn't. Readers need it too, and it's often the economic journo's job to give them a nudge in the right direction. For instance, $100 million seems a lot of money—and to even the richest individual among us, it is—but it's only about 0.1 per cent of the federal and state governments' total spending each year, and it's often necessary to put it in that context for the reader. More generally, I send the reader a signal of whether I expect him to regard a figure as high or low—'as little as 10 per cent' or 'as much as 10 per cent'—which makes it much easier for him to catch the drift of my argument.

Never reluctant to exaggerate, politicians have taken to quoting the value of their budget measures 'over four years' (the number of financial years shown in the budget's 'forward estimates'). Regrettably, political journalists seem to share the pollies' interest in quoting the biggest, most impressive numbers possible. But people are used to evaluating figures in annual terms, which was why it was better in the old days when Treasury would calculate the value of measures in their 'first full year'. So economic journos have to do better than their political colleagues. If it's not possible to establish the annual value of a measure (and label it 'about $X billion a year') then the multi-year value must *always* be labelled 'over four years' or whatever.

Unlike economists, economic journos have to be careful with the metaphors they use to describe movements in certain indicators to ensure they don't confuse people. It makes more sense to more people to say the nation's terms of trade have improved or deteriorated rather than gone up or down. Similarly, it's better to say the productivity of labour has improved by X rather than risen by X. And it's much less confusing to say home loan affordability has deteriorated or improved rather than gone down or up.

Then there's the matter of graphs. The news media love presenting information graphically because it breaks up the text and some people find graphs an easier way to take in the story. Some people do, many don't. So when I've used graphs I've always taken care to tell people just what it is the graph is telling them: 'As you see from the graph, . . .'

With news reports, the graph is often initiated by the news desk rather than the reporter, with the reporter (who's the only person in the process with a full understanding of the story the graph is illustrating) supplying the requisite figures to the artist who prepares the graph. Unfortunately, most artists are much stronger on art than they are on statistics, so it's surprisingly common for stories to be accompanied by graphs that are wrong in some way, don't fit the story, or even laugh at it. Nothing could be better calculated to confuse and annoy our more attentive readers. So I have an iron rule for my boys: as the only certified numerate party involved, I hold *them* responsible for all errors made by artists. Their responsibility for their story doesn't end until they've checked and corrected any graphic that accompanies it.

It's entirely legitimate to adjust the scale on a graph to ensure the latest wobble—the subject of the story—is visible to the naked eye. Even so, there's much scope for using graphs to misrepresent the 'relative magnitudes', as Holmes put it. I remember a state commission of audit that made much of the increase in debt the new government inherited. It produced a small graph of the progress of the debt where the line started in the bottom left-hand corner and shot straight up and across to the top right-hand corner. By manipulating the vertical and horizontal scales in a different way to the naughty boys at the audit commission, I could have produced a graph that used the same underlying figures to produce a virtually flat line across the middle of the graph. The seminal work on the misuse of graphs is Edward R. Tufte's *The Visual Display of Quantitative Information*.

Before we leave the subject of numbers, a cautionary tale for the purveyors of impressive figures. It's well known people aren't particularly moved by, say, a story reporting the death of 5000 people in a flood in Bangladesh, or even a story saying unemployment has risen by 10,000 in the past month. In the philosopher Peter Singer's book about personal giving to worthy causes, *The Life You Can Save*, he quotes well-known psychological research about the largest number of people in a news story that readers are able to empathise with. It turns out to be *one*.

This explains why so many overseas aid agencies have a photo of just one person in their ads, why they use sponsorships of individual children to raise money, even though that money will probably go to the whole family or even the village. It also explains why so many news stories about government policy changes are built around a 'case study' *and photo* of just one person or family.

How to be readable

Economic journalists may have special responsibilities for the use of numbers, but this heightens rather than exempts them from the need for a good writing style. Every journo's goal is to produce what's known in the trade as 'the good read'. Remember, we're talking journalism, not literature. The foundation for a good read is 'the easy read'. In journalistic terms, the easy read comes from how you write the story, whereas the good read adds an intrinsically interesting subject. The ultimate test, of course, is whether you can use good writing to produce a good read without very promising material.

The first element of an easy read is a quick read. The reader has limited time and, in any case, may not be giving us her full attention. We have a few readers whose job requires them to keep up with the news, but most of our readers are volunteers and they stop reading when they stop enjoying the experience, such as when they find it too much of a slog. The key to a quick read is a conversational style, simply because this involves the natural rhythms all of us find so familiar and comfortable. And a big part of a conversational style is punctuation—in particular, lots of commas. Unfortunately, a view has developed among subeditors that commas should be kept to a minimum because they slow the reader down in his haste to get through the piece. This is a misconception. The way to punctuate a sentence is to speak it aloud, and insert a comma at every pause. Breaking the sentence up in this way—including bracketing off subsidiary clauses and so forth—actually helps people take in its meaning more quickly.

Because the quick read is such an important part of the easy read, the greatest crime in readability is to write a sentence the reader has to stop and reread to gather its sense. This can happen when you use unfamiliar rather than conversational sentence constructions, as well as when you write ambiguous sentences. A common source of ambiguity arises when trying to describe relationships with two nouns rather than one in the same sentence—when there are too many 'its' or 'theys' in the sentence. An easy solution is sometimes to make one noun singular and the other plural. But the general rule is that good writers develop a sixth sense that automatically scans every sentence for potential ambiguity, and recasts the sentence to remove the ambiguity before moving on to write the next one.

Another dimension of the quick read is the short read, of course. Brevity is regarded as a great virtue in journalism, and rightly so. It's not just that newspapers are chronically short of space and are seeking room for more stories, it's also that the reader is short of time to read. Journalists know that shorter pieces are much better read than longer ones, so journos do need to keep their writing as tight as possible. And when you scrutinise each sentence for superfluous words, it's surprising how many words you find that could be cut without any loss. You ask yourself the sub's question: can we live without it? Often the answer is yes.

But while brevity is a virtue, so is clarity. And as every economic journo's economic education should tell her, conflict between desirable objectives is common, meaning you have to seek the best trade-off (the best combination) available. In a clash, clarity trumps brevity. Short but incomprehensible isn't a winner. As I used to say early in my career when seeking a bit more space, I can get it down to one sentence if you want me to, but only an economist will be able to understand it. Where sufficient space to do justice to the subject just isn't available, the answer is to tackle a smaller subject or to limit yourself to only some dimensions of the subject.

Another contributor to the easy read is adequate signposting, to ensure the reader follows the direction of your exposition and never loses his way. Whenever the argument changes direction—when you are acknowledging a paradox, contradiction, complication or qualification—you signal it with 'but', 'however', 'paradoxically' or, one of my favourites, 'even so'. There's a race of journalists who consider it bad form to use such words, especially in a news report, but this betrays an incomprehension of what we're doing.

Next, sentences. They should be of varying length, but with a preponderance of short ones and few long ones. If a sentence threatens to get too long, just insert a full stop and start again with an 'and' or a 'but'. Forget all primary-school notions that there's something wrong with starting a sentence with a conjunction. Of all the columns I've written over the years, the intro of which I'm proudest was just three words: I like dentists. Not as good as the Bible's shortest sentence: Jesus wept.

Verbs in the same sentence should all have the same tense. The convention in journalism is for the reporting of events—which have already happened—to be done in the past tense, though a report of the content of a book may be in the present tense. The convention also dictates that any explanation or background information added by the journalist be distinguished from the reported facts by being written in the present tense.

Some journos are excessively precious about altering quotes, but I take a more pragmatic approach. Provided you never change the person's meaning, I don't hesitate to, for instance, spell out a set of initials. And when you intervene to correct someone's grammar you're actually avoiding doing their reputation an injury. Many people don't speak as formally as they write, and we're often reproducing speech in writing.

Speaking of initials, a relatively recent style change at Fairfax has pretty much banned references to organisations by their initials. For instance, not only is the name of the IMF to be spelt out in the first reference, it's to be referred to as 'the fund' in subsequent references. I think it's an excellent rule because so many people find initials-strewn stories so off-putting. Why call the Reserve Bank the RBA when you could call it the Reserve? Why say CEO when you can say chief executive?

The younger generation is a bit shaky on the difference between active and passive voice, but it's important to write in the active voice and use the passive only occasionally for special effects. The difference is simple: A did B is active; B was done by A is passive. Now you know why bureaucrats use passive and journos use active.

From sentences to words. Good writing draws its strength, vigour and colour from strong verbs and nouns, not fancy adjectives and adverbs. Verbs should be as vigorous as you can make them. 'He strolled/skipped/ran home' beats 'he went home'. You can't avoid using the verb 'to be', but it's weak and you should search for something stronger, though this is not to say the dollar should 'plunge' or 'soar' every time it moves. Nouns should be as specific as you can make them, not general. Grandiose adjectives and adverbs are the stuff of beat-ups.

Everybody has two vocabularies: one consisting of the words they know and use regularly and another, much larger one of words whose meanings they know but rarely use. There's no margin in using words whose meaning is obscure to most people. So a good writer looks to use words on that second list—familiar but less clichéd.

The second of George Orwell's six rules for writing is 'never use a long word where a short one will do'. Short, Anglo-Saxon words almost always beat longer, Latinate words. Short words both save space and are more comfortable for the reader. So say 'before' rather than 'prior to', 'about' rather than 'approximately', 'thus' rather than 'therefore', 'spending' rather than 'expenditure', 'job' rather than 'employment', 'start' rather than 'beginning'. Don't consume an ice-cream; eat it.

His fifth rule is 'never use a foreign phrase, a scientific word or a jargon word if you can think of an everyday English equivalent'. Don't say 'data' when you can say 'figures', 'per annum' rather than 'per year', or '$X thousand per capita' when you can say 'per person' or even 'a head'. Avoid poncy foreign plurals such as 'bureaux' or 'indices', 'referenda', 'premia' or 'fora'. And if you must use Latin words such as data and media, remember they're plural.

Avoid business jargon like the plague (not to mention clichés). Never say 'ongoing' and only say 'going forward' in jest. Pompous pollie-speak is just as bad. Never address an issue, only ever a public meeting or an envelope. Avoid academic jargon such as 'moreover'; say 'what's more' or 'as well' or just 'and'. And don't use weasel words like 'problematic'.

Just because a word ends in 's' doesn't make it plural. Economics, politics, ethics and many more are all singular. Some authorities frown on 'elegant variation'—avoiding repeating the same word—but the practice is so common readers have come to expect it. When I engage in repeated repetition I do it for effect. A good rule for writers is: don't tell, show. Don't promise to tell a 'funny story'; tell it and let your hearers decide if it's funny.

Don't get smart with the meaning of words. I once was accused of exaggerating when I said some practice was burgeoning. I protested that the dictionary meaning of the word was 'budding', not growing like mad. But I was in the wrong. Words mean what most people take them to mean, not what dictionaries say they mean. (I make an exception, however, for disinterested versus uninterested.) Similarly, I don't believe in arguing with subs. What you wrote may be strictly correct, but if it didn't make sense to the sub it's not likely to make sense to the reader. And the only sensible decision rule for journos is that if you wrote something the readers misunderstood, it's always your fault and never theirs. When a professional communicator fails to communicate she's fallen down on the job.

It's important to serve the reader and always take account of the reader's point of view. That doesn't mean telling people what they want to hear, it means viewing events from the reader's perspective. Until recently, for instance, morning-paper journos wrote about things that had happened that day but, knowing what they wrote wouldn't be read until the next morning, they always described those things as having happened yesterday. But since these days many news reports are published on the website on the day they happened and then republished in the following day's paper, Fairfax has switched to the rule of simply referring to the day the event happened or is expected to happen. A loss.

Even so, the broader principle remains: you do the calculations on the reader's behalf. You don't say something will start next month and leave it to the reader to work out that next month starts next week. You don't say something will happen on 28 April when you could say 'next Tuesday'. You don't say an indicator fell from 10 to five, you do the calculation and say it halved to five.

Once you've mastered all that, you only need to find something good to write about.

CHAPTER 10
THE SCIENCE OF JOURNALISM

If one morning I walked on top of the water across the Potomac River, the headline that afternoon would read: 'President Can't Swim.'

Lyndon Johnson

Let me tell you about two cavemen, Ig and Og. They're out in the wild when they come upon a bush with berries they haven't seen before. Ig immediately eats a handful, but Og just puts a few in his dillybag. Ig and Og come upon a cave. Ig bowls straight in, but Og doesn't fancy the dark cave, so waits outside. Ig finds a few old bones but nothing more interesting. As they walk home, they hear a rustling in the bush nearby. Ig ploughs on, but Og stands frozen until the rustling stops. Clearly, Ig is brave and Og's a wimp.

I'm indebted to John Lanchester of the *New Yorker* for that story, and here's the point: all of us are descended from Og and none of us from Ig. Why? Because Ig died an early death before he could father any children. He ate poison berries, was killed by a bear he disturbed in its cave or was bitten by a snake. Natural selection has caused us to be people with strong negative emotions such as fear and anxiety because these alerted us to danger, thereby helping us to survive and propagate.

Jonathan Haidt, a professor of psychology at New York University, says an important principle of design by evolution is that bad is stronger than good. 'Responses to threats and unpleasantness are faster, stronger and harder to inhibit than responses to opportunities and pleasures.' Our brains have been hardwired to emphasise the negative. But here's the trick: we are people living in the space age with Stone Age minds. We've spent 99 per cent of our history as hunter-gatherers.

It was a mere 10,000 years ago that humans first began farming and only 5000 years ago that half the world's population had stopped being hunter-gatherers. But 10,000 years—500 generations—is far too short a time for our brains to have evolved in response to our changed environment. The Australian Aborigines help to prove this. They spent at least 40,000 years cut off from other humans but are physiologically identical to other races.

The point of civilisation—all the economic and social development, the unbelievable advances in technology—is to remove from our environment the threats that plagued us as hunter-gatherers. These days, a supermarket that sold poison berries would be strung up by the health department. We've managed to corral the wild animals so that they're a long way from where we live. Local councils have building standards intended to minimise the risk of our homes collapsing around us and killing us. Insurance policies protect us from loss should our homes burn down.

Governments and charities swing into action when an area is destroyed by a cyclone. Multiple efforts are made—from car design rules to seatbelts to random breath testing to speed limits—to reduce the risk of us killing or maiming ourselves on the roads.

Occupational health and safety laws are designed to minimise the risk of us killing or injuring ourselves while we earn our living. The whole welfare system is designed to ensure we don't go hungry even though we're too young, old, sick or burdened with children to work—or just because we can't find a job. Medicare ensures we don't die in the gutter because we can't afford to go to hospital.

In short, modern society is designed to remove the need for us to worry about our survival. So much so that some of the risks of modern life actually arise from the lack of adversity. We become obese and contract diabetes because it's so easy to avoid exercise and because the fattening foods to which our bodies are attracted are now abundant.

Why bad news is good news

But despite the greatly reduced threat to life and limb, we still have hunter-gatherer minds that continually search our environment for things to be fearful of. See where this is leading? Our overactive fear mechanism explains some important features of modern life.

In particular, it explains how the news media select news. News is anything the public finds interesting. But the stories the media judge to be 'newsworthy' are preponderantly negative—bad news about natural disasters, accidents, crime, problems in the economy, stuff-ups by governments, arguments with other countries and all the rest. Why so relentlessly negative? Because that's the kind of news the media have discovered most excites the interest of their customers. Why are we more interested in bad news than good? Because of the way our minds have evolved. Most of us find change disturbing, so the media focus heavily on changes of all kinds—particularly changes for the worse, but also good changes, such as a tax cut.

Many people assume the news media's role is to bring us a balanced summary of what's happening in the world around us. Perhaps it should be, but that's *not* the way the media see it. Their summary is deliberately unbalanced. They highlight and give an exaggerated impression of the extent of bad news because people find this interesting, while ignoring the non-bad news because it's boring—unless it happens to be good news that's particularly outstanding or unusual.

This negative bias isn't restricted to the non-fiction news media. The fiction entertainment media are also more negative than positive. Why do teenagers flock to horror movies? Why are cops and detective shows so popular on telly? Why do the mildest little old ladies read whodunits with another murder in every other chapter?

Because it satisfies some unconscious need to exercise their fear muscles. But TV programs portray more violence and chaotic relationships than exist in real life, and studies by psychologists find that people who spend a lot of time watching television tend to overestimate crime rates and show more anxiety and less trust in others.

In his book *Informing the News*, Thomas Patterson, of Harvard, says such responses are a consequence of what psychologists call the 'surveillance function'. People seek reassurance that the world, both near and far, is safe and secure, he says. This explains why the policy problems of greatest interest to citizens are those that directly affect their daily lives or the lives of those like them. It's why people give little thought to energy policy until petrol prices rise. It explains why extreme weather events, natural and human disasters and the onset of war rank highly in the public's news preferences. 'It's also why people take more interest in Main Street economic issues, like high gas prices, than in Wall Street economic issues, like stock price manipulation,' he says.

But this explanation of people's unquenchable interest in bad news carries a subtle warning for overzealous news outlets. The punters may be compulsive in their surveillance of their environment for threats, but that doesn't mean they're hoping to find a lot of them. They're actually seeking reassurance that their world is free from too many worries. So when the media overdo the negativity—when, by diligent selection they pile up all the bad news and ignore most of the good, giving their customers a quite distorted picture of the world around them—they shouldn't expect much gratitude.

Our preoccupation with the search for threats has to be reconciled with another truth well established by psychologists: optimists far outnumber pessimists. Despite all the threats we're aware of, the great majority of us harbour a surprisingly positive view of the state of the world and our ability to survive and prosper. Indeed, it's clear we take our optimism to quite unrealistic lengths. One of the most documented findings in psychology is that the average person claims to believe extremely flattering things about themself.

For example, a large majority of people think they are more intelligent, more fair-minded and less prejudiced than the average person. A survey of a million US high school seniors found that 70 per cent of them thought they were above average in leadership ability, and only 2 per cent thought they were below average. A survey of university professors found that 94 per cent thought they were better at their jobs than their average colleague.

We're inclined not only to adopt self-serving beliefs about ourselves, but also comforting beliefs about the world. For instance, polling in the US indicated that although only 25 per cent of the population believed the country as a whole would be better off financially in the coming year, 54 per cent thought *they* would do better.

This suggests most of us have considerable ability to deflect the bad news the media serve up to us. But it also raises the possibility that an audience of incorrigible optimists may eventually reject those news outlets that attempt to serve them a diet of unrelenting negativity. And if almost all outlets have shifted their mix of stories heavily in favour of bad news, this may help explain why people are turning away from print and broadcast news.

It's in the paper so it doesn't have to be true

Journalists know, and mass media scholars have confirmed, that many people have a quite exaggerated view of the news media's ability to influence public opinion and behaviour. The 'direct effects' theory of mass communication—also known as the magic bullet or hypodermic needle theory—argues people tend to believe whatever the media tell them.

But studies show people's minds are not blank slates on which the media write. Most people's upbringing and experience leave them with many preconceived views on how the world works and should work, and the media's messages have to make it past these filters. Leon Festinger, the psychologist who discovered cognitive dissonance, said that 'a man with conviction is a hard man to change. Tell him you disagree and he turns away. Show him facts and figures and he questions your sources. Appeal to logic and he fails to see your point . . . When presented with evidence—unequivocal and undeniable evidence—that his belief is wrong he will emerge not only unshaken but even more convinced of the truth of his beliefs than ever before.'

In short, most people read for reinforcement of their existing views, not for enlightenment. They tend to read those news reports and columnists they expect to fit with their existing views and avoid those they expect to challenge their views. When they do read stuff that conflicts with their preconceived notions it causes them to dig in rather than reconsider. One thing this means is that the news media's greatest effect on the world is to increase people's confidence in the rightness of their views. It thus probably tends to reinforce rather than challenge the conventional wisdom on the issues of the day. This happens partly because of the audience's reaction, but also because of journalists' inclination—conscious and unconscious—to see things from their audience's point of view and tell people what they want to hear. The most honest—and revealing—name for a newspaper is *The Mirror*.

So the news media tend to play along with what psychologists call 'confirmation bias'. Whereas the scientific method tells us we should search for evidence that *disproves* our theories, humans prefer to do it the other way, seeking out—and remembering—events and facts that seem to confirm the rightness of our existing beliefs. Contrary evidence we explain away or soon forget.

People are always accusing the media of bias—by which they usually mean partisanship—and no doubt there's a fair bit of it about. But bias is much more in the mind of the reader than most readers realise. In the early 1980s Robert Vallone and other psychologists at Stanford University showed a group of undergraduates a number of news reports by the three US television networks of the Beirut massacre of many Palestinians and Lebanese, which some people alleged the Israeli forces had allowed to happen. Some of the students began with pro-Israeli views, some with pro-Arab views and some with mixed feelings. Those with pro-Israeli views perceived a marked pro-Arab bias in the clips, whereas those with pro-Arab views perceived a marked pro-Israeli bias. Those without firm preconceptions perceived only a slight pro-Arab bias.

As a columnist who's regularly accused of bias I know exactly how this remarkably contradictory finding could come about. The journo tries to call it down the middle, noting the points which seem to favour one side and those that favour the other. Trouble is, partisan readers ignore the points that go their way as no more than a statement of the obvious truth, but vigorously object to points going the other way as blatantly untrue. It's not always the case, but readers who accuse the media of bias are often revealing a lot more about their own biases than the journo's.

It's mistaken, however, to go from believing the media are hugely powerful in their ability to influence the way their readers think to believing they have little influence on anything. As we've seen, they do reinforce people's existing views and hence the community's prevailing views on problems and their solutions. There's evidence they have a significant effect in setting the public policy agenda—when they focus on some issues at the expense of others, they do leave their audience with the impression these are the issues that matter most. When politicians respond to the media's demands for action on these issues, the media's agenda-setting role is reinforced. What's much less clear, however, is whether the media's choice of agenda items is driven by their proprietors' ideological leanings or by their attempts to enhance their commercial success by selecting those issues most likely to stir up their readers. These days, even where certain newspapers take a strongly ideological line in their choice of stories, their motive is more likely to be commercial—pick a segment of the audience and tell them only what they want to hear—than purely ideological.

My father raised me to be contemptuous of fashion. It came as quite a shock when, well into my career at the *Herald*, I realised that signalling and promoting changes in fashion—in economic thinking, not just hemlines—is one of the media's major roles.

Humans are a storytelling animal

Journalists habitually refer to their news items as 'stories' or even 'yarns' and like to think of themselves as (non-fiction) storytellers. They do this because it's what the profession has always done. But whether or not they realise it, what we do is an industrialised version of what people have been doing since they lived in caves. Storytelling satisfies an urge whose origins lie deep in our evolutionary past.

The eminent American biologist E.O. Wilson says storytelling is a fundamental human instinct. Evolution has wired our brains for storytelling. In *The Storytelling Animal*, Jonathan Gottschall says 'we are, as a species, addicted to story. Even when the body goes to sleep, the mind stays up all night, telling itself stories'.

You can say we like telling and listening to stories because we enjoy them, because we find them entertaining. The question, however, is *why* evolution has programmed us to enjoy storytelling so much. Short answer: stories are the way humans make meaning out of the seeming chaos of life. Gottschall says the storytelling mind is a critical evolutionary adaptation which 'allows us to experience our lives as coherent, orderly and meaningful'.

We are also, of course, a pattern-seeking animal. 'The human mind is tuned to detect patterns, and it is biased towards false positives rather than false negatives,' he says. 'Our hunger for meaningful patterns translates into a hunger for story. The storytelling mind is allergic to uncertainty, randomness and coincidence. It is addicted to meaning. If the storytelling mind cannot find meaningful patterns in the world it will try to impose them. In short, the storytelling mind is a factory that churns out true stories when it can, but will manufacture lies when it can't.'

My guess is non-fiction stories came before made-up ones—or perhaps there was a time in human existence when we didn't draw a sharp distinction between fiction and non-fiction—but the neuroscientists tells us that stories we know to be fictional and those we believe to be true light up just the same parts of the brain when we hear them. And whether or not the stories are true, they offer feelings for which we don't have to pay. According to the writer Janet Burroway, they 'allow us to love, condemn, condone, hope, dread and hate without any of the risks those feelings ordinarily involve'. According to the psychologist Keith Oatley, stories are the flight simulators of human social life.

Because storytelling is embedded in the brain, stories aren't optional, they're essential. According to the film producer Peter Guber, narrative is more than a literary device, it's a brain device. And stories *should* be powerful: they helped us share information long before we had a written language. Guber says stories are the most effective form of human communication, more powerful than any other way of packaging information. Telling purposeful stories is the most efficient means of persuasion in everyday life, the most effective way of translating ideas into action or motivating people.

Our brains sync up when we tell stories. A team of psychologists at Princeton led by Uri Hasson had a woman tell a story while in a functional MRI scanner so they could monitor the parts of her brain that lit up as she spoke. Then they had a group of volunteers listen to the story through headphones while their brains were scanned. Their brains lit up in just the same pattern as hers had. The more the listeners understood the story, the more their brain activity mimicked hers.

Daniel Siegel, a professor of psychiatry, says storytelling is an *integrative* process. 'It not only weaves together all the details of an experience when it's being encoded but enhances the network of nodes through which all those details can be retrieved and recalled. Research shows we remember details of things much more effectively when they are embedded in a story,' he says. Others say much information is stored, indexed and retrieved in the form of stories.

Guber says the first rule of telling stories is to give the audience an emotional experience. 'Stories must give listeners an emotional experience if they are to ignite a call to action,' he says. And by far the most effective and efficient way to do this is through the use of metaphor and analogy. 'More than mere linguistic artefacts, these devices are key components of the way we think, building blocks of the very structure of knowledge. In their swift economy, they evoke images and turn on memory, with all its rich sensory and emotional associations, bringing the listener into the story, cognitively and emotionally, as an active participant,' he says. Pamela Rutledge, director of the Media Psychology Research Centre in Los Angeles, adds that 'we perceive and remember something based on how it fits with other things. One way the brain sorts things is by metaphors'.

A report in the *New York Times* tells us that the way the brain handles metaphors has received extensive study. Some have found that figures of speech such as 'a rough day' are so clichéd they're treated simply as words and no more. But researchers from Emory University have found that when laboratory subjects read a metaphor involving texture—such as 'the singer had a velvet voice' or 'he had leathery hands'—their sensory cortex, responsible for perceiving texture through touch, became active. Other research has found that words such as 'lavender', 'cinnamon' and 'soap' elicit a response not only from the language-processing areas of our brains but also those devoted to dealing with smells.

April Vannini says in the *Sage Encyclopedia of Communication Theory* that 'from the moment stories are selected for telling, to the way in which they are introduced, shared and commented on, individual narratives are placed within larger frames of moral propriety, decorum and common popular knowledge that stipulates notions of right and wrong, true and false, and aesthetically valuable and valueless'.

Perhaps because of all these discoveries about the cognitive significance of stories, interest in the role of storytelling is spreading to disciplines that formerly would have had a soul above such seemingly frivolous topics—though they often prefer to use the more upscale term 'narratives'. Professor Robert Shiller, of Yale, a behavioural economist who's one on the most innovative thinkers about macroeconomics, argued in the wake of the global financial crisis that the ups and downs of an economy are substantially driven by stories.

'Such narratives, especially those fuelled by accessible human-interest stories, are the thought viruses whose contagion drives the economy,' he writes. 'The contagion rate of stories depends on their relation to feedback, but plausible stories have to be there in the first place. The narratives have persistence in that they affect our views. The story that drove the worldwide stockmarket bubble that peaked in 2000 [the 'tech wreck'] was complex but, put crudely, it was that bright, aggressive people were leading the way to a new era of capitalist glory in a rapidly globalising economy.

'This narrative seemed plausible to casual observers because it was tied to millions of little human-interest stories about the obvious successes of those friends, neighbours and family members who had the vision to participate enthusiastically in the new environment. But it is hard today to recreate such a narrative given so many stories of trouble.'

Gottschall writes that 'business executives are increasingly told that they must be creative storytellers: they have to spin compelling narratives about their products and brands that emotionally transport consumers'. 'Political commentators see a presidential election not only as a contest between charismatic politicians and their ideas but also as a competition between conflicting stories about the nation's past and future. Legal scholars envision a trial as a story contest, too, in which opposing counsels construct narratives of guilt and innocence—wrangling over who is the real protagonist.'

Closer to home, Bernard Keane, of the crikey.com.au website, offered the Rudd government as early as 2008 the free advice that it needed an overarching narrative. 'What's so important about narratives?' he asked. 'The news media crave them. They make sense of events and provide a framework for understanding. They guide what is emphasised and what is skipped. And they entertain . . . If the government doesn't provide a narrative [which the Rudd government conspicuously failed to do], the media will provide one or more for it.'

But what of the one fact-based occupation that has always been happy to see themselves as purveyors of stories? Journalists are being both urged and tempted to make their 'stories' more story-like. News outlets hold seminars to teach reporters how to tell their stories in a more narrative form. It's not as silly as it sounds. The archetypal 'inverted pyramid' formula for news stories—in which the story is summarised in the first paragraph and then facts are listed in order from most important to least important—is anything but story-like.

At another level, however, as the competition intensifies both among proliferating news outlets and between news outlets and the ever-multiplying rival ways for people to entertain themselves, journalists are being tempted to respond by upping their stories' entertainment count. The venerable British journalist and media commentator John Lloyd has written about the temptation to replace hard news and analysis with entertaining news. 'That does not just mean replacing politicians with celebrities—though it can mean that. It also means making the news narratives conform more closely to fictional stories; making a premium of drama, conflict and confrontation; giving pride of place to crime and social disorder or, conversely, to heart-warming versions of domestic life. And it means making even unpromising politicians into celebrities—by emphasising scandal, personal habits and controversy.'

Journos like to believe everything they report is new. In truth, and as this consideration of the nature of storytelling reminds us, what they regard as new is often just a new example of a familiar story, one the journos know the audience loves to hear again. Sometimes a new, offbeat angle is ignored so the story can be forced to fit a tried-and-true formula. Keane says 'most news stories—even sports stories—are, in essence, minor variants on stories we've heard a thousand times over: crime doesn't pay, the recklessness of youth, the folly of single motherhood, bumbling bureaucrats, out-of-touch politicians and so on'.

And this discussion of the way humans use stories to make sense out of the chaos around them should remind journalists of the pitfalls facing those who want the stories they tell to remain strictly non-fiction. Thomas Patterson, author of *Informing the News*, observes that journalists' primary tools—observation and interviewing—leave much scope for them to get the story wrong. 'Aspects of public life that are not in the line of sight get less scrutiny than those that are,' he says. This leads to the prevalence and predictability of what social psychologists call 'fundamental attribution error'—the tendency of an observer to exaggerate the significance of a 'salient' (prominent, easily seen) actor or event. President Bush campaigned hard for the election of certain Republican senators and most of them succeeded, so Bush is given most of the credit. When journalists write that 'the market moved because of X' or 'the company failed because of Y' they're almost certainly misrepresenting the truth. Economists' term for such explanations is 'ex-post rationalisation'. Drawing unwarranted conclusions is something the rest of humanity does all the time, but is that a good enough excuse for professional truth-tellers? Patterson cites another common pitfall faced by news storytellers—'framing bias'—but we'll give framing much more careful scrutiny in a moment.

Industrial-strength gossip

Stories the world over are almost always about people with problems, according to Gottschall, which suggests a lot of the stories we tell each other are gossip. Gossip has a bad reputation, but as the US news anchor Barbara Walters has said, 'Show me someone who never gossips and I'll show you someone who isn't interested in people.' And not many of us fit that category. Gossip is the casual exchange of information about people who are absent. The information doesn't have to be negative, nor does it have to be mistaken, but it's often both. A story that Jane looked lovely at her wedding isn't as interesting as that her uncle made a spectacle of himself at the reception. But since I wasn't actually present, I could have got the details wrong.

Anthropologists tell us gossip is virtually universal in human societies and estimate that personal stories and gossip account for up to two-thirds of our conversation. There's little reason to believe women indulge in it more than men do. So it's clear that, though excessive and uncharitable gossip does tend to be frowned on, we all do it. We all do it because we all enjoy doing it but, again, the question is *why* we've evolved to enjoy it so much.

What evolutionary advantage did it confer on us? The Oxford evolutionary psychologist Robin Dunbar—proposer of 'Dunbar's number', the calculation that the size of the human brain limits to about 150 the number of stable social relationships a person can maintain—argues gossip sessions may have evolved from the social grooming observed in other primates. He says gossip aids the social bonding within groups. To survive, individuals need alliances with others, but as groups get larger it becomes harder to physically connect with everyone. Gossip became a social interaction that helped the group gain information about other individuals without personally speaking to them. It enables people to keep up with what's going on in their social network and also creates a bond between the teller and the hearer as they share information of mutual interest and spend time together.

Related theories suggest gossip allows people to monitor individuals' reputations for being co-operative and reliable. This may help explain why studies show people do indeed take more interest in adverse information. I've often thought that the financial markets, whose electronic trading would these days allow traders to be widely dispersed geographically, remain concentrated in a few

CBD streets because traders need access to the kind of negative information about other traders that no one would be prepared to commit to any recorded medium.

Gossip also gives us information about social norms and guidelines for behaviour. We find out what kinds of behaviour we should avoid because most other people disapprove of them, we learn what social sanctions are imposed on people who offend group norms, and we use gossip to punish those who offend our own views of acceptable behaviour. So gossip can be seen as essential to the existence of 'social capital'.

If gossip is an inescapable and important part of life and community, it shouldn't be surprising if a fair proportion of the 'stories' carried by the news media could be classified as gossip. Nor would it surprise if the news media's increased competition using more overt forms of entertainment had led to an increase in the gossip component. To some extent the news media—and the pure entertainment media—simply represent an institutionalised or industrialised version of the storytelling and gossip-spreading that has always occurred at the informal and amateur level.

Of late what we've been getting a lot more of from news outlets is gossip about celebrities—people made famous by the mass media, sometimes without the possession of great personal merit. In his book *Psychology of the Media*, David Giles suggests an evolutionary explanation for our interest in celebrities may be that intricate details of their lives allow us to learn about potential hazards in the social environment—what might happen if we cheat on our partner, what kinds of outfits are likely to earn us admiration or provoke derision, and so on.

Evidence that interest in celebrity gossip is greatest among the young, and declines as we get older, adds some credibility to this theory. And the theory is not inconsistent with my own long-held view that the media's discussion of celebrities' private lives represents the industrialised provision of gossip to people whose busy lives in big, impersonal cities leave them with too few real friends and acquaintances to gossip about.

But for those who fear the news media's difficulty competing in the digital world leave them with little choice but to increase their diet of soft news such as celebrity gossip, Thomas Patterson's *Informing the News* has good news. The political scientist Michael Robinson used data to look at more than 1300 different news stories that 200,000 Americans actually consumed between 1986 and 2007. The focus was on conventional news outlets, not celebrity gossip magazines. His methodology was designed to minimise 'social desirability bias'—the tendency of survey respondents to overstate 'good' behaviours and understate 'bad' behaviours.

Robinson ranked a list of 14 story subject categories according to how many respondents were following each category 'very closely'. The categories 'celebrity lives and deaths' and 'celebrity scandals' came last with close interest from only 17 and 16 per cent of respondents, compared with the top-ranking category of 41 per cent 'war and terrorism'. Robinson divided his 20-year sample into three sub-periods, but found little change in the popularity of celebrity stories over time. His findings were similar to an earlier, Harvard study.

Everything is in the frame

For many years many practitioners believed in the possibility of 'objective journalism'—presentation of the facts of the matter free from subjective judgements by the journalist. Perhaps some journos still believe in it, but a moment's thought exposes its impossibility. Every stage of the process by which journalists bring a news story to their audience involves the application of subjective judgement on their part. They collect many more facts than they could use, then select the relatively small number they *will* use. They decide which facts they'll incorporate in the 'lead'—the first sentence of their report—and hence the 'angle' they'll adopt in their reporting of the story in an effort to make it as interesting and important as possible. Then they decide the order in which other facts will be included in the story, knowing those that are higher up will be read by more people than those lower down.

An editor will decide whether the story is actually used—whether it's among the most interesting stories available given the limited space or time available. The editor decides how much prominence to give the story: an early page or a later page, where on the page it will appear, how much space it will be given and whether it's accompanied by a photo or other graphic. (In an electronic news program the editor will decide the story's position in the bulletin and how much time it's given.) The story will be 'subbed' by a subeditor, who will make small or extensive changes to the 'copy' and write the headline that summarises its content as attractively as possible.

That's objective journalism? I'm often sceptical when editors defend themselves by claiming their critics are trying to 'shoot the messenger'. How many messengers do you know who read all the letters before deciding which they'll deliver and which they won't, which they'll abbreviate or rewrite, which they'll shout from the rooftops and which they'll whisper?

It turns out the cognitive psychologists have a lot of light to shed on the inescapably subjective choices journalists make in their reporting of the news. They do so with their concept of 'framing'. It's a remarkable thing, but the way humans react to situations or propositions is heavily dependent on the way they're 'framed'—the way they're packaged, the context in which they're put. We can react differently to the same proposition depending on how it's framed. A classic example: even doctors say a 90 per cent success rate for operations is more acceptable than a 10 per cent failure rate.

When you become conscious of framing you realise we're surrounded by it, with many people using it to manipulate our reactions to things. For instance, almost all advertising involves framing—drawing unspoken links between the product you're trying to flog and some attractive situation or emotion. Their not-so-subtle message is, buy my margarine and you'll have a happy, healthy family.

Political spin is a form of framing. It's about portraying situations or decisions in ways that reflect more favourably on the pollies involved. Their opponents, of course, try to frame the same situations or decisions in a more negative light. Framing is the reason you should be sceptical of the results interest groups quote from the opinion polls they commission. It's too easy to influence the answers you get by the way you frame the questions you ask—including the questions you ask in the lead-up to the key question.

It's wrong, however, to conclude framing is a practice of the unscrupulous, those who wish to manipulate us in some way. The deeper truth—in fact, the great discovery of cognitive psychology, as Barry Schwartz and Kenneth Sharpe point out in *Practical Wisdom*—is that just about the only way we can get our minds around anything is to compare it with something we already know about. Years ago, my boss Vic Carroll reminded me of the classical rule of rhetoric that argument by analogy is invalid. Sorry, turns out that the only way we learn is by comparing things we don't understand with things we do understand. This doesn't mean every analogy-based argument is correct, of course, just that there's no other way to argue.

The term 'frame' is itself a metaphor. Schwartz and Sharpe say it's a wonderful metaphor because it emphasises our capacity to take the chaos of the social world around us and organise it in an understandable way. 'In framing the scene, we are setting the picture off from its surroundings, excluding what is on the outside and defining what is inside as special and worthy of attention. Frames tell us what is important and help us establish what should be compared with what,' they say.

So it's all very well to say we should be able to see and evaluate things as they 'really are', unbiased by the way they're packaged, but it's just not possible. All context is framing and, stripped of their context, facts are meaningless. 'Framing is pervasive, inevitable and often automatic. There is no "neutral", frame-free way to evaluate anything,' according to Schwartz and Sharpe.

Despite the potential of our dependence on framing to lead us to bad decisions, it also provides us with the *possibility* of choosing wisely. It's up to us how we choose to frame things. So our task when we make decisions is not to avoid being influenced by frames, but to choose the *right* frames—frames that help us to evaluate all that's relevant. And judging what the right frame is will depend on the purposes of our evaluation and impending decision.

That brings us back to journalism and Patterson's contention that the second common pitfall faced by news storytellers is 'framing bias'. He says framing is 'the process by which reporters select certain aspects of a situation and build their stories around them, as opposed to other aspects of the situation. The effect is to prime the audience to see the situation through the frame that the journalist has selected.

'For example, although every congressional debate includes co-operation and conflict, journalists tend to report such debates through a conflict frame, which highlights the conflictive aspects and subordinates the co-operative aspects, thereby leading people to view such debates as embodying conflict rather than also involving co-operation.'

In fashioning their stories journos *have* to pick an angle; they simply can't avoid framing. When they seek to remove the spin from politicians' speeches and press releases they are, unavoidably, substituting their own spin. But they need to be more conscious of their own role in the framing process and more thoughtful about whether the frames they choose to use are those that do least to mislead their readers and most to serve the readers' needs.

Patterson implies reporters rely on too limited a number of frames. 'Stories on policy issues, for example, tend to be told either through a problem frame—which highlights the nature of the policy issue—or through a strategic frame—which highlights the political manoeuvring surrounding the issue. The problem frame dominates when issues are addressed in broad terms, usually at an early stage in their development. When issues become politicised, however, the strategic frame takes over,' he says. In our context, when the debate about pros and cons becomes hard to explain, it's easier to shift to 'race calling' (strategic framing)—whether the government has the numbers to get the bill through the Senate.

Race calling can suppress the factual information citizens need to make sense of the political world. Patterson says factual information is also suppressed by journalists' reliance on 'episodic frames'—which highlight only the facts of an event—instead of

'thematic frames'—which include also the event's causes and consequences. In other words, daily news outlets tend to report the bit that's just changed—the latest episode—without putting the new development into the context of 'the story so far' and why it matters.

I've often thought that fewer reports of incremental developments in a continuing story and more 'position papers' on particular policy issues would frame the news in a way that allowed readers to make more sense of it. If I'm right, journalism needs less devotion to 'the way we've always done it' and more attention to what the scientists can tell us about why our readers work the way they do and, indeed, the deeper reasons *we* do the things we do.

CHAPTER 11
SECOND THOUGHTS ABOUT THE JOURNALISTS' ETHOS

Journalism: a profession whose business is to explain to others what it personally doesn't understand.

Lord Northcliffe

I've loved almost every minute of my newspaper career, but the longer I've been a journalist the more critical I've become of journalism, news gathering and 'the media'. Perhaps the biggest problem with the profession is its lack of reflection on what it's doing and why it's doing it. There's no shortage of effort or ambition, no lack of willingness to compete with the others, but there *is* a tendency to do things the way they've always been done and see journalism as a traditional craft or even an art, rather than something to be analysed.

Almost all journalism is undertaken by commercial firms anxious to make a profit, and even when it's done by public agencies such as the ABC, the spirit of competition with the commercial sector is so strong that, in practice, there's little difference in the values and behaviour of journalists from profit and not-for-profit organisations. So journalists are *selling* the news they gather, and if they don't attract enough customers they'll be in trouble with their bosses and, ultimately, may find themselves out of a job. They rarely dwell on this, however, and no journalist sees herself as doing something little different from selling soap. All of us see journalism as also having a higher purpose, something we're quick to appeal to whenever we fear government policies threaten the freedom of the press. Often that higher purpose is expressed in the metaphor of the news media as 'the fourth estate', playing an indispensible role in keeping governments accountable to the public.

I readily agree journalism must have a higher purpose. I've always sought the best trade-off I can reach between commercial success on the one hand and doing an intellectually respectable and worthwhile job on the other. It took me too long to realise this higher purpose was best expressed as Serve the Reader—to focus on the readers and their needs, providing them with the information they need (sometimes without them knowing they need it) in a clear, concise, accurate, easy-to-grasp and interesting, even entertaining, form. Isn't that the objective of every journalist and editor? In principle it may be, but too often in practice it ain't.

Good competition and bad

Over my four decades in the business of daily journalism, conditions have become ever more competitive. In recent times the cause has been the way the digital revolution has shifted classified and display advertising and readers from newspapers to internet sites and other digital 'platforms', in the process greatly reducing the amount we can charge for advertising. But the game was getting more competitive long before then, not because of any growth in the number of newspapers—the reverse, in fact—and only partly because radio and television became more active in broadcasting news. Mainly the problem was the greater competition from all the many more things people could do with their leisure time. Long before newspaper circulations began actually falling they were failing to keep up with growth in the population.

All this may explain why news gathering has become less serious and more entertaining, why even the 'quality' newspapers are reporting more crime and the doings of celebrities, devoting much space to leisure activities such as food, wine and entertainment guides, and directing political and economic reporting more to 'race calling'—who's up, who's down—than to debating policy issues.

At another level, however, it doesn't adequately explain why journalists and their editors still think of 'the competition' almost wholly in terms of what their opposite numbers are doing. Newspaper journalists compare their stories with what other papers have printed; radio and TV journalists compare their bulletins with other stations' and networks' bulletins. I think this narrow approach to competition comes not so much from commercial pressures as from the instinctive human competitive spirit, which is as much in evidence among journalists and their editors as it is among football players.

Why is this a problem? Because it neither meets the commercial imperative nor, more seriously, adequately serves the reader. What motivates journalists is the journalistic ethos—the profession's long-held beliefs about what constitutes journalistic success and what doesn't. Old-school journos know and young journos soon learn which stories are 'newsworthy' and which aren't, what behaviour wins approval from your peers and bosses and what doesn't. Competition is an integral part of the journalistic ethos. Journos on the same news outlet compete to find the stories that will be given the most prominence—that will lead the front page or lead the bulletin, or lead page three rather than page four. Did I have a win or did you? Then everyone from the editor down compares today's paper with those of our rivals. Did we have a story they missed? Did our story on rumblings against the PM beat theirs or did theirs beat ours? How many exclusive stories did we have on the front page compared with them? Did they run something on page one that we relegated to page five? To everyone bar whoever decided on the page five placement, that counts as a loss. Did we devote more pages—or more minutes of the bulletin—to coverage of last night's budget or did they? Who had the smartest, snappiest headline summarising the budget's reception?

To some extent competition between journalists and news outlets is a good thing, keeping people on their toes and encouraging the pursuit of excellence. Editors consciously foster competition between their journalists to 'get the best run'. Papers or TV channels with a monopoly in their district rarely excel. When Rupert Murdoch launched *The Australian* in 1964, its beautiful design and much better editing eventually obliged the stodgy and complacent *Sydney Morning Herald* and *The Age* to transform their performance. What I wonder is whether the impetus for reform came from fear of losing readers or from simple journalistic rivalry. My guess is it was the latter posing as the former.

But though the absence of competition is a bad thing, it doesn't follow that the more competition the better. And the competitive spirit so integral to the journalistic ethos—and so central to the enjoyment successful journos get from their job—does as much to hinder as to advance journalism in its pursuit of the two goals of commercial success and service to the reader. Of course, though there is scope for conflict between those goals, it's more likely that emphasising the readers' needs will bring commercial success.

As the social researcher Hugh Mackay famously taught, the key to competition is to focus on the customer, not your competitors. And that's precisely what's wrong with the journalistic ethos: the besetting sin of journalists and editors is that they compete to impress other journalists and editors. It's their status within the profession they care about most, not serving the reader. Journalism is too incestuous.

Too often the competitive spirit comes at the expense of the readers, not their benefit. When one journalist breaks a story, their opposite numbers are notoriously reluctant to follow it up. They think of the humiliation they will suffer before their peers by tacitly acknowledging their rival's success; they don't think of their duty to ensure their readers—who are unlikely to have read their rival's story—are informed of an important development.

There's nothing reporters and their editors value more highly than scoops—exclusive stories. Much effort is devoted to uncovering them at the expense of more mundane reporting, and much prominence is given to them even if they're not all that world-shattering. What reporters and editors rarely if ever ask themselves is how much value *readers* attach to scoops. Do they care that a story is exclusive, or even know it's exclusive? Do they consciously—or even unknowingly—value a news outlet more highly because of its greater number of exclusives? Personally, I doubt it. These days media outfits do a reasonable amount of market research, but do they check the commercial value of scoops? To my knowledge, never. Journalists and their bosses esteem scoops so highly they don't want to risk being told they're being self-indulgent.

It's true that—whether or not they realise it—readers are greatly served by scoops that bring to light information governments are seeking to conceal, provide new insights about how the world works, or reveal wrongdoing that wouldn't otherwise be known of. But most exclusives fall far short of those high ideals. Sometimes they're no more than sketchy and inaccurate speculative stories about policy measures soon to be officially announced. Often they're self-serving leaks from interest groups, including governments and others, giving selected journalists a head start on reports or decisions they are about to make public. Are such 'exclusives'—known in the press gallery as 'drops'—worth the effort and attention given to them? I doubt it.

Another respect in which rival-focused competition doesn't deliver benefits to readers is its tendency to be risk averse. Judgements about newsworthiness—which stories readers will find most interesting—are highly subjective. When judgements about the placement of stories differ between news outlets, there's always a tendency to feel the others got it right at our expense. So it's not surprising there's a great temptation to second-guess your competitor's reaction to a story. If I do the same as I expect my rival to do—play up this story, but play down that one—I minimise the chance of being caught out. But I also minimise the choice available to both lots of readers, not to mention abdicating my responsibility to do what *I* judge to be best for *my* readers.

If my competitor is doing the same thing I'm doing, we've both got ourselves locked in a game that's lost touch with our readers' interests and will be hard to break out of. It's this risk-averse competition that leads to the media's herd behaviour: all the news outlets covering much the same stories and coming to much the same conclusions about what's important and what isn't.

Economists refer to such behaviour as a 'collective action problem': even if we realise what we're doing doesn't make sense, we're each afraid to stop doing it for fear of giving our opponent an advantage. Editors of the quality papers often compete to see who can devote the most pages to covering the latest natural disaster or major government report. Winning such a game impresses their journalists and other editors, but it means even the losing editors provide their readers with far more stories on the topic than they're likely to want to read. When I pointed this out once to an editor who was a former colleague, he said, 'You might be right, Ross, but don't ask me to be the first to stop doing it.'

As I explained in chapter 10, journalists are right in believing their readers find bad news more interesting than good news, and so are right to give a fair bit of prominence to threats, problems, crises and controversies. But I believe the intensification of competition—and particularly the popularity of risk-averse competition where my rival's predilection for bad news leaves me determined not to be outdone—has led too many editors to go overboard on the bad news, giving their readers more negativity than they can handle. It may sound paradoxical, but it remains true that the great majority of people—including media consumers—are instinctive optimists. They want to go on believing that, despite some problems, the world's not such a bad place and the future will be better than the present. Serve such people a daily diet of unrelenting depression and too many of them will, rather than slitting their throats, stop reading your paper.

Media manipulation

The intensity of competition between news outlets makes them susceptible to manipulation by interest groups, particularly governments, which these days devote much attention, staff and taxpayers' dollars to 'managing' the news media in their reporting of policy and politics. Journalists need to come up with a continuous stream of scoops (no matter how dubious) and ministers' press secretaries are happy to oblige them—provided their offering is given sufficient prominence and is run uncritically. By contrast, should a journalist come up with an unauthorised scoop a minister finds embarrassing, his press sec's efforts to downplay the story will find a receptive audience among the journalist's rivals, who are looking for reasons to avoid writing follow-up stories.

Although much information about government policy decisions is provided in formal documents or at press conferences, much background information is provided informally by ministers and their staff. This leaves press secretaries with leverage to punish journalists who've written stories the minister's office regards as unduly critical or to reward journalists who are more accommodating. Should that office restrict the supply of information to a journalist from one outlet, this will put it at a competitive disadvantage to other outlets. But so great is the competition between journalists that should one journalist fall into disfavour, another journalist from the same outfit will happily take his place. In other words, the intensity of the competition is so great that governments have little difficulty playing journalists and their outlets off against each other.

There was a time when the practice of locking up journalists while they absorbed the voluminous budget papers before their release was justified by the need to keep market-sensitive information confidential until after the financial markets have closed. But such a need has long passed. These days, the markets are open almost continuously. So why does the expensive and cumbersome lockup arrangement persist? Why doesn't the treasurer announce his budget in the early afternoon, giving the media plenty of time to digest it before evening news bulletins and morning papers? Why do so many journos from the outlet's state capital head office have to journey to Canberra to attend a single Parliament House lockup?

Because the lockup has been transformed into the chief device governments use to manipulate the media's initial reaction to their budgets. Journalists are kept cut off from all contact with the outside world for about six hours before being let out at 7.30pm as the treasurer starts to deliver his brief speech in the House, televised to the nation. This leaves the media little if any time to find out what experts think of the budget. But the treasurer and the Treasury experts will have been available throughout the lockup to answer any questions the journos have.

In the days when Paul Keating was still in the process of perfecting the lockup as media management device, I remember one senior Treasury officer I knew saying to me conversationally, 'Pretty hard to find much to criticise, eh?' It's become standard practice for governments to leak the budget's bad news in the days before its announcement and leak smaller items of good news that might have been overlooked on the night, but carefully keep under wraps one nice big act of generosity for the media to discover and get excited about as they prepare their budget coverage in the lockup. In recent years the abuse of the lockup has reached the point where government press people leak to radio and TV reporters outside the lockup budget items they may broadcast *during* the lockup.

The obvious question is why the media don't rebel against this highly manipulative and inconvenient arrangement. Because no editor dares refuse to play ball, fearing their competitors would happily undercut them. It's a similar story with one of the main devices governments (and, with less success, oppositions) use to control the media's coverage of election campaigns. Those senior journos covering the leader are herded around on a campaign bus or plane, attending a lot of shopping centre walks, factory visits and photo opportunities, being given little information about the itinerary, little contact with the leader and little time to study policy documents before the press conference at which they're made public. To my knowledge, only once has an editor, from Brisbane's *Courier Mail*, declined to send his senior people on such a goose chase, arguing they could be more usefully employed covering the election from home base. Why was he game to take a stand? Because the *Courier Mail* is the city's only daily newspaper.

A classic example of the way government media manipulators are able to turn the media's obsession with both competition and timeliness against them, and thereby limit the publication of embarrassing information, arose in 2011. Two gallery-based 'FOI editors', who had been getting lots of scoops from freedom-of-information requests, complained bitterly that Treasury had starting frustrating their efforts by releasing the documents they sought publicly (rather than giving the requester first dibs) and, what's more, doing so late on Friday afternoons, when it was too late for stories to be written for evening TV news bulletins or even Saturday papers. If you couldn't get the information exclusively, why would you bother applying? And if the information couldn't be written up on the Friday, who'd be interested in writing it up for Monday?

Lack of reflection

Journalism suffers from its practitioners' adherence to longstanding attitudes and practices and their lack of reflection on *why* they do the things they do. They imagine the journalistic ethos to be the epitome of journalism's higher purpose, unaware that many of their values make sense only from a commercial perspective. Many journalists disparage media market research about readers' preferences, little realising their long-held views about what constitutes a good story and what doesn't are merely the handed-on guesses of long-gone editors about what the readers seem to like. That is, fossilised amateur market research from the days before professional market research.

The value journalists attach to scoops that bring readers news (often inaccurate and incomplete news) a day or two before it becomes common knowledge can be justified only in terms of their employer's commercial interests, not any higher purpose. Whether or not their view is justified, editors imagine gaining a reputation for being first with the news will add to their sales. A case in point is the arrest of the Australian businessman Stern Hu in China. One of my boys, John Garnaut, won the profession's Walkley Award for being the first to report this story, which would hardly have failed to come to light within a few days. I told him he didn't deserve a Walkley for such a modest achievement, but he did for his years of exceptionally high-quality reporting and interpreting of China's rise (an achievement that would never win such approbation from his peers).

A related element of the journalistic ethos is the considerable value attached to timeliness: the earlier some development is reported the better. By definition, journalists believe, news has to be new. While it's still judged to be new, their appetite for the story is almost unbounded, but their enthusiasm wanes quickly as the unfolding story loses its novelty. For a reasonably significant development, a typical pattern would be for a paper to run too much for anyone to absorb on the first day, a bit of follow-up information on the second day, less on the third, a wrap-up feature story in the Saturday news review section and then nothing much again.

It may well be that readers are keener to hear about things when they've just happened. It may even be it doesn't take all that long for them to lose interest in the topic and be ready to hear about something new. If so, these are essentially *commercial* considerations editors would want to accommodate. What doesn't make much sense are the extremes to which journalists take their concerns about newness. Often, an interesting item that *could* have been reported on day one but wasn't for some reason will be judged 'old'—and thus not newsworthy—by day three or even day two. Where's the logic in that?

There's a stigma to reporting things your peers may judge as 'not new' or 'off the pace'. And columnists often feel they can't write about a particular topic without a 'news peg'—without being able to link the topic to some event that happened, ideally, the previous day or, at most, the same week. What's missing from this obsession with timeliness and the literal definition of newness is any thought about the readers' preferences. How can something be 'old' if journalists know about it but the reader doesn't? How can we be sure readers lose interest in topics as quickly as journos do? Why couldn't it be after the dust has started to settle that readers are most interested in reading an assessment of what the event amounts to and its lasting significance? And how could it possibly be that a subject considered of sufficient interest to be worthy of a column is only worthy if something to do with the subject happened this week? Are readers' interests *that* transient?

And what about the truth that there's not much new under the sun? I think a fact is new if it's likely most readers have forgotten it. In any case, they say all novels fit one of seven eternal storylines.

The truth is that many 'new' stories are merely new versions of old familiar stories. Another truth is that journos often select the facts of a 'new' story to make it fit what they know is a favourite formula. When I was writing a book on happiness I maintained a Google search on the word. There was an unending stream of news stories from around the world headlined Money Does Buy Happiness and, in roughly equal measure, Money Doesn't Buy Happiness.

The 24-hour news cycle

There's no denying there is among the news media's audience—a section of it, anyway—a great impatience to know the latest 'breaking news'. When something really notable happens—the disappearance of Malaysia Airlines' flight MH370, for instance—this is understandable, but there remain some people prepared to listen to or watch continuous news, or regularly check a news media website, presumably mainly out of boredom. But vanishing aeroplanes or resigning premiers are comparatively rare. I remember turning on CNN in a European hotel room to find I was staring at an empty runway somewhere in Spain where, a voice informed me, a plane was believed to have run off the end. For as long as I could stand it, I watched that lack of colour or movement while the unseen presenter and his expert guests speculated about what might have happened. I remember thinking: why don't you guys find out what happened and why, then tell me; my interest in the story isn't as great as you seem to assume. It was Jon Stewart, host of US TV's *The Daily Show*, who said, 'At a certain point you realise that there's not enough happening to justify 24 hours of news. They should just show a snow cone melting until something happens.'

There may be a market for incomplete, inaccurate, undigested news, but I can't imagine it's a particularly lucrative one, and it's not one I want to serve. It seems true, nonetheless, that the growing preoccupation with 'breaking' news is helping to shorten the media's already short attention span. When you're repeating the news every hour—or expecting people to keep revisiting your website in search of the latest—you never dwell on anything for long, and have an insatiable appetite for some source to present you with some new news. Since you're producing 24-hour news on a shoestring, you don't have the resources to go out and get your own news, of course. Another consequence is to make you dependent on continuous feeding with 'announceables' by governments and other interest groups trying to use the media for their own ends.

And so to the subs' table

But if reporters aren't sufficiently reflective on how what they do advances their stated objectives, the same is true of sub-editors. Their 'revealed preference', as an economist would say, seems a strange combination of insisting things still be done the way they always were and insisting they be done according to the latest stylistic fashions—fashions that seem driven by artistry rather than research, or even clear thinking about means to ends. I mentioned in chapter 9 the fashion of keeping punctuation to a minimum, which *may* be intended to avoid slowing the reader down but, taken to extremes, has the opposite effect. Of late the subs have also taken to keeping capital letters to a minimum.

Another wrong-headed subs' fad is not to hyphenate compound adjectives. It doesn't seem to have occurred to them that the point of hyphenating run-of-the-mill phrases is to make it instantly clear which words qualify the adjective and which the noun. This hastens comprehension—or, as the psychologists would put it, 'cognitive ease'. Consider this one: 'The states collect about half their own source revenue from payroll, conveyancing and land taxes.' Source revenue? What's source revenue? And all because someone thought it smart to stop hyphenating 'own-source'.

As Lynne Truss wrote in *Eats, Shoots and Leaves*, 'punctuation is essentially a courtesy. The writer uses punctuation to save the reader from puzzling over his intended meaning. Why should the innocent reader be lumbered with all the work?' Just so. And how does inadequate punctuation advance either our commercial objective or our higher purpose?

As for the enforcement of long-established attitudes and practices, one attitude is that a quality newspaper must be written in a quite formal (that is, stilted) style, and a conversational style eschewed. I've spent much of my career suffering subs trying to sabotage my efforts to speak simply and comfortably with the reader by painstakingly filling out my contractions. The written word loses much, relative to the spoken word, because of its inability to convey verbal emphasis and tone of voice. The 'emoticons' used in emails are an attempt to reduce this problem. The device I use is to put key words in *italics*—whether they're the word you'd naturally emphasise in a sentence to make its meaning clear, or the word that makes sure the reader easily grasps some technical comparison I'm making.

Trouble is, old-school subs tend to disapprove of italics and often try to minimise their occurrence. Why, for goodness sake? Because in the days of hot metal, a word in italics would slow the production process down while the linotype machine shifted from the tray containing ordinary type to the tray containing italics and then back again. But hot metal went out 30 years ago. See what I mean about old habits dying hard? Then there's the minor matter of the % sign. Although it's long been used in graphs and tables, it's never used in copy. We always spell out 'per cent', never even abbreviating it to 'pc'. Why? The reason is lost in the mists of time. Maybe it's just formality, but my guess is it was thought that not everyone would know what % meant. Maybe not then, but surely they would today. My broader point, however, is that subbing needs to be less about subjective notions of artistry and more about ensuring the practices we enforce are those most calculated to advance our objectives.

A better journalists' ethos

Well, so much for my critique. If I'm so smart, what better approach would I propose? Remembering Mackay's Dictum—the key to competition is to focus on the customer, not your competitors—my answer is that we should change our ethos to Serve the Reader. This doesn't mean going populist, serving up happy schlock or telling readers only what they want to hear. It means doing our utmost to ensure readers are fully and accurately informed about all they need to know, and that we don't knowingly allow them to be misled by vested interests, with the message delivered as clearly and pleasantly as we can manage.

This change of ethos should empower our editors to fail to match the competition whenever they have reason to believe readers would be better served by doing something differently from the way it's always been done. They would be free to encourage their staff to innovate—something particularly desirable as the industry adjusts to radically changed and still changing technology—taking care to ensure there was no punishment of people whose experiments didn't work.

The Serve-the-Reader ethos is what editors need to empower themselves to solve their collective action problem and stand up to media management by politicians. They should stop allowing political leaders to lead their senior reporters around by the nose during election campaigns, stop taking part in budget lockups that lack real justification, and stop turning a blind eye while ministerial press secretaries punish gallery reporters who write stories their political masters find inconvenient. They should reconsider the competition-driven obsession with timeliness that says a story considered perfectly fit for presentation to readers on Friday is somehow unpublishable by Monday. The overriding question must always be: do our readers need to be told about this? It would be good to see editors adopt an attitude that any story the politicians tried to bury on a Friday afternoon—or under the cover of a terrorist attack—should be singled out for special treatment no matter how many days had passed before this became possible. If the pollies went to all that trouble, it's a safe bet the readers would be interested in being told the story.

We need to stop focusing so much on our competition with other news outlets and be more conscious of our broader competition with all the other ways for our readers to spend their leisure time. This does mean we need to keep our efforts entertaining. But though we should maintain a reasonable proportion of lighter stories—human interest, funny happenings and so forth—it doesn't mean dumbing down the news, obsessing about trivia, avoiding the serious, making political and economic reporting only about race calling, or beating up every story. Those are the easy, lazy ways to attempt to make our stories more entertaining. The harder way is better writing, the easy read and the good read.

What we've had too much of in recent times is *passive* journalism, where we wait to be fed by governments and interest groups with axes to grind, where the news agenda is set by everyone but the journalists, where we uncritically pass on to our readers self-seeking claims provided they're sufficiently disturbing or controversial, and often don't bother passing on news that lacks controversy but is still worth knowing.

It would be instructive for news outlets to measure the proportion of news initiated by the outlet rather than arriving via press releases, press conferences and the like. What we need more of—and what would be a great motivator of journos—is *active* journalism. This would involve more getting out and searching for our own stories, with the search directed by the issues and concerns we know to be of importance to our readers, or believe ought to be drawn to their attention.

To borrow some business jargon, it would involve adding more value to our news reports. We'd cast a far more critical eye over press releases and claims made at press conferences. We'd add more context and background to our reports. We'd follow stories for longer. We'd follow-up old announcements by politicians and others: whatever happened to the plan to do X by 2015? In other words, we'd hold authority to account in a way we rarely do at present. Politicians and their press people would hate this, but we'd be focused on the needs of our readers, not our contacts. When industry groups claimed some government action would 'destroy 10,000 jobs', we'd come back later to ask why it hadn't happened. We'd be playing our part in keeping the bastards honest.

Active journalism would involve the media playing a greater auditing role in checking the claims made by politicians and interest groups before passing them on to our readers. Rather than broadcasting wrong or dubious factual claims with the excuse that 'we didn't say it, he did', we'd protect our reputation and stop abusing our readers' trust by seeking comment from independent experts or, better, using our own expertise. This would mean employing more qualified and experienced reporters, of course, but I'm convinced greater expertise is central to the survival of quality journalism.

While we of course would continue to report many *opinions* we disagreed with—this exercise isn't about suppressing debate—we'd stop passing on without qualification *factual* assertions we knew to be wrong or which needed checking. We would stop generating more controversy than actually exists by portraying every issue through an adversarial frame. Nor would we be so obsessed by controversy that we neglected to bring to our readers' attention occasions when it suits both sides of politics to agree on something quickly and quietly. We never neglect to report politicians' pay rises, but we allowed many readers to go to the 2013 election not knowing both sides had agreed to increase the Medicare levy—that is, every rate of tax—by 0.5 percentage points, something neither side wanted to advertise.

We'd avoid the pseudo balance and even-handedness that leads to false equivalence. We wouldn't give one person saying the world was flat equal space with a genuine authority saying it was round. Some outlets have done this with climate change; we should make sure we don't do it with vaccination, even though that would make it a more sensational story.

The passive way to report an unfolding story is with a daily description of any new development. But the truth is, most readers don't follow most issues so closely they're able to make much sense of incremental developments. And though the world and the news cycle may have sped up, Thomas Patterson reminds us in *Informing the News* that what hasn't sped up is human capacity to think things through. So active journalism, by contrast, would be less incremental and more thematic—that is, more explanatory. More 'position papers', if you like, summarising the story to date and adding more background and context. More explanation by more qualified and specialised journalists, adding how and why to the reporters' who, what, where and when. There's no shortage of news, but a great shortage of assistance in making sense out of the chaos rather than adding to the confusion.

Such an approach would favour *comment* and analysis over *opinion* and analysis. It would favour analysis of facts over dogmatic expressions of opinion; light over heat. In the political realm, it would seek to clarify the choices available to voters. It would get closer to what so many readers fondly (but wrongly) imagine the media do: provide them with a representative picture of what's happening in the world beyond their view.

The world being the fallible place it is, all economic indicators present us with a combination of 'signal' and 'noise'. So in the reporting of economic stats, active journalism searches for and reveals the signal rather than headlining the noise. It eschews the meaningless period-to-period volatility even though this makes for more sensational stories.

Investigative journalism—with its guaranteed scoops and record of prompting royal commissions and other official inquiries—is something every journo is proud of, though few are engaged in and many wish they could get into the investigative unit. Active journalism would take a broader approach to investigative journalism, in two senses. It would encourage all reporters to take a more critical approach to the stories they write, anxious to avoid propagating anything that could mislead their readers. A good motto would be: every journo an investigative reporter.

But investigative journalism needs to be broader in the sense that there are many more issues than wrongdoing by politicians and conmen that could usefully be subjected to in-depth investigation. The economic world—with its administered prices for electricity, gas and water, compulsory third-party and workers compensation insurance—is, as the Bible says, 'white unto harvest'. Such investigations would be much closer to readers' hearts and pocketbooks. And exposing the sophistry in the 'independent modelling' used by governments and interest groups to bamboozle the public would almost amount to a full-time job.

Other specialists could be usefully employed in what I call 'forensic journalism': searching the public record—including annual reports, budget documents, auditor-general's reports, the *Government Gazette* and official statistics—for news stories in the manner of America's late I.F. Stone or our own Tim Colebatch of *The Age*.

A news outlet that gave primacy to serving the reader would take a far more analytical approach to scoops. It would start by exposing journalists' veneration of any story that can be claimed to be an exclusive to the scrutiny of market research aimed at establishing how conscious readers are of scoops and how highly they value them, then try to assess whether their commercial value justifies all the effort and expense journos put into finding them.

Then it would assess their contribution to journalism's higher purpose. In this it could employ the US media academic Jay Rosen's classification of scoops into four types. His first category—'the enterprise scoop'—is the type every journo likes to think of when she hears the word, and whose contribution to the public good not even I would question, 'where the news would not have come out without the enterprising work of the reporter who dug it out.'

Type two is 'the ego scoop', 'where the news would have come out anyway—typically because it was announced or would have been announced—but some reporter managed to get ahead of the field and break it before anyone else'. Rosen says such scoops are of no value from the readers' point of view. In Australian political reporting the name for such exclusives is a 'drop' because the story is leaked to a particular journo, or group of journos, by the government's press office as part of its media management. Whether intended or unintended, these drops come at a high price: the recipients—or would-be recipients—are in thrall to media manipulators.

Type three is 'the traders scoop', where a report from a business or economic journalist allows alert traders on the financial markets to steal a march on their less-alert colleagues. Such exclusives are of some monetary value to a few traders, but are of no social value.

Rosen's fourth type is 'the thought scoop', where a story contains new insights, coining terms, defining trends or apprehending some new trend before anyone else recognises it. When you can look at all the dots everyone can look at and be the first to connect them in a meaningful and convincing way, that's something. Rosen says this is the most under-recognised type of scoop. Just so. It's the type I aim for and envy most when others achieve it. And it's the type we could expect to see more of if we moved to more active journalism.

The Serve-the-Reader ethos would put timeliness into more sensible perspective. It's obvious readers want to be told the news as soon after it happens as possible but, except in cases of the most genuinely sensational breaking news, they're not in the tearing hurry it suits journos to assume they are. It suits them because timeliness is a relatively easy way to compete. We should stop timeliness being used as an excuse for poor quality and not give it priority over getting the facts right or providing adequate context. If stories are worth drawing to the attention of our readers we shouldn't put them on the spike merely because they're a few days old. If a competitor has beaten us to a story we shouldn't hesitate to follow them up if the story is worth knowing and is unlikely already to have come to the attention of many of our readers.

Greater attention to serving the reader ought to halt and reverse the competition-driven pressure to make the news more and more negative. It's only as depressing as it is because we consciously bypass good-news stories in our preference for more and more bad news. Just as mothers insist their sugar-, fat- and salt-loving children eat a balanced diet including fruit and veg, so sensible, reader-attuned editors provide their customers with a mix of good news and bad. Just as the veggies heighten the pleasure from dessert, so a measure of good news actually serves to increase the impact of the bad news.

Readers could use a lot more heartwarming stories about individuals putting service before self, charities achieving success in fighting disadvantage, even government programs that are working. Some journos seem to think writing nice things about people is unprofessional or maybe even unmanly, a sign you've been suckered by your contacts. While there are still so many things that are wrong with the world, only a toady would acknowledge that a few things are going right, they think. I guess it's an instinctive defensive reaction against all the PR people looking to place positive stories about their company or government.

But the readers' interests should come first and there's no reason to believe they have an aversion to good news (as opposed to an undoubted special interest in bad news). Business journalists ought to write up success stories—particularly small-business people who've done something notable—as well as championing the interests of shareholders over company managers and coming down hard on big businesses that rob people of their savings or otherwise screw up. They shouldn't be too proud to draw their readers' attention to the improved financial product some bank has come up with, even at the price of giving the bank a free kick.

And while we're lifting the fatwah against good-news stories, we should resist the machismo-driven resistance to neutral stories, otherwise known as 'news you can use', news to 'cut out and keep'. It may not excite any journalistic breasts but it does interest our readers to be given information such as which services will be open over the holiday period and much else.

As I trust I've convinced you by now, putting service to the reader first and moving to active journalism should make the news *agenda* liberating rather than constricting, as it is at present. We should be putting items on the agenda rather than reserving that privilege for everyone but ourselves. It's an approach that involves harder work by better-qualified journos, but that ought to be something that recommends it. And it's an approach that gives a longer-term focus to our work, something likely to improve our battered reputation for accuracy and trustworthiness.

CHAPTER 12
FUTURE OF JOURNALISM: A BATTLE PLAN

As Clay Shirky notes, 'You're gonna miss us when we're gone!' has never been much of a business model.

Eric Beecher

The future of quality, independent journalism is highly uncertain. Will newspapers survive much longer? Doubt it. Will Fairfax Media survive? The odds are against it. Will quality journalism survive? Yes, but probably in a different form.

Newspapers, joined by the rest of the news media, have always played an essential role in ensuring our democracy works well. Just as governments need oppositions to keep them on their toes, so the fourth estate's role has been to hold the actions—and inactions—of politicians up for public scrutiny and thus make them accountable to the electorate.

This is why, according to Eric Beecher, media entrepreneur and former editor of the *Herald*, the story of how newspapers fell victim to a commercial market failure is more significant than just the demise of an industry business model. It has the makings of a 'civic catastrophe'. 'That's because the serious journalism of influence in

Australia, apart from the government-funded ABC, resides mainly in four newspapers—the *Sydney Morning Herald*, *The Age*, the *Australian Financial Review* and *The Australian*,' he says. 'Between them, these four mastheads provide most of Australia's coverage of politics, justice, economics, business, science, health, welfare, public policy, international affairs, arts, culture and ideas.'

Three of those four papers are owned by Fairfax, although News Corp—whose ownership of six capital-city tabloids in addition to the *Oz* gives it almost two-thirds of the metropolitan and national daily newspaper circulation, leaving Fairfax with a quarter—is in just as much trouble as Fairfax.

The threat, of course, comes from the digital revolution and the papers' loss of revenue and readers to the internet and the manifold websites, 'platforms' and rival activities it has spawned. Any journo could tell you how the press got to its present dire straits, but they won't tell it the way I, as an economic journo, will. It's an economic story, about markets and the technological change they promote and adjust to. It's an old, old story while also being, in its specifics, something much more disruptive than we've seen before, affecting newspapers throughout the developed world.

The economics of newspapers

For everyone other than those whose livelihoods it disrupts, and those oldies who (like me) much prefer to read their news on pieces of paper, it's a change whose benefits in many respects far outweigh its costs, as is usually the case with new technology. What makes this change so much more worrying is the strange fact to which I've referred, that such a vital role in the good functioning of our democracy—and in the cultural life of the nation—could reside in the hands of one profit-making industry. As Thomas Patterson remarks in *Informing the News*, a book I've made much use of, 'the press is unusual in that it is a private business with a public trust.'

Of course, this is hardly the first technological change the press—or the rest of the media—has had to negotiate. The good news is that, so far, it has adapted and survived, though in ways not envisaged at the time the threat emerged. I remember reading about the consternation of American press people in the nineteenth century after the laying of the undersea telegraph cable from Europe. Until then, their business model had been to be the first aboard ships arriving from Europe, collect all the newspapers and use them to write their own stories. With the foreign news now coming by telegraph, they'd lost their monopoly over it. How would they ever survive? They found a way.

I'm old enough to remember the anxiety caused by the arrival of television in Australia in the mid-1950s. First on the block would be the picture theatres—which, remember, showed newsreels along with their movies. It's true many suburban cinemas closed and cinema-going was never as widespread again, but the cinema chains packed down and survived and the much later advent of the multiplex—a classic example of the pursuit of 'economies of scope', where the same facility is used to produce a greater number of products—has seen cinemas and cinema-going thrive.

Next for the chop after the advent of television was radio. It's true radio was never the same again. No longer did people sit around in their living rooms listening with rapt attention to serials and quiz shows. But radio became something you listened to while doing something else around the house, and a little more technical change allowed radio to find a new role as something you listened to while driving. The arrival of the transistor radio made radio listening a more movable, individual rather than fixed, group activity. Radio hardly dominates the electronic media scene the way it did before television, but it's doing well enough.

Newspapers have had to weather the arrival of each of these electronic alternative forms of entertainment and news dissemination. Newspapers lost their effective monopoly over news from the moment in 1939 that the ABC began gathering its own news rather than reading out articles from the papers. The introduction of television soon made the evening news bulletin the main source of news for many people. Then the move to hourly radio news bulletins completed the process by which newspapers ceased to be in the breaking news business. By the time people picked up their papers next morning they already knew the substance of most of the news contained in it. Perhaps *this* helps explain journos' and editors' obsession with scoops. But should you listen to a breakfast radio or TV news program before opening your morning paper, the likelihood is you'll already have heard a report of the best of those exclusives, often without attribution to the print source.

Though most of my years as a print journo have involved a continuous fight to keep readers and prevent a decline in circulation, since the arrival of the internet it's become a much greater struggle to respond to the loss of both readers and advertising revenue. Up to that point, the problem was only partly the loss of customers to the electronic news outlets. It was also a loss of customers to the ever-growing range of ways for people to spend their leisure time apart from reading the paper. Both factors explain the demise of afternoon newspapers in the late 1980s and early 90s. But there was no loss of people needing to place a classified ad, nor firms needing display ads to push their wares.

It's our precipitous loss of advertising revenue to the internet, much more than our loss of readers, that's now threatening the survival of quality journalism. With newspapers—particularly (former) broadsheet newspapers such as the *Herald* and *The Age*—it's legitimate to ask which came first, the news or the ads? Did editors who wanted to publish news need ads to help pay their way, or did business people who wanted to sell advertising space need to wrap news around the ads to attract the readers who would give the ads an audience?

It's a chicken-and-egg argument. Newspapers have *always* been about advertising. It wasn't until 113 years into its almost 175-year history that the *Herald* took classified ads off the front page and replaced them with news. Many readers, who regard the cover price or subscription they pay as hefty enough, imagine themselves to be paying for their paper the way they pay for everything else they buy. In truth, what newspapers call 'circulation revenue' has only ever accounted for 25 or 30 per cent of total revenue. Newspaper people see it as covering the cost of the newsprint and not much else. It's probably true to say that, until quite recently, managers kept cover prices artificially low—and offered deep discounts on subscriptions—in an effort to keep circulations up and thereby justify the high prices they were charging advertisers.

So newspaper journalism has always been paid for primarily by advertising revenue. Broadsheet newspapers the world over have always derived much of their revenue from classified advertising, but this was especially true of the *Herald* and *The Age*. Beecher says that, before the digital onslaught, they were generating as much as 56 per cent of their revenues from 'classies'—far more than papers such as the *New York Times* and the London *Daily Telegraph*.

The plain truth is the *Herald* and *The Age* had near monopolies in their city's classified advertising market, which they exploited to the full, charging advertisers huge premiums above their cost of production—what an economist would call 'economic rent'. According to Beecher, this gave them profit-to-revenue margins of close to 90 per cent. Now you know why classies were long referred to as 'rivers of gold'. The point to note, however, is that little of that gold made it to the Fairfax bottom line. Newspaper profits were comfortable, but never excessive. Rather, the gold paid for the quality journalism (with a fair bit of overmanning among printers and journos thrown in).

Many rivals sought a share of our golden river, but with little success—although towards the end the *Trading Post* did manage to capture our ads for second-hand household goods, the 'rats and mice' of our business. As a rule, however, the 'barriers to entry' to the classified marketplace—the high cost of printing plants and high cost of physical distribution—were prohibitive. Our tabloid rivals lusted after a share, but never got far because we were too well entrenched. Every seller wants to advertise in the place where all the buyers are; every buyer knows to come to the place where all the sellers are. So our near monopoly was largely a natural one—though, with other newspaper proprietors, we did take the precaution of tying up the newsagents with agreements that were probably illegal under the Trade Practices Act had anyone in Canberra thought it politic to take on the media barons.

It took me a lot longer to realise it, but newspapers in general also enjoyed a near duopoly in display advertising. With some leakage to radio, magazines (most of which the newspaper companies owned) and outdoor advertising, if you were an Australian company wishing to advertise your product you had two main choices: an ad in a newspaper or an ad on free-to-air television.

Television got the bigger bite, but our share was hardly small. The premiums we charged wouldn't have been anything like those for classies, but they would have been significant—protected by the premiums the TV channels were extracting.

The first stage of the digital revolution actually benefited newspapers. The move from typewriters to computers and, far more significantly, from hot metal to cold type significantly reduced the cost of producing and printing papers. We no longer needed compositors, and far fewer printers overall. By seizing the opportunity presented by the new technology to break the physical link between the publishing and printing functions and move new, purpose-built printing plants to greenfield sites nearer the edge of the city, the companies were able to walk away from generations-long restrictive work practices and, indeed, break the power of the printers' union. That the advent of much-cheaper offset printing also reduced a barrier to entry into the newspaper business hardly worried anyone.

From there on, however, the news from the digital revolution was all bad for newspapers. Alan Kohler, leading business journalist, entrepreneur and former Fairfax editor, says he began warning in the early 90s that the internet would mean the drying up of the classified rivers of gold. The penny dropped for me when he wrote in a column in 2002 that 'the classified advertising cash flow that has long subsidised quality journalism has also peaked. Fairfax's problem is . . . that quality journalism is fundamentally unprofitable . . . it is subsidised by classified advertising'. Beecher is still bitter that when, by invitation, he delivered this message to the Fairfax board in 2004, he was sent packing.

After Young Warwick Fairfax lost control of the family company and then the Canadian newspaper proprietor Conrad Black chose not to stick around, Fairfax became the plaything of the share market and the big end of town. Beecher complained that 'in the absence of either a proprietor or a majority shareholder . . . Fairfax has been run by a board with one distinguishing feature: lack of industry knowledge or expertise. The board has never understood the scale of the challenge posed by the internet. It never saw the size of the looming crisis and never made plans for a worst-case scenario. If it had, the mindset of the whole company, from chairman to copy kid, might have been radically different. The company would have tried new and different strategies to adapt. Some would have failed and some succeeded, but simply acknowledging the dilemma would have made a huge difference to the outcome'.

Even when a merger with Rural Press turned out to be a reverse takeover, bringing John B. Fairfax back as our biggest shareholder in late 2006 and making Brian McCarthy, an experienced newspaper man, Fairfax's chief executive two years later, it didn't help. Neither man understood the challenge we faced. To be fair, the history of business tells us such inertia is common. Philip Meyer writes in *The Vanishing Newspaper* that 'the disruption of existing business models by substitute technology is an old story in American business . . . The old businesses hang on too long to their accustomed ways of doing things and become ripe targets for upstart competitors who are not burdened by tradition'. This is why I say the odds are against a big, venerable, lumbering company such as Fairfax successfully making the transition to the brave new digital world.

Even so, it really is surprising all those Fairfax suits couldn't see how outgunned we were by the arrival of the internet. When you're classifying small ads on a big piece of paper, you can do so on only two criteria: you divide them by broad subject matter—the main ones being homes, jobs and cars—then list them alphabetically under each classification. By contrast, a website can classify its ads any number of ways, and change the classification criteria at will. Show me, for instance, all the houses you've got for sale in this suburb or part the city that are within this price range, have at least three bedrooms and are no more than 10 minutes from the station. Not all that many? OK, let me relax a few of those criteria and see how many more that brings me. And get this: now I've picked a dozen that sound promising, use a little video to show me round each place before I take the trouble of driving out to see them in the flesh. According to Beecher's figuring, a decade ago the *Herald* and *The Age each* carried around 200 pages of classified advertising a week. By 2013 that was down to some 50 pages and still falling.

Most people around Fairfax like to lay most of the blame for Fairfax's fumbled response on Fred Hilmer, academic and former McKinsey management consultant, who was chief executive for seven years until 2005. Hilmer was offered the chance to buy the infant websites that soon came to dominate the online classified markets for homes, jobs and cars, but declined. He thought their sale prices too high relative to their value and got that badly wrong. As has been trumpeted from the rooftops, Hilmer declined but Jamie Packer and his mate Lachie Murdoch didn't.

The journos lament that if only Hilmer hadn't missed getting those key sites and capturing the bulk of the classies we were losing from the paper, how different our prospects would be today! I don't disagree, but this is where it helps to know a bit of economics. What most journos don't understand is that, though we'd be better placed today had we captured the key sites, we'd still have a big hole in our revenue. Natural monopolies are a product of the existing technology; when the technology changes sufficiently, the monopoly disappears. When you move classifieds online, the high barriers to entry in the paper world evaporate. The costs of setting up an online classifieds website aren't prohibitive. And whereas in the physical world long-established players have a huge advantage over new entrants—how much will it cost them to make their arrival in the market known to potential customers?—in the virtual world the biggest and the smallest sites sit side by side.

As a buyer I may start with the biggest and best-known site in the category, but it costs me just a few clicks to check a much smaller site while I'm at it. Or I can use a category search engine that searches for what I want on all the relevant sellers' sites and ranks them by price or some other criterion. In other words, the lower barriers to entry in the digital classies market mean the scope for charging prices well above costs has pretty much gone. If you happened to own the biggest and best-known site you could charge a bit of a premium—users will pay a little extra to deal with an outfit with a good reputation—but nothing like what we used to charge in the old days. (In passing, note what a huge improvement the digital revolution has brought to *users* of classified advertising: a far better product for a much lower price.)

It's a similar story with display ads. The barriers to entry that gave free-to-air television and newspapers a near duopoly, and allowed them to charge a premium for their ads, have come down with vastly increased competition from online sites—many of them nothing to do with the distribution of news—and other manifestations of the digital revolution. Free-to-air networks' margins and revenues are down, with the move to pay TV just the first of their problems.

According to figures collated by Franco Papandrea, of the News and Media Research Centre at the University of Canberra, over the 11 years to 2012, newspapers' share of the total Australian advertising market dropped from 37 per cent to less than 22 per cent, while online's share went from nothing to 25 per cent. (Note that these dollar-based shares understate the degree of shift in the *volume* of advertising because the prices for advertising online are so much lower.)

The other major casualty of the online onslaught were magazines and classified directories, with their share of the total market almost halving to 10 per cent. Now with the biggest share, of 30 per cent, television seems little affected so far, though this share *includes* pay TV. Radio's share was little changed at 8 per cent.

In 2012, more than half of the total *online* ad revenue of $3.3 billion a year was earned by search engines and directories, leaving 26 per cent for general display ads and 20 per cent for classified ads. But get this: of all the online ad revenue, the newspaper companies' share was just 8 per cent, according to Papandrea's figures.

Now let's look just at newspapers' total advertising revenue. Over the 11 years to 2012 it fell by roughly 6 per cent to about $2.9 billion, while the nominal size of the economy doubled. Need more to convince you newspapers have a problem? Narrowing it down just to Fairfax Media, over the four years to 2012 its total operating revenue *from all sources* fell by almost 21 per cent, whereas the economy *grew* by about 25 per cent.

There's a well-known rule of thumb among newspaper people around the developed world that for each $1 you lose in conventional advertising revenue you gain 10 cents in online ad revenue. Actually, the latest estimate from America's Pew Centre says it's nearer 7 cents. This isn't saying the prices papers are able to charge for a digital ad are a tenth or a fifteenth of the price for an equivalent conventional ad. Thankfully, it's not that bad. The comparison also takes account of the many newspaper ads that move online but not to a newspaper-owned site. But now the American rule of thumb has progressed from 'digital dimes' to 'mobile pennies'. That is, as people shift their news reading from the site to their mobile app, the ad revenue potential is further diminished.

Before we move on, let's just consider what these changes mean not for newspapers or journalism, but for the advertising industry and advertisers. They show that, while the economy was doubling in size over the 11 years to 2012, the estimated total spend on advertising rose by just under 50 per cent. It's possible, of course, that this slow growth during the period was explained by a significant fall in the *quantity* of ads being placed. To my knowledge there are no figures that could tell us. But I'd be surprised if this were the case. If we make the conservative assumption the quantity of advertising increased moderately, the most likely explanation for the relatively slow growth in the total spend would be the much lower prices charged for the growing share of ads placed on the internet and the dampener this placed on the ability of non-online advertising carriers to keep raising their prices in line with economy-wide inflation and a growing demand for advertising.

This brings me to a journos' nightmare I've been having for the past few years. What if the shift of advertising online—where it's often possible for the old scattergun approach to be replaced by ads far more tightly targeted to the known interests and buying habits of the viewer and where it's now possible for advertisers to pay on results—meant the businesses of Australia were able to do all the advertising they wish to do at some fraction of its former cost?

If there's any truth to that nightmare—and I fear there is—it spells an immense challenge for the preservation of quality journalism. It also suggests the most underwritten—and probably understudied—aspect of the digital revolution is the upheaval it's causing in the advertising industry. It must be in a bewildering state of flux as it determines just how the new digital world works and how best to exploit the radically changed opportunities now opening up but with, as yet, an unknown end-point.

But my duty as an economic journalist compels me to repeat the point: what may be a nightmare for journos and newspaper people, and a wild ride for advertising people, is also an unmitigated boon for businesses spending on advertising—and their customers, who bear the cost of that advertising in the prices they pay.

It's the marked fall in newspaper advertising revenue, which may well have a lot further to run, that constitutes the greatest threat to the future of quality journalism. If we'd kept the revenue while losing some readers we'd have a lot less to worry about. Of course, there is a loose link between ads and readers. We've always used our ability to attract readers to then attract advertisers, as well as to justify the high prices we were charging for ads. To a small extent with classified ads, it worked the other way—as we were reminded when we started losing them. Someone with a classie in Saturday's paper would buy a copy just to check their ad had made it, or to check the competition it was up against. At first it was mainly ads that we lost to the net, but then our papers started losing readers too—although not just readers who preferred to read their news on a screen, also those readers who found things to do in the digital world they regarded as more entertaining than reading news.

Of course, the internet has greatly increased the competition each newspaper faces from other papers' websites. Before the internet, every newspaper enjoyed what economists call 'natural protection'. Newspapers were too bulky and their news too perishable for there to be much trade in papers beyond their own areas. When I spent a term at Cambridge University on a press fellowship in late 1983, I would scour the British media for news of Australia with only the slimmest pickings. The Fairfax office in London would post me copies of the *Herald* that were about a fortnight old. These days, as everyone knows, you can be anywhere in the world and use a computer, iPad or smart phone to monitor the *Herald* website or tablet app as often as you like. And of course, at home in Oz you can read newspaper websites from your former home town in Melbourne and, indeed, any Australian city or any of the English-speaking world's big-name papers. The internet has made news a much more tradable commodity. Before now, pretty much the only trade in news stories was a wholesale trade between newspapers and other news outlets.

Eventually, of course, even Fairfax couldn't avoid responding to the digital challenge. The loss of revenue became so rapid in the late noughties that, had we not, we'd be out of business already. To be fair to Hilmer, he did get a digital division going in the late 1990s. (And he did offend his journalists by referring to them as 'content providers'—a term that wouldn't ruffle many feathers today.) At least relative to News Corp, we did put a lot more early effort into building up websites for the *Herald* and *The Age*, making our newspaper stories freely available as well as adding news from other sources, videos and so forth. This early move has given us an advantage, with each of the *Herald* and *The Age* sites up there today rivalling the lately arrived combined (and *free*) news.com.au site for the crown of having the most users. The plan was always to build the biggest news sites and then figure out a way to 'monetise' them, and that's how it's gone: millions of hits, but not enough millions of revenue.

We've had plenty of cost cuts and redundancy rounds, with the first big one coming with the closure of *The Sun* in 1988. But the serious, thought-through organisational response to the digital challenge didn't start until a new chairman, Roger Corbett—Beecher's bête noire—brought back the hugely experienced Fairfax editor Greg Hywood as chief executive in 2010.

When you're a stock-exchange-listed public company, expected to earn an adequate return on the shareholders' capital invested in the business, it follows as a matter of arithmetic that your revenue must exceed your costs and, should revenue fall sharply, your costs must fall just as sharply. As an accountant turned economic writer, I've never had a quibble with this logic. And after Kohler pointed out it was the huge premiums from our classified ads that had always paid for our quality journalism, I've had no trouble accepting that, as we lost our advertising revenue, we'd also have to cut the cost of our journalism. Would this involve a loss of quality? Inevitably—though it doesn't follow that ever dollar saved would involve a quality loss. I'm sure we began the process with fat to cut.

Beecher says that, until recently, the three main Fairfax papers plus the *Oz* employed about 1500 journalists, whereas by mid–2013 it was closer to 1000 and, he speculated, could be as few as 500 within two years. As I noted in chapter 4, the redundancies at Fairfax have all been been voluntary, with surprisingly generous payouts.

The successive rounds of redundancies—with more to come, I have little doubt—have involved a fair amount of work intensification, but Hywood has used several devices to limit the loss of quality. The main one has been greatly increased economies of scope, with the three Canberra bureaus merged into a smaller number of journos writing stories to be run in the three papers—*Herald*, *Age* and *Canberra Times*—and on the three websites and other digital platforms: tablet apps and smart phone apps. The *Herald* and *Age* business sections were first merged under the rubric of BusinessDay, then combined with the *Fin* as part of a new

Fairfax Business Media 'vertical' headed by my boy Sean Aylmer. There's also been a lot more swapping of copy between the *general* sections of the three papers.

Another, highly publicised attempt at reducing labour costs without too much loss of quality has been the outsourcing of most of the papers' subediting, first to Pagemasters—an Australian Associated Press (AAP)-owned business that also does contract work for News Corp—and then to Fairfax's own 'sub hub' in New Zealand. Outsourcing may involve a net reduction in the number of people used to do the work, but for the most part the savings come from lower salaries and benefits, plus tighter working arrangements. Does having subbing done in another city—or another country—involve a loss of quality? Yes, but I can think of worse ways to cut costs.

An objective of the redundancies has been not only to reduce staff numbers but to lower the average salary of the remaining workers. I've long argued to any editor who'd listen that just because we were letting senior and middle-level people go, we shouldn't stop recruiting and training the very best trainees we could find. Indeed, the more bright young things we had coming up, the more relaxed we could be about letting more expensive, middle-level people go and the more we could avoid the expensive business of filling vacancies by poaching good people from other papers.

The sad truth is that the long era of flowing golden rivers left us with salary levels way out of kilter with our newly straightened circumstances. (We've also had to compete, to an extent, with the generous salaries paid by News Corp, subsidised by a river of gold flowing not from classies but from the American company's cable TV and movie business—now staunched by the separation of 21st Century Fox from the 'new News Corp'.) I foresee that the Ross Gittinses of 10 or 15 years' time won't be paid the equivalent of what I'm paid. *This* bit doesn't worry me; I'd have done it all for much less money and I don't doubt my successors would too. The rewards from having your opinions broadcast to the world are a lot more than the money they pay you.

Though cost cutting on the editorial floor has long been commonplace at Fairfax, Hywood is the first chief to really make major cost-saving changes to all other parts of the empire, many of them far removed from news production. He's making big savings on the printing side with the closure of our plants at Chullora in Sydney and Tullamarine in Melbourne. Broadsheet-size newspapers are justified not so much by tradition as by that being the most cost-effective way to run classified ads. When the classies go, the financial rationale for broadsheet goes with them. And printing plants built to cope with at least 200-page Saturday papers go hugely underutilised. So the move of the *Herald* and *The Age* to tabloid ('compact') size is explained purely by the savings to be had by closing Chullora and Tullamarine and having the papers printed on existing, tabloid-only presses owned by the Rural Press part of the empire.

The transition of news from paper to digital platforms has necessitated a move to a more meaningful 'metric' of our readership—and hence, appeal to advertisers—than traditional newspaper circulation figures. I'm not convinced the two are comparable in terms of quality, but newspaper readership figures—calculated by applying a certain multiple to the circulation figure—are far exceeded by the number of readers of our site and other digital platforms. In consequence, the change in circulation has become less crucial. So Hywood, rather than his News Corp rivals, has led the way in abandoning the various expensive fudges both companies have long used to inflate their circulation figures, exploiting loopholes in the rules of the Audit Bureau of Circulations.

We've stopped paying a fortune to truck a few copies to far-distant country towns and stopped dumping thousands of free copies at sporting matches and the like (though not stopped offering free copies at airport gates—when people are trapped in an aluminium tube for an hour or two they tend to read their papers very thoroughly; I know I do). This coming clean has saved us money—the variable cost of printing papers is quite high—but also meant sharp falls in circulation figures, causing them to overstate the true decline in circulation. Even so, there's no denying the genuine decline in circulation has been marked as readers drift off to digital news sites and other uses of their leisure time.

So much for what we might think of as the negative—though unavoidable—response to the digital challenge. What have we done that's more positive? Well, we did act reasonably early to set up our own online classified sites for homes, jobs and cars—and promote them in our papers—though with mixed success. The main contribution of David Kirk, who succeeded Hilmer as chief exec in 2005, was to dilute the newspapers' effect on Fairfax profits by acquiring other businesses, particularly digital-transaction websites such as (the notably profitable) New Zealand Trade Me, Stayz holiday rentals and RSVP online dating.

Hywood started with cost cutting, then moved on to the revenue side in search of more revenue and new sources of revenue. He began jacking up the papers' cover prices, presumably on the assumption that, with diehard give-me-paper-or-give-me-death readers coming to predominate, their demand would be 'price inelastic'—not terribly sensitive to price rises.

He finally turned away from the conventional wisdom that 'they won't pay for anything on the internet' to join News Corp, the *New York Times* and many other newspapers in asking online readers to pay a price for ready access to their journalism. In distinction to News, however, our approach has been more softly, softly. Our 'metered' approach allows people 30 looks a month before asking them to subscribe and, even then, our paywall is 'porous' in that people following links from Google or Twitter or suchlike aren't blocked. Presumably, the intention is to gain subscription revenue without damaging our attractiveness to online advertisers by losing too many clicks. But it's clearly an approach that can be adjusted—tightened—over time in the light of experience.

Hywood is also trying to develop new sources of revenue from such things as hosting events (marathons, conferences and the like) and 'content marketing' (writing copy for news-like ads by businesses) and helping small businesses with their marketing arrangements.

That's fine as far as it goes—not very—but Hywood's most radical, forward-looking move has been to change the focus of our news-gathering effort, making it 'platform neutral' and 'digital first'. Until he instituted this reorganisation of methods and mentality in 2012, journos continued to prepare their stories for publication in the next day's paper, and the digital people were free to make any use of it they wished thereafter. Now the norm is for stories to be published online as soon as they're written—and very quickly subbed—then 'reverse published' in the paper the following day. This is possible because the overlap between people using our site and those reading our paper is surprisingly small. (This explains why the words 'yesterday' and 'today' are now rarely found in our stories, having been replaced by 'on Tuesday' and 'on Wednesday'.) Another change is that even reporters not specifically assigned to the website's breaking-news team now spend a fair bit of time writing immediate stories for the site, writing follow-ups as the story unfolds during the day, and then working up something more profound for use in tomorrow's paper. (See what I mean about work intensification?) Journos are meant to be 'platform neutral' in that they write their stories for use on any or all print or digital platforms and don't much care which.

Though as a habitually distrustful old-school journo I shouldn't say it, from the beginning of these reforms Hywood and his former offsider, Jack Matthews, were good at ensuring their journos and other staff were kept fully informed about the (increasingly evident) threats to the company and its journalism's survival, as well as their response to that threat and the reasoning behind it.

It was long part of the Fairfax journos' ethos that *we* write the stories, and leave it to the managers to worry about advertising, money and bottom lines. Our contribution to the company's commercial success went not a centimetre further than the circulation figures. For journos to worry about the views of advertisers would be unethical. It was a good way of working, inculcated by Sir Warwick and the Fairfaxes. On a couple of occasions—a few involving Neville Wran—old Wocka walked away from revenue rather than submit to pressure from powerful advertisers.

There was an inbuilt, permanent creative tension between editors and advertising managers, with the general manager adjudicating any irresolvable disputes. I remember mentioning to my boss Chris Anderson that the ad manager had rung me to let me know a bank that did a lot of business with us was quite unhappy with my column that morning. Anderson's face went white-hot as he said, through gritted teeth, 'Leave—it—with—me.' I knew he was going back to his office to ball the man out for daring to speak directly to one of his journos.

While the river of gold was gushing, this dogmatic division of church and state was something we could easily afford. But as the technological challenge has become more threatening, we journos have had to become less bifurcated in our refusal to think about advertising revenue and the company's bottom line, while still leery of worries about the hurt feelings of particular advertisers. Thanks to our top managers' improved communication efforts, I think most Fairfax journos now have a good understanding of the technology problem, accept the link between the company's financial fortunes and our future as journalists, accept that quality journalism matters more than particular platforms and understand how the company is going about trying to securing our future.

Late in 2011 I cracked a much-envied invite to one of the fabled lunches hosted by the Sydney art dealer Ray Hughes upstairs at his studio. Turned out he—and his son Evan—had a message for me. A few months earlier, the *Herald* had run a startling Saturday front page depicting a sharp fall in the sharemarket with a jagged line plunging from the top to bottom of the page and a huge headline screaming 'World on the brink'. As striking front pages go, it was a masterpiece. But first Hughes, then his son, took me aside to say that, after that front page, they hadn't sold a painting for a fortnight.

At the time, I believed there was nothing much fundamentally wrong with the economy—whatever might have frightened the sharemarket—but there was a lot of pessimism around and if Australians wanted to talk ourselves into a recession, we could. So I passed on the Hughes' feedback to the boss, Amanda Wilson, reading her a little lecture on how it was neither our duty nor in the interests of journos hoping to avoid further rounds of redundancies to exaggerate the economy's problems and maybe scare off more advertisers. To my surprise she accepted my advice—she'd agonised over that page—and asked me to repeat the message to the paper's regular senior editors' meeting. I did, arguing 'not that we should tell our readers everything in the garden is rosy, but that we should report what's happening soberly and responsibly, taking care not to exaggerate'. We should report the bad news, but we had no obligation to jump to conclusions about how much worse things might get. My point in telling you this story is simple: a board table full of hard-bitten editors listened to my arguments with little demur. Five years earlier I'd have been hounded out of the room.

Hard facts about a hard future

You may not be exposed to it, but a lot is being written about how the digital revolution is changing newspapers and the news media. It's being written by academics and entrepreneurs far more knowledgeable than me, but I'll try to summarise it for you. Remember, this is the biggest paradigm shift (a word I don't use lightly) in the dissemination of information—and hence news—since the invention of the printing press.

The revolution is far from over, so the situation is still very much in flux. No one knows where it will end up, partly because we're still exploring and exploiting the potentialities of the technological change that's already happened, partly because there's probably more technical change to come in short order, and partly because businesses' innovations in response to those potentialities will themselves change the path we follow and where we end up.

So there's a lot we don't know—a lot we can't know because it's in the future. But there are some things we do know, though never immutably. There are some propositions we can be reasonably sure are right, mainly because we can see trends that have been proceeding for some time and don't look like reversing. I've tried to boil down what we know to nine propositions.

1. The supply of news is increasing. By this I don't necessarily mean that more newsworthy things are happening, nor even that more stories are being written, though both could be true. Rather, I mean there are now many more mediums through which news can be received—newspapers, radio, free-to-air television, pay TV, websites, tablet apps and smart phone apps—as well as many more individual news providers in most of those media categories. A single *Herald* or *Age* news story can now be read on at least four platforms—paper, site, tablet and smart phone—plus our *Brisbane Times* and *WA Today* sites and often the sites of innumerable Fairfax regional papers.

As well, someone who lives in Sydney or Melbourne can now read the online versions of virtually any or every English-language newspaper in the world, plus a lot of the big-name British and American news magazines, such as the *New Yorker* or *The Economist*. A key but less known fact is that, though there are now many digital news suppliers not associated with newspapers, the great majority of the news stories to be found online have been written by newspaper journalists and those working for the established wire services, such as Reuters or AAP. Ninemsn and Yahoo7 are among Australia's top news sites, but how many of their stories do you imagine they wrote themselves?

What's more, it's possible to learn the substance of a particular newspaper news story without going anywhere near a newspaper-owned site. A lot of digital users get their news from news 'aggregators' such as Google and Yahoo, which use a loophole in the copyright law to steal the newspapers' thunder without paying—while often including a link to the real thing. (Where users don't avail themselves of the link, they get to see the aggregators' advertisers' messages, but not our advertisers'. And even the many news-seekers who come to us via search engines or recommendations on social media see other outfits' ads as well as ours. This does much to explain why the newspaper companies' share of online advertising revenue is so small.)

So, in the words of US academic Jeff Jarvis, one consequence of the digital revolution is that 'a media system built on scarcity is being replaced by one based on abundance'. Great for the customers, not good for the news media.

2. The demand for news is declining. Newspaper circulations are now falling sharply, but that's not the half of it. For decades, most people got most of their news from the evening news bulletins on television. They had little choice, since all of the limited number of channels showed their news at the same time. But the advent of cable TV in the US and later, pay TV in Australia, with their much wider ranges of channels to pick from, has made it easier to avoid television news, and many people have. In earlier generations, young people caught the news habit by watching the evening news with their parents on the family set. Now, even if parents are watching the news, their kids can watch something else in another room. According to American research quoted by Patterson, compared with their peers who grew up without cable, those from cable households were 40 per cent less likely to follow the news regularly after leaving home.

It's true a lot more news is consumed on the internet these days, particularly by young people, but this hasn't stopped the decline in news consumption overall. Still in the US, Patterson says 'younger adults are now far less likely than older adults to follow the news closely, even when internet-based news is taken into account. Although the web offers thousands of news sites, most young adults don't visit such sites regularly or hang around long when they do'. Even so, youngsters are only part of the story of Americans' 'flight from news'. 'Within *every* age group, Americans devote less time each day to news than was the case even a decade or two ago,' Patterson says.

There's little reason to doubt that American trends will be matched here, if they aren't already. On the net, people tend to use search engines to focus their news consumption on particular items of breaking news they've come to hear about, or focus on particular topic areas. This means they don't consume nearly as many news items as they would have under the pre-digital ways of delivering news. Using US figures from 2009, Google's chief economist, Hal Varian, calculates that the average user spent little more than 70 seconds a day looking at internet news sites, compared with the 25 minutes a day spent by the average newspaper reader. 'There's a reason for the relatively short time readers spend on online news: a disproportionate amount of online news reading occurs during working hours,' Varian says.

Against this, Joshua Gans, a young Australian professor now working in North America who's an expert in digital economics of international standing, says Varian's figures are per outlet. And since we don't know how many news outlets the average user visits, it's not certain the overall consumption of news has declined rather than just been spread more widely. His work raises another question: how do you define news? He says Facebook is the largest news organisation ever. Its users consult it regularly for news of their friends' doings. Old-school journos may scoff at the notion that this kind of trivia is 'news', but the likelihood remains that, for many people, Facebook is sufficient to satisfy their recurring urge to know 'what's happening?'.

There's now a wider gap between heavy and light consumers of news. While cable and the internet have made it easier for those interested to consume great quantities of news, they've also made news easier for the less-interested to avoid. Why does the *overall* demand for conventionally defined news seem to be declining? Mainly for the reason I keep stressing: the ever-growing competition from other ways for people to spend their time. But also, according to Patterson, because the media's attempt to fight the decline has backfired. He says an American study from 2011 found the rise in infotainment to be one of the leading causes of the long-term decline in the size of the traditional news audience. He blames the fixation with celebrities, disasters and crime, and the habit of 'decontextualising' events as well as the shift in political and economic reporting from policy issues to race calling.

3. Newspapers' days are numbered. Just about everyone at Fairfax Media Ltd accepts this—as witness, our change of name from John Fairfax Ltd, revealing our preference for being seen as a media company rather than a newspaper company—though there seem to be some at News Corp who are still in denial. That most newspapers won't last forever is easily demonstrated in the print media's marked and continuing loss of total revenue—down 26 per cent over the four years since its peak in 2008—and their decline in circulation. The total circulation of metropolitan and national dailies fell heavily with the demise of afternoon newspapers in the late 1980s and early 90s and continued a steady decline until 2008, when the rate of fall accelerated. The fall in 2012 was particularly sharp and continued in 2013.

Their high printing and distribution costs mean newspapers are a particularly expensive way of disseminating news, so their revenue and circulation figures won't have to fall much further to have the transformed 'media companies' pulling the plug.

A big part of the problem is generational: the reading of newspapers is skewed towards older generations. According to research commissioned by the Australian Communications and Media Authority, in 2010–11 the reading of newspapers was highest for those aged 65 years and over (86 per cent) and lowest for those aged 14 to 17 (52 per cent). Those proportions wouldn't be regular readers, however, more occasional flick-throughers. American evidence says younger adults are much less interested in politics than their parents, which makes them less interested in reading newspapers, and every Aussie parent knows that even if their kids *are* interested in the news they'll read it online, rarely on a dead tree. It would be comforting to think that newspaper reading is a habit young people acquire from their parents once they've matured. Sorry: though I spent much of my career hoping that was how things worked, Meyer quotes American research showing it's never worked that way. The proportion of daily newspaper readers has been getting progressively lower in each of the four generations born since 1928. So the claim that the paper-reading habit is dying out is literally true.

But though almost everyone in the business knows newspapers' days are numbered, no one knows what the number is. It will be determined by when the newspaper products reach the point where the reconceived 'media company' would lose less money if it were to cease producing them—after taking account of the continuing costs of generating news 'content' for their digital products and the limited saving in corporate overheads the cessation would bring about. (This, by the way, gives the lie to the frequent rumour that a decision by Fairfax to cease producing the *Herald* and *The Age*

Monday to Friday is imminent. It's true the company's monthly accounts show these *weekday* 'products' losing money, but this is an artefact of conventional accounting practices. If you ask the accountants the right question—would ceasing production save us money?—the answer is: no, it would actually cost us money. Why? Because of the continuing costs I've mentioned. I fear the day will come when newspaper-only revenue declines to the point where that answer changes but, at time of writing, it hasn't happened yet.)

The view in the US is that, though virtually all the nation's many newspapers will disappear, its four biggest or best papers—the *New York Times*, the *Washington Post*, *USA Today* and the *Wall Street Journal*—will survive. Does that mean at least some of *our* best four—the *Herald*, *The Age*, the *Fin* and the *Oz*—will survive? It's a nice thought, but I ain't banking on it.

4. In a digital world, the only big cost is content. Accountants divide the costs of producing a product into two categories: fixed and variable. The fixed costs are those you'd incur even if you produced only one unit. The variable costs are those that are generated by each extra unit you produce. Simplifying, you achieve economies of *scale* by producing as many units as you can before having to incur the extra fixed cost of building a bigger plant. By spreading the fixed costs over a greater number of units you lower the *average* cost per unit (while leaving the variable cost per unit unchanged). Similarly, you achieve economies of *scope* by using the same plant to produce a wider range of products. The additional product categories don't add to fixed costs, but do average them over a greater number of products of various types, meaning that if you can sell the additional products at prices even only a little above their variable costs per unit you're ahead on the deal. It was this that made deciding to produce the *Fin* (or a Sunday paper) on the *Herald* and *Age*'s presses attractive financially.

Tutorial over. Like most manufactured products, newspapers have high fixed production costs—the presses, the journos' salaries and other editorial expenses—and high variable costs: the paper, the ink and, to some extent, the cost of delivering the paper to newsagents. With digital news, however, it's very different. You do have the fixed costs of setting up and staffing a website and servers, but these are small relative to the fixed costs of physical production plants. You also have the continuing fixed cost of mainly journos' salaries necessary to generate the content for digital delivery. But your subsequent, variable costs are almost non-existent. The news you put on your site can be consumed by one user or a million at virtually no extra cost. Similarly, you can seek economies of scope by putting the same story on any number of different sites—not to mention tablet and mobile apps—at virtually no extra variable cost.

This means that, particularly by comparison with newspapers, the cost of producing and distributing news through digital channels is quite low. This, of course, is a big part of the reason the established news media have so many new competitors on the internet (particularly when they can appropriate our news at no cost to themselves). But it also means that, as digital-only news outlets, we don't need to attract nearly as much revenue as we used to to make an adequate return on capital. Which is some cause for hope.

5. The mass media is becoming less mass. Meyer says the internet is just the latest in a long line of advances that contribute to the 'demassification' of the media. As long ago as the early 1970s, the American sociologist Richard Maisel could see evidence of this: theatre was spreading to smaller spaces off-Broadway, newly built cinemas had fewer seats, publication of technical books was growing faster than fiction books, less-regular magazines were doing better than monthly and weekly magazines and community newspapers were holding on to readers more effectively than metropolitan papers.

In his paper 'Doing Well and Doing Good', Patterson notes that, with all the extra digital platforms and multiplying sites and apps, the audience for news is fragmenting. He says audiences will continue to fragment as new entrants contend for audience share. But then he makes a significant—and, to general newspapers, not particularly welcome—point: 'as the histories of radio and cable television indicate, a highly fragmented market rewards those who appeal narrowly to a particular audience segment.' In radio's early days, he says, the strongest stations were those that offered general programming. But over time, people became more selective and radio became a niche medium—talk stations, country music stations, oldies stations, top-forty stations, all-news stations and so on.

'When information sources are abundant, people tend to gravitate towards those that offer a differentiated product. The way in which people navigate cable television is an example. Although there may be many available channels, the typical user concentrates on six to eight of them, returning again and again to these channels and staying tuned when something of interest appears,' he says.

Now for his commercial message (with which I just happen to agree): as markets continue to fragment, news strategies are almost certain to target either the hard- or soft-news consumer. 'Demand for hard news should be stronger because of the larger size and narrower preferences of hard-news consumers. The strategy that is likely to fail is one that targets both soft- and hard-news consumers.' A recent US study found that, in local TV markets, newscasts that emphasise either hard news or soft news had higher average ratings than those pursuing a middle course. So, new rule: don't try to be all things to all persons. In *Informing the News*, Patterson says studies indicate that targeting increases an outlet's credibility with its users, which results in increased loyalty.

For myself, I'd expect that the huge range of digital news outlets will eventually pack down, with some unsuccessful outlets quitting the market and a relative handful of continuers accounting for most of the traffic. Humans are creatures of habit: we tend to find something we like and stick to it. We're also social creatures, so what we tend to like, lots of other people do, too.

Along with this trend to fragmentation and specialisation, a related trend is 'unbundling'. One part of this is the unbundling of classified ads from news—they have separate sites—but there's also a tendency for different news topics—sport, business, politics—to each have their own sites rather continuing to be part of one big news department store, so to speak.

Finally, there's an important trend that doesn't fit the 'demassification' label: the 'commodification' of news. In modern usage, a commodity is an undifferentiated product. The product I'm selling is little different from the one you're selling—perhaps because they both come from the same wholesaler. There's a lot of this undifferentiated product available on the market, which means you can't charge much of a margin above cost—especially if some outlets are giving it away.

6. Editors have lost a lot of their power. Before the revolution, the editor was king. He (or occasionally, she) was the ultimate judge of what the audience wanted and would be given. When you're playing it by ear, what the punters want could have a fair bit of what-I-think-they-should-be-given mixed in—not always a bad thing. After the revolution, two things have changed.

First, there's no more guesswork about what the punters want. In its various manifestations, the internet provides continuous, instantaneous market research: how many people clicked on a particular story and how long they stayed reading it. If a story doesn't get many hits in the first 15 minutes, pull it down and try something else. If stories about celebrities or photos of women with plenty on display get lots of hits, put more up. So the choice of story shifts from the editor to the customer. You beaut.

Second, whereas the conventional media always presented their news in carefully selected packages—called bulletins or newspapers—it's now possible for consumers to pick and choose. They choose from the multiplicity of outlets, they choose which stories to read on a particular site, they choose which big-name journos they wish to follow and they can set up arrangements that say 'only alert me to stories about these three topics'. So whereas editors used to determine what stories went into the package that was sent to everybody, now individual consumers can mix and match to put together their own personal package.

Vested-interest alert: one thing this does is increase the importance, and hence value, of star journos. More than ever before, editors need to surround themselves with stars (or 'brands', as they're starting to call journos with their own following). That's the point, of course. Journos with a following will mean more users making visits to your outlet part of their self-chosen package.

Research suggests editors were surprisingly weak at second-guessing what the punters wanted. One study found that newspaper editors overestimated readers' interest in sport and fashion, and underestimated interest in national, international and government news. But, equally, there are dangers in responding too mechanically to users' clicks. One involves the interpretation of data, which we'll get to in point 9. Another involves judgement, the short term and the longer term. If you'll forgive a little sexism, I'll plunge on. If you always give the punters exactly what they want, will they respect you in the morning? I see it as an application of the mother-at-tea-time effect. What the kids demand is fat, salt and sugar. But if that's all you give them, when they've grown up, will they accuse you of being a bad mother? Every mother knows that if you make them eat a reasonable ration of greens along with their meat and dessert, things will end up well in various respects. Quickly, cue next proposition . . .

7. Brands have become more important. Humans are creatures of habit and, as well, they find too much choice confusing. That's what brands are for. From baked beans to newspapers, they help you sell more. Brands offer the promise of a known quantity and consistent quality. With a good brand you won't be dudded; something wrong with it, we'll readily exchange it or give you your money back. If there's some trick to working the product, you already know how to do it and don't have to keep learning new tricks. Tried switching from Vegemite to Marmite? You get to feel at home with the brands you like, even become loyal to them. Humans are like that. Remember the eternal debates between Holden men and Ford men?

Media brands have always been important, and hence valuable, but with the breakdown of old monopolies and the huge increase in mediums, sites and apps they become more important and valuable. Brand is reputation. Every grocery or handbag manufacturer understands the importance of both protecting their brand and working to enhance it, knowing this leads straight to the cash register. Brands evoke emotions—positive or negative. Brands are closely linked to social status. There are working-class brands, middle-class brands and upper-class brands. Guess what? Upper-class brands have higher profit margins than lower-class brands.

Unfortunately, too many editors aren't as brand-conscious as they should be. When the *Herald* announced it was turning 'compact', we published a letter from a woman asking how, when that happened, people would know she wasn't reading the *Daily Telegraph*. Too many of our editors thought that a great joke rather than a valuable warning. It meant that when we went tabloid, we had to make sure our readers didn't think it meant we'd gone tabloid, if you take my meaning. Touchy-feely, perceptions—they matter.

I fear the quality press has failed to protect its brands the way it should have. When you've got sagging circulation, it's too easy for short-sighted, less brand-conscious editors to think the answer is to move a little down-market with more soft news—especially when you've got punters clicking away madly on the soft stuff on your site. As for *enhancing* the brand, what do you mean? Getting more scoops?

Cut to a speech in 2014 by the editor-in-chief of London's *Telegraph*, Jason Seiken: 'The most valuable asset of any news organisation is its brand principles—integrity, honesty, reliability and trust.' These are 'immutable and non-negotiable'. You try to create a culture where 'everything else is open to experimentation and change'.

8. The last monopoly is local news. One way of looking at the digital revolution is that it's broken down a lot of monopolies in various classes of advertising, but also in journalism. As we've seen, the internet has whipped away the natural protection that prevented much trade in newspapers, even between parts of the same state. On the net, our news stories are open to legal pilfering by news aggregators. Analogue free-to-air TV channels were protected by the limited width of the spectrum.

But there's one monopoly that can't be taken from metropolitan news outlets: in-depth coverage of their home town. National and international sites just don't have resources—or the degree of user interest—to cover particular cities, regions or states with any degree of depth. And when your home town happens to be a state capital city, that's quite a large topic: all the big-city problems of transport, congestion, house prices, planning, utilities, local entertainment and restaurants, plus all the state government issues of health, education, roads, law and order, and community services.

9. We have entered a data jungle. So tread carefully. News outlets—newspapers in particular—have gone from a dearth of information about their customers to an avalanche. In the old world it was easy to ask readers what type of news they wanted, but not to get reliable answers. Their answers were subject to 'social desirability bias'—the tendency of survey respondents to overstate what's regarded as good behaviour and understate bad behaviour. In the digital world, however, you don't ask, you measure users' behaviour. It's what economists call the users' 'revealed preference'—you judge what people want not by what they say, but by what they do.

Great. But it ain't that simple. We may have a lot more 'data' to play with, but we still have to judge how useful it is and draw the right conclusions from it. Jock Given, media professor at the Swinburne Institute for Social Research, says the information age has a paradox: more sophisticated tools enable us to know so much more, but the increasingly complex behaviour permitted by the net technology means there's so much more we need to understand. 'Digital users are easier to track but harder to follow,' he says.

There are two main reasons for wanting to know what users are doing: determining their news preferences and demonstrating to advertisers how much they have to gain from using your site. From the beginning, much attention has been paid to counting clicks, otherwise known as page views or page impressions—how many times people click on a particular page, or your site's total number of PIs in a month. This has given rise to much dubious effort to generate clicks using 'clickbait', which someone defined as 'men from Mars, breasts from heaven and celebrities behaving badly'—in short, any superficial thing that tempts users to click on it. Trouble is, this measure takes no account of how long people spend looking at the page. According to the boss of Chartbeat, an internet measuring company, 55 per cent of page impressions last fewer than 15 seconds. So it's wrong to imagine a page clicked is a page read.

A somewhat more sophisticated measure is UAs, 'monthly unique audience'—the number of individuals who visit a site during a month. It's thus a measure of the *breadth* of a site's audience. Advertisers like it because it measures actual people, so—for the moment, at least—it's become the industry standard. Trouble is, it doesn't measure repeat visits. Someone who visits the site once in a month counts the same as someone who visits 100 times.

A better measure is UBs, 'daily unique browsers'—the number of web browsers or other devices visiting a site during a day. The average number of daily UBs in a month is a better measure of users' loyalty to a site, though it overstates the number of individuals using it because someone using more than one device to visit the site on the same day—a PC at work, a smart phone on the train and an iPad at home, for instance—gets counted more than once.

Other measures are the average time spent on the site by users per month—say, for the *Herald*, an hour and 40 minutes—and the average session duration for each single session during a month—say, for the *Herald*, 16 minutes. Another proposed measure is 'attention minutes', calculated by multiplying page impressions by the average time spent per page. Yet another measure seems to be used to aid decisions about how long stories should be kept on the site: the story's page impressions in the past five minutes, which takes some account of how long people are staying on the story.

All very educational. I'm no expert on internet 'metrics', but I *have* spent decades playing with statistics, and this has left me convinced of the wisdom of a couple of principles. One is, make sure you know exactly what it is a particular metric is measuring—it may not be what you think. Another is, make sure you know the conceptual limitations of the measure you're using—every metric has them.

And remember one of my mottos: the world's a complicated place. That's partly because human motivations can be complicated, even contradictory. I may say I want plenty of foreign news, for instance, but not actually read it much. Does that mean I wouldn't mind if you cut back your foreign news coverage? Not necessarily. What I may be after is the respectability or status that comes with reading a classy masthead known to all—but particularly the people I know—to be upscale. Or try this one: two men get onto a website; one is looking for the latest column by Laura Tingle, the other is after Peter FitzSimons' column. But if you put a sexy photo in their way they're both likely to take a quick perve. Metrics: Tingle, one hit; FitzSimons, one hit; sexy photo, two hits. So both came to your site to see a sexy photo, did they? Then increase the sexy photos and cut back on the columnists.

Securing journalism's future: A battle plan

Everyone in journalism dreams of the day when some other newspaper—no doubt led by a great entrepreneur, no doubt

American—comes up with the new business model that allows journalism to survive and prosper in the digital world. When that great day dawns, every other newspaper/media company in the developed world will fall on the new formula, the skies will clear and it will be back to, and on with, a digitally modified business as usual.

Or maybe not. What history suggests is more likely is the slow emergence of a new way of doing journalism, not simply a neat transition to a bunch of new, digital platforms. The likelihood is that it will be new, lean news organisations that come to dominate the news industry, perhaps sitting behind the old big brand names they've bought at the old behemoths' liquidation sale. Or maybe they'll develop their own brand names, partly because the old brands became so tarnished in their declining years and partly because of a desire to trade on their newness and not to be associated with the old, boring way of doing things.

If the present big brands do survive, it will be because of the alacrity with which they've been willing to change long-held views about how journalism is done, making their transition to the new approach fast enough to avoid financial collapse before their last newspaper-ad customers had moved on.

The journos' dream is that the discovery of a new business model merely involves finding a new way of paying for journalism as it's always been done. I fear it will involve radical changes to the journalism as well as the funding. In the new world of cheaper classifieds and cheaper display ads then, unless we find some wonderful new source of funding, the journalism will have to cost less. That means a different journalism.

Here's my best thinking on how we can make it from here to there. I'll approach the task from the perspective of Australia's four main quality newspapers, but particularly the *Herald* and *The Age*. It's a 10-point battleplan.

1. Ensure the paper dies of old age, not neglect. With the revenue it still generates—at time of writing, it's still by far the greatest part of the news-related revenue that the company generates—the paper is the only thing that will keep us solvent until we find the new, profitable combination of journalism, advertising, subscription or other revenue. While we do need to become 'digital first' and focus on all the changes we need to make to survive and prosper in the new world, we mustn't neglect to give good service to our loyal, subscription-paying readers and those advertisers who still find it profitable to use our pages. This includes retaining sufficient expertise to solicit and appropriately price newspaper advertising. The time will come soon enough when advertising and subscription revenue is insufficient to cover the considerable cost of printing and distributing the paper and only then will it be time to give up and move on.

Meanwhile, the commonest complaint journos hear about the paper is that there aren't enough stories in it worth reading. I take this to mean that the kind of people still reading the paper aren't much impressed by our efforts to attract readers by making the news softer and more entertaining. If so, the readers are right. We have an intelligent readership who want solid, well-written, engaging fare, not frippery. I think our latest crop of editors now understands this, but once adverse impressions have taken hold it can take a long time to dispel them.

2. Get on the front foot with digital advertising. If advertising is to play a significant role in financing digital news, we need to take it a lot more seriously than we are. We seem to have a dearth of senior advertising specialists playing influential roles in our decisions about how the business should change. We have experts on how to chase clicks, but not on how to turn clicks into money. Rather than waiting for the advertising market to sort itself out and decide what it wants—or for some other media company to show us what to do—we should be doing our own thinking about how we can provide advertisers with something of value to them that they can be persuaded to pay a lot for. Rather than conforming to sub-standard 'industry standards' we should be developing our own measures, which better capture the value that our kind of journalism and our kind of readers offer certain classes of advertisers. To the extent that we can't resist the trend to 'programmatic advertising'—the automated buying of ad space—we should be finding ways to sell at a premium.

3. Encourage readers to pay for their journalism. The commercial news media have been reliant on advertising for most of their revenue since the beginning. But it's now open to question whether advertising revenue will remain adequate in a world of digital advertising and, though we should do our best to ensure its continuation, we need another string to our bow. In principle, there's no reason people shouldn't pay the full price for the news they consume, just as they pay for the books they read and most other things they need. In practice, however, there is a long tradition of paying nothing for radio and television news and only nominal prices for newspapers. It may take some time to 'reframe' news as something worth paying for—especially since news, of varying quality, will remain free from various sources—but we should persist with asking people to pay for it directly and in seeking new ways to frame the imposition of a price. It's notable that the invention of apps saw people who'd stoutly refused to pay for anything online willing to pay for them. The reason for persisting with digital subscriptions—and for slowly raising their price—is the prize: it would be hugely liberating for news media organisations to simply sell their product direct to customers in the same way most businesses do. Selling our product directly puts the emphasis on ensuring we're giving our readers value for money, which can only be a good thing. If they aren't prepared to pay subscriptions, maybe they're prepared to pay per view—tiny payments per article read, known as 'nano-transactions'. And remember, digital news is a lot cheaper to produce than dead-tree news.

4. Know what we're on about. Journos could take the attitude that everyone needs to make a living, the news media provide us with a living, so we should do all we can to ensure this continues for as many of us as possible. I know it's easy for me to say at my age but, while that's fine for people who make their living selling soap, it's not good enough for the fourth estate. The news media have a vital, irreplaceable part to play in the effective functioning of democracy. We must ensure we continue to discharge that duty and are not diverted into easier ways to make a living. Beside that objective, the survival of Fairfax as a company and the preservation of many jobs for those who want to work in journalism pale into insignificance.

In the report 'Post-Industrial Journalism', prepared for the Columbia Journalism School, the authors describe the kind of journalism that must be preserved for the sake of society: journalism that 'exposes corruption, draws attention to injustice, holds politicians and businesses accountable for their promises and duties. It informs citizens and consumers, helps organise public opinion, explains complex issues and clarifies essential disagreements.' They add that such journalism is equally irreplaceable in the effective functioning of market economies, not just democracies.

'Not all journalism matters, of course,' they continue. 'Much of what is produced today is simply entertainment or diversion.' But it's 'hard news' that distinguishes the iron core of journalism from just another commercial activity. 'There will always be a public appetite for reporting on baseball, movie stars, gardening and cooking, but it's of no great moment for the country if all of that work were taken over by amateurs or done by machine.' It's the hard core of journalism that must be preserved, even if this involves accepting the loss of many journalists' jobs.

5. Play to your strengths. The great strengths of the *Herald* and *The Age* are their brands—their reputation for trustworthiness and even up-market respectability—and their audiences of 'ABs', advertising-speak for the top two socio-economic groups. It's the strength of our brands, as much as all the effort we've put in, that has given us two of the top news websites in the country. The ABs are attractive to advertisers because of their higher levels of disposable income. But they're also attractive to serious journalists because, not by chance, they also represent the best-educated people in the community, the ones most likely to be interested in the hard news that has always been Fairfax's strong point. The ABs have the wherewithal not only to buy from our advertisers but also to pay a subscription should they choose. I fear that, in our earlier attempts to arrest our falling circulation and in our efforts to keep our websites on top, we've lost sight of the truth that the ABs have always been—and should remain—our target market. We've been trying to correct our supposed weakness—lack of appeal to Cs and Ds—rather than playing to our strengths.

Our other, newly recognised strength is our possession of what I've described as the last monopoly: local news. Fortunately, this is an opportunity we've already cottoned on to. *The Age* has always given a high priority to reporting and analysing Melbourne and Victorian news, and in recent years the *Herald* has done this in Sydney, too. News about city and state governments, and all the vital services they are responsible for delivering to our readers—roads and public transport, education, health and hospitals, and law and order—must henceforth constitute a very large part of our news task. If *we* don't do it thoroughly, who will? The *Herald Sun* and the *Daily Telegraph*? A few TV channels and radio stations? We'll have little competition from them and none from the big national and overseas news sites.

6. Stop chasing clicks. At the time Fairfax began establishing its websites it may have been a sensible strategy to make everything freely available and aim to be the biggest and best news site in the country, in the confident hope that some way of 'monetising' all those hits would eventually turn up. There's no doubt the first part of the strategy has worked a treat; we really do have two of the biggest sites, despite formidable competition. But it's time to question the second part: we've built it, but the advertisers still haven't come—at least, not bearing enough monetary gifts. It's possible we just haven't tried hard enough to convert all those clicks into advertising dollars, but the more likely explanation is that clicks just aren't worth much. In which case, why are we putting so much time and effort into chasing them? Isn't there some better game we could be playing?

The bosses of our websites readily acknowledge the limitation of clicks—page impressions—as a measure of anything a potential advertiser might be attracted to. But the truth remains that chasing clicks is what our web bosses do—with all their emphasis on SEO (search-engine optimisation, which means choosing the wording of headlines we know will get our stories listed high up in the online searches users do) and other tricks—and encourage our journalists to do. The truth is it's become a cop-out: a game we play because we're good at winning it, not because winning it does much to help us pay our way.

The commercial goal of journalism used to be maximising circulation, so it's been easy and tempting to simply switch to the new commercial goal of maximising clicks. As I argued in the previous chapter, journos love competing in competitions and convincing themselves they're doing well in the comp. And the clicks comp is so much more alluring, with all its hard numbers, its instant feedback about what's being clicked on, its daily reports on which stories got the most hits and monthly reports on how the top news sites rank click-wise. Journos enjoy competing for its own sake: give them a comp where performance is so easily, regularly and objectively measured and they'll happily go on playing that game every day until the money runs out and they're out on the street.

Managers need to call a halt to this game and direct their journos' energies to goals more consistent with our commercial imperative *and* our higher purpose. We need to sharpen our focus on ABs, developing our thinking on how we should go about holding and attracting AB digital subscribers and delivering our ABs to potential advertisers. Then we need to develop the 'metrics' that measure our success in attracting and holding the ABs. Only these measures should be used to motivate the troops. We should certainly stop showing staff measures that encourage them to keep trying to attract fleeting clicks from non-ABs.

But there's one important qualification: particularly in distinction to the newspaper, we need to attract *younger* ABs and soon-to-become ABs once they've climbed a little higher on the corporate ladder. If you like, we're after the children, even the grandchildren of our newspaper readers. Aim at the well-educated and money is more likely to follow. What we need to remember is that the younger generation is likely to be more broad-minded and less stuffed-shirt than their parents. More interested in social issues such as same-sex marriage, but also more interested in celebrities and suchlike. What needs to change is the approach: not Gosh, have you heard the latest, but Why do you think there's been so much interest in Kim Kardashian doing X.

7. Start doing less with less. So far, as ever-falling advertising revenue has required round after round of redundancies, we've been trying to do more with less. Despite an ever-shrinking staff we've tried to do all the news-gathering we've always done, albeit with a decline in quality. Actually, we've tried to do more than we've always done because the advent of the websites has lured us back to the breaking-news business we haven't been in since the arrival of radio and television news bulletins. With this new emphasis on getting stories up on the site within minutes of them breaking, then updating the story as the day progresses, what gets underdone is anything that requires more time for digging and thinking. But this is the wrong way round. We're putting more effort into attracting fleeting clicks from people who probably aren't ABs, while putting less effort into the better backgrounded, more explanatory and analytical stories that ABs find more satisfying.

Clearly, this can't go on much longer. We can't allow our coverage of the whole waterfront to become ever thinner. With redundancies likely to continue, it's time we made hard decisions about what we continue doing and what we can no longer afford to do.

8. Get out of commoditised news. All the experts tell us news has become a commodity, meaning in the digital world it has become widely available and all much the same, thus making it worth little to advertisers and users. Fine. That makes it the obvious thing we should stop doing. Not all of what we think of as news has been commoditised, just the bit we call breaking news or, as I prefer, instant news. Commoditised news is the quick and dirty, who-what-where-and-when journalism provided by AAP and other wire services.

There's no point in us continuing to compete with the wire services to provide instant news. Our version may be marginally better but, even if it is, can enough users tell the difference? We end up competing with the many rival suppliers of commoditised news—most of them too canny to actually produce it themselves—on the basis of who's best at search-engine optimisation, at writing headlines that bring you to the top of the stories found by a Google search. But that's a wasting game. It won't be long before all our rivals have learnt how to write headlines as optimising as ours. No, give it up. If we still want to put instant news on our sites we should do it simply and cheaply by running wire copy ourselves.

9. Stick to our core competencies. The experts also keep telling us the days of the one-stop shop for news are over; we can no longer be all things to all people. It's a question of packaging. Newspapers have always put together a comprehensive selection of news and presented it to their readers as a package: you want to know what's been happening? Here is it. But that's not how it works on the internet, we're told. People used to like to get all their news from one source because of the time and expense involved in gathering news on particular topics from a range of sources. In the virtual world, however, all that has changed. Everything you want to be informed about is out there, just a click away and probably free. So each user puts together their personal package: I want to be alerted by the best specialist site to any developments on this subject and that. I'm a fan of this columnist who writes on this topic, so I'll visit your site when you alert me that she's written another column, but on this other topic I like a rival outfit's columnist so I visit its site to keep up-to-date on his version of events. These days there's less browsing and more 'intent'—I know what I want, so I go straight to it.

I'm not certain this analysis applies as much to sites seeking to attract AB subscribers and AB advertisers as it does to sites seeking to maximise their clicks. I'm not sure it applies as much to the older readers who'll eventually join the online throng as it does to the younger readers who're already there. And I'm not sure most people avail themselves of the thousands of sites available, or they soon settle for regularly visiting a relative handful. The alternative theory to the no-more-department-stores contention is that there's still a place for the 'trusted generalist' new source.

But, be that as it may, since we're almost certain to have a lot less money available to spend on the journalism we produce, we have to stop doing something, and the obvious things to stop doing are those subject areas which have never been our strong suit relative to our online competitors. It would be hard to justify the expense of maintaining foreign correspondents, for instance. It then just becomes a question of whether we should run the (cheaply available) coverage from superior outlets such as the *New York Times* or vacate the foreign news topic completely. We would be guided in such decisions by our knowledge of the topics of most interest to our AB customers.

10. Move to a value-added model of journalism. A value-added model would buy in the who, what, when and where of routine stories so we could focus on adding the harder, more informative, more valuable bits our AB readers are looking for: the how and why; the context and background information, the analysis and comment. Less time spent on the basics of routine stories leaves more time for digging up exclusives. Finding *genuine* scoops should do much to discharge our higher purpose—and meet Lord Northcliffe's dictum that news is 'something someone somewhere doesn't want printed'—even if does less to advance our commercial interests than journos happily assume.

Value-added news involves more depth and less breadth in our news coverage. It's more thematic and less episodic, providing busy readers with a summary of more important developments and what they prove (which, by the way, makes it harder for news aggregators to pinch). It is topical, but more of it is initiated by our journos who've discovered matters of importance our readers need to be informed of, and less of it is initiated by press releases or merely conforms to the agenda-setting of politicians, businesses and other power-holders. It helps to close the gap between what the media does—report the unusual and exceptional—and what our readers assume we do: provide them with a balanced picture of what's happening in the world beyond their personal experience.

Value-added news accepts that the age of the general reporter is over. We're compelled by circumstances to employ fewer journalists, so those we do employ have to be more specialised in the lesser range of topics we now choose to cover. Journos need to be more academically qualified in their area of specialty, meaning they probably need to be more highly paid than general reporters are at present. As well as being knowledgeable and able to write with authority on their subject, they need to carry their erudition lightly, writing with clarity and seeming simplicity at a level appropriate to our audience of readers who, while well-educated in some other field, aren't expert on the writer's subject.

With specialisation and an ability to write well goes the potential to become a journalist with a personal following—someone who's a 'brand' in themselves. Such journos are the antithesis of commoditised news. A smart strategy would be to put together a team of as many personal brands as possible, to have a name-brand at the head of all the various topic areas the outfit decided to stick with. That sounds expensive, but only if you try to put together a bench of name-brands by poaching established stars from other outfits. A smart news outlet develops its own name-brands by selecting the best at entry level, training and mentoring well, giving those who shine the chance to grow and promoting their work when its quality merits wider notice. Train them and treat them well and you stand a good chance of keeping them.

A news outlet that focuses on a smaller number of longer, thematic, analytical stories in core areas such as politics, economics, business and 'local' has the potential to be a terribly earnest, boring rag. But it doesn't have to be provided there's sufficient emphasis on good writing, not taking ourselves too seriously and a good mix of light and shade, hard and soft, with good news to leaven all the bad. Implicit in this is that our coverage of politics and economics should be a lot more about policy and a lot less about race calling, such as leadership speculation and the ups and downs in economic indicators. Does more discussion of policy sound boring and of little interest to our readers? That's because to date it's been written more by generalists than specialists, who lack the ability to distinguish between the key features and the peripheral details, who are distracted by the finer points their political contacts are arguing over, who have been trained to search out the new rather than how to explain things simply and clearly and, above all, because we've allowed ourselves to lose the vision that policy discussion must always be tied back to the concerns and the experience of our readers. Make it relevant to our readers' lives—which ain't the same thing as simply gratifying their prejudices and pre-judgements—and they'll read it with interest.

A variation of the value-added model if the outlet was following the 'trusted generalist' approach would be for some non-core topic areas to be headed not by a resident expert but by a curator, whose job would be to pick from all the bought-in copy the very best selection for our readers, one that conceivably could be better than that provided by any of the various individual news sources to their own readers.

To get to practical details, I see the newsroom being divided into a relatively large number of small topic teams, each led by the resident expert, assisted by one or two less experienced journos, plus a research assistant and a lot of equipment (each of which would be a lot cheaper than a journalist). The younger journos would monitor the wire services' coverage of the topic, often putting stories online untouched, but where justified rewriting them and adding background. The team would use video reports, infographics and data mining to enhance their news coverage and explanatory journalism.

In such a way the role of the journalist would be redefined to meet the ideal espoused by the authors of the report on post-industrial journalism: the journalist as 'truth-teller, sense-maker and explainer'. Such a greatly reduced and refined conception of the journalistic task ought to preserve and even enhance the quality press's contribution to the effective functioning of our democracy and our market economy. And we just might be able to make such a contribution commercially sustainable.

INDEX